Clientelism, Social Policy,
and the Quality of Democracy

Clientelism, Social Policy, and the Quality of Democracy

Edited by
DIEGO ABENTE BRUN
and
LARRY DIAMOND

Johns Hopkins University Press
Baltimore

© 2014 Johns Hopkins University Press
All rights reserved. Published 2014
Printed in the United States of America on acid-free paper
2 4 6 8 9 7 5 3 1

Johns Hopkins University Press
2715 North Charles Street
Baltimore, Maryland 21218-4363
www.press.jhu.edu

Library of Congress Cataloging-in-Publication Data

Clientelism, social policy, and the quality of democracy / Edited
by Diego Abente Brun and Larry Diamond.
pages cm
Includes bibliographical references and index.
ISBN-13: 978-1-4214-1228-3 (hardback)
ISBN-10: 1-4214-1228-4 (hardcover)
ISBN-13: 978-1-4214-1229-0 (paperback)
ISBN-10: 1-4214-1229-2 (paperback)
ISBN-13: 978-1-4214-1264-1 (electronic)
ISBN-10: 1-4214-1264-0 (electronic)
1. Patronage, Political—Developing countries—Case studies.   2. Democratization—
Developing countries—Case studies.   3. Developing countries—Politics
and government—Case studies.   4. Political sociology.   5. Comparative
government.   I. Abente Brun, Diego.   II. Diamond, Larry Jay.
JF2111.C54 2014
324.2'04—dc23   2013018543

A catalog record for this book is available from the British Library.

*Special discounts are available for bulk purchases of this book. For more information, please
contact Special Sales at 410-516-6936 or specialsales@press.jhu.edu.*

Johns Hopkins University Press uses environmentally friendly book materials,
including recycled text paper that is composed of at least 30 percent post-consumer
waste, whenever possible.

CONTENTS

Javier Auyero
University of Texas

Ernesto Calvo
University of Houston

Christopher Chambers-Ju
University of California, Berkeley

Kanchan Chandra
New York University

Linda J. Cook
Brown University

Larry Diamond
Stanford University

Kent Eaton
University of California, Santa Cruz

Paul D. Hutchcroft
The Australian National University

Juan Pablo Luna
Catholic University of Chile

Beatriz Magaloni
Stanford University

Rodrigo Mardones
Catholic University of Chile

Carlos Meléndez
University of Notre Dame

María Victoria Murillo
Columbia University

Simeon Nichter
Stanford University

Martin Tanaka
Pontifical Catholic University of Peru

Nicolas Van de Walle
Cornell University

As we approach the fourth decade of the Third Wave of global democratization, global democratic progress remains at something of an impasse. Although the Arab Spring raised hopes for a new burst of democratic transitions, most Arab states remain mired in authoritarianism or stuck at various stages of transition that will probably work their way toward democracy only gradually, at best. Since 2005, the rest of the world has witnessed not a springtime of democracy but a democratic recession, in which levels of freedom have fallen for several consecutive years and democratic reversal has become more common. In fact, the rate of breakdown of democracy during the period 1999–2011 was nearly twice the rate of the preceding twelve-year period. In all, nearly a third of the democracies that have existed since the Third Wave began in 1974 have broken down.

There are many reasons for the failure of democracy, but one of the most significant factors is bad governance. This can take many forms, but the underlying phenomenon is that state structures do not work fairly, efficiently, effectively, and transparently in their attempts to deliver public goods that are needed for socioeconomic development. Additionally, the individual benefits that collectively constitute social policy, such as income support, health care, educational access, jobs, and job training, are not allocated based on need or ability. Rather, in each of these instances and in many other realms of public policy, something intervenes to undermine the fair and efficient distribution of public resources. Usually, that "something" prominently includes political clientelism, a persistent pattern in which officeholders exchange state benefits for political support and loyalty.

As several authors make clear in the chapters that follow, clientelism is as old as politics itself, and it may in some respects be "functional" for the growth of democracy in that it provides a means for parties to mobilize support and for candidates to build resilient constituencies. Yet to the extent that clientelism distorts the distribution of state benefits in low-income and lower-middle income democracies in particular, it may exacerbate inequality, since anti-poverty programs are among the most commonly targeted for clientelistic (rather than truly need-based) distribution.

These practices produce the double misfortune of making it more difficult to lift the poor out of poverty, which makes those democracies that are already the most fragile even more vulnerable to collapse. Hence, the logic of political clientelism—which is another way of saying favoritism based on political ties—seems directly in tension with the Weberian ideal of an impersonal, bureaucratic state efficiently delivering state benefits to those most in need of them, or at least to those for whom they are explicitly intended.

When group ties distort the distribution of state resources, more egregious personal considerations are often not far behind. Thus, individual corruption is often the handmaiden of clientelism. Both are departures from the model of the rule-based, bureaucratic Weberian state. And when politicians mobilize votes on the basis of particularistic ties—as patrons exchanging state benefits for continued political support—then voters become clients rather than citizens, and they are unable to use their vote to hold politicians accountable for their overall performance on behalf of the constituency or the country. If voters look the other way at inefficiency and unfairness because the system seems to work for them personally—and thus in a sense it is "fair" enough—then they are also likely to look the other way when the politician rewards himself in office with a generous share of "patronage" for himself. As a result, in systems where distribution happens largely through patron-client networks, more resources often leak out through corruption than through clientelism per se. If clientelism provides a means in the short run—however suboptimal—of stabilizing politics and providing politicians with reliable bases of support, in the longer run it badly damages the rule of law, the accountability of government to citizens overall, and thus the quality of democracy. The result is often strong bases of support for certain individuals who corner control over the distribution of resources, but widespread general cynicism about parties, politicians—and democracy itself.

There is also a further cost to pervasive clientelism: in multiethnic societies, ethnic resentments and conflicts will be stimulated, because the bonds that tie clients to patrons tend to be forged along ethnic lines. Just as the winners in the distribution game belong to certain ethnic groups, so do the losers. This is one reason that political violence is so common in states where public resources get appropriated to fuel and lubricate patron-client machines. It is also a reason that most political scientists—and civic activists—believe that democracy is better, fairer, and more sustainable when there gradually develops alongside it a Weberian bureaucratic state rather than a corrupt and clientelistic one.

To explore more systematically how political clientelism works and evolves in the context of modern developing democracies—and with particular reference to social policies to reduce poverty—the International Forum for Democratic Studies of the National Endowment for Democracy (NED) organized a two-day conference in Quito, Ecuador, on November 5 and 6, 2010, along with our local host, the Ecuadorian think tank Grupo FARO. The conference brought together approximately twenty scholars and practitioners from around the world, including several from South America and the Andean region in particular. The international character of the meeting was intended to generate a discussion that was not excessively self-referential and that enabled participants to learn from a wide range of experiences across cultures, political contexts, and historical legacies. Participants were thus expected to benefit from both regional and international perspectives and from theoretical analysis and empirical research as well as from practical experience. The conference was structured with an eye toward learning from successful experiences and developing a set of best practices for possible reform and change. The regions included were Latin America, Africa, Southeast Asia, and Eastern and Central Europe.

We do not pretend that this volume addresses all the necessary questions, much less that it provides all the answers that we would want. Yet in an era when democracy increasingly seems suspended between the age-old practice of clientelism and a growing demand for better, more efficient and just governance, we think our effort to bring together fresh research and thinking by some of the best social scientists working on these countries and regions is timely and compelling. From these rich and instructive case studies we can, and in fact do, begin to glean the larger comparative lessons that can help countries transcend the natural sociological reflex toward clientelistic ties and build that most elusive of all political structures—a fair, efficient, and accountable state, based on impersonal criteria and the rule of law. As Diego Abente Brun writes in the introduction, this is indeed "a challenge that demands the concerted effort of reformist politicians and effective civil society organizations."

LARRY DIAMOND

This book began with a conference in Quito, Ecuador, co-sponsored by the International Forum for Democratic Studies of the National Endowment for Democracy and Grupo FARO, a leading public policy think tank in Ecuador. We would like to extend our sincere thanks to both institutions, and to the Network of Democracy Research Institutes, which the Forum coordinates and of which Grupo FARO is a member.

We extend our special gratitude to the Executive Director of Grupo FARO, Orazio Belletini. His enthusiasm and dedication made it possible to assemble this stellar group of scholars to address the issues included in the volume. Our thanks go as well to the staff of FARO, especially Andrea Ordónez Llanos. We also thank Marc Plattner, co-director of the International Forum at the time, who helped to design the conference and to guide and enrich the conference discussions.

We also want to acknowledge the important intellectual contributions to the conference made by Christian Gruenberg. His insistence on incorporating the gender dimension into the analysis to take into account the double burden imposed on women, in their doubly marginalized roles both as clients and as women, remains a critical issue that deserves to be studied in depth. We regret that considerations of space and the ultimate coherence of the book volume did not enable us to include his chapter in this publication.

A debt of appreciation is also due to the Ford Foundation, which provided much of the funding needed for the meeting; to the Center for Democracy, Development and the Rule of Law at Stanford University for additional funds; and to the Taiwan Foundation for Democracy, which funded the participation of scholars from Southeast Asia.

The International Forum for Democratic Studies at NED also contributed some funds and above all considerable work by its staff. For that we thank Maria Fleetwood and Melissa Aten. In addition, Ryan Doherty, a research associate at NED, spent considerable time editing the manuscripts, and Sukanya Banerjee, also a research associate at NED, did a superb job of helping to assemble the final manuscript. Without her generous and rigorous contribution in the final editing, it would have taken much longer for this volume to see the light of day.

Our gratitude goes as well to Johns Hopkins University Press staff: to Suzanne Flinchbaugh for her support and patience, to Juliana McCarthy, and most especially to Elizabeth Yoder for her great work as editor.

Clientelism, Social Policy,
and the Quality of Democracy

Evaluating Political Clientelism

DIEGO ABENTE BRUN

During the Third Wave of democratization, almost all countries in Latin America and a large number in Africa and Asia became consolidated democracies in the sense that democracy became broadly accepted as "the only game in town." Yet the democratic systems in many of these countries remain characterized by poor quality and failure to adequately address the social and economic challenges they face, a deficiency that persistently erodes their own legitimacy.

Some of the factors that explain this lack of government effectiveness relate to aspects of what can be called state capacity: institutional strength, technical expertise, and quality of the civil service. Others have to do with the role of political institutions—especially the executive and the legislature—and the modes of political intermediation between them and the population at large as they impinge on the effectiveness of the policymaking process. One such mode of intermediation, political clientelism, is particularly deleterious.

In the past decade this concern has resurfaced with intensity. Accustomed, as scholars were, to think of clientelism as a relic of the past, or as a feature of the least-developed societies, or of the less-developed areas of rapidly modernizing countries, it was thought of as a passing phenomenon, a feature that would quickly disappear like "the pimples of adolescence." But as Javier Auyero showed us ten years ago, in the most modern and advanced Latin American countries the "pimples" were back—and with a vengeance.[1] Later works by Steven Levitsky, Levitsky and Helmke, Stokes, and Remmer offered further confirmation of this disturbing trend.[2] Soon it became clear that clientelism was flourishing or reviving not only in Argentina but also elsewhere in Latin America as well as in Africa, Asia, and even in postcommunist Europe. It was no longer found only in rural areas but was present in urban settings as well. Besides, as Kitschelt and Wilkinson argued, clientelism also proved to be alive and well in developed societies.[3] Thus, the last decade witnessed an explosion of studies on this subject, and these days it is rare to attend a professional conference that does not feature at least a dozen or so panels on the matter.

By and large, political clientelism is more prone to thrive precisely in that area of public policy most neglected in the past and most relevant in the present: social policy, and especially anti-poverty policy. Indeed, it is the generalized emphasis on anti-poverty policies that contributed additional importance to the study of clientelism. In turn, the fact that social policies are, will, and should remain at the forefront of the public policy agenda makes this inquiry all the more relevant.

This volume examines the experiences of a number of Latin American countries as well cases in Africa, Eastern Europe, and Southeast Asia. Its objective is to highlight the specificities of each case as well as the commonalities between them. Rather than responding to a pre-established and rigid theoretical framework, authors address questions considered most important for the analysis of their cases, some emphasizing an ethnographic approach and others privileging a more politico-institutional analysis. The theoretical exercise is an inductive one, and in the conclusion Beatriz Magaloni pulls together different elements into a unifying framework that can serve further studies.

Our contributors' questions include:

- Parties. What role do parties play in the expansion or contraction of clientelistic practices? Do all parties behave alike, regardless of their nature, or are there differences worth noting? These questions are addressed particularly in regard to the cases of Argentina, Chile, and Africa.
- Rules. To what extent can clientelism be attributed to a set of rules that favor it, and if and when rules change, do they have a significant impact? This is a question raised in the study of Colombia.
- Caste. How does caste affect the mechanics of clientelistic relations? The question is dissected in the analysis of India.
- Regime type. Are there differences attributable to types of political regimes, and if so, which ones and where? The study of the African case throws important light on this regard.
- Socioeconomic structure. To what extent does the complexity of economic development affect clientelism? The study of post-communist countries helps us clarify this.
- State bureaucracies. What role does strong versus weak state bureaucracy play? The cases of Chile and post-communist Europe illustrate this question.
- Exploring causes, proposing alternatives. Is clientelism a necessary evil? Can countries "outgrow" out of it? What are the alternatives for combatting it? This a question discussed throughout the volume but especially in the conclusion.

The Study of Clientelism in the Discipline

The study of clientelism in the political science discipline began in the 1970s as part of what Susan C. Stokes has called the first wave of clientelistic studies, mostly, although not only, related to the historical period of decolonization and nation-building.[4] Some of the most important contributions include James Scott; Steffen Schmidt, J. Scott, J. C. Lande, and L. Guasti; Eisenstadt and Lemarchand; and Gellner and Waterbury.[5]

In his path-breaking 1972 article in the *American Political Science Review,* James C. Scott pointed out that the difficulty of Western political scientists to elucidate the nature of the political process in the Third World was grounded in the fact that they tended to rely either on a horizontal class model of association and conflict or on factors such as ethnicity, language, and religion. While the first model could not account for situations in nonindustrial areas where political loyalties cut across class lines, the second failed to account for patterns of conflict and cooperation among primordial groups. The answer, Scott argued, was to focus instead on informal, leadership-centered, clientelistic relationships that evolved from the village level but permeated "nominally modern institutions such as the bureaucracies and political parties." Simultaneously, the expansion of the national economy and national political parties resulted in the transformation of the basis, but not the logic, of clientelism, "creating new bases of patronage and devaluating old ones."[6]

In an important later study, Martin Shefter examined the question from the point of view of the logic of political parties, highlighting an interesting distinction not only in terms of the locus of analysis but also in terms of the cases studied.[7] What makes political parties choose programmatic instead of clientelistic incentives to entice voters to support them? Under what conditions do they pursue one or another strategy? As a response to what he termed the "neoclassical" theory of patronage, Shefter emphasized that the social basis of the political system was but one of the elements to take into account. Other important factors were the resources available to the parties as well as the parties' relations with other constituencies, its own core of activists on the one hand, and the elites on the other.[8] This approach prefigured Stokes's second wave, associated with the processes of democratization and re-democratization, which includes the works of, among others, Stokes, Nichter, Calvo and Murillo, and Wantchekon.[9] The first perspective, more structural and sociological, and the second, more decisional and political, are different but not mutually exclusive and, as will be seen, underlie the chapters of this volume.

Furthermore, the already large body of extant literature has often used loosely and sometimes interchangeably concepts such as clientelism, patronage, and pork-barrel politics. It has also defined clientelism variously as a dyadic *relationship,* a *network* of dyadic relationships, and a one-shot vote-buying operation.

It is necessary, therefore, to give some clarity to a variety of concepts often used interchangeably. It is important, for example, to differentiate clientelism from pork-barrel politics. The latter is not dyadic and therefore is neither divisible nor excludable. Pork-barrel politics revolves around narrowly constructed but public goods, such as a bridge, a road, or a hospital in a district that benefits groups of people or territories and all the individuals in those categories benefit equally. The benefits of these types of politics tend to be more difficult to withdraw once granted and center around the material rewards more than the relationship.

Patronage is a more fuzzy category, because it can be particularistic (generally in the form of jobs), in which case it resembles clientelism; or it can be group-based, in which case it resembles pork barrel. As in the previous case, benefits of these types of politics tend to be more difficult to withdraw once granted and thus tend to promote political loyalty more than political dependence.

Patronage and pork-barrel politics, although thought of as belonging to the same species, exhibit specific differences and are admittedly less detrimental to the quality of the democratic system. Similarly, distributive politics, as Juan Pablo Luna and Rodrigo Mardones highlight, is still another distinct category and tends to have a far wider reach. Yet an important caveat is that even what may be designed as a distributive policy, say a conditional cash transfer, may be implemented clientelistically, as in Argentina, or in a more universalistic way, as in Chile and in Brazil, according chiefly to the nature of the parties in power and the capacity of the state.

The most widely used recent definitions of clientelism were put together by Stokes and Kitschelt and are fairly similar. According to Stokes, clientelism is a method of electoral mobilization defined as "the proffering of material goods in return for electoral support, where the criterion of distribution that the patron uses is simply: did you (will you) support me?"[10] For Kitschelt, "clientelistic accountability represents a transaction, the direct exchange of a citizen's vote in return for direct payments or continuing access to employment, goods, and services."[11] Without pretending to engage in a lengthy conceptual debate, for the purpose of this volume the concept of political clientelism will be used to refer to

- a set of asymmetric dyadic relationships that consists of the exchange of private and occasionally access to club goods and/or political influence to ensure that even non-excludable public goods reach their beneficiaries in a relatively expeditious manner in exchange for political support and/or loyalty that include but are not limited to voting

- that persists over time and tends to take the form of extended networks
- but that as result of the generalization of electoral politics may also take the form of a one-time interaction.

This definition relies on the existing literature cited above but only loosely, since disagreements are endemic and consensus exists only at a fairly broad level. Also, the reader will notice that "club" goods can only be dyadic when one thinks of one pair of the dyad as a group and thus will tend to think of the relationship as non-clientelistic. Yet on closer inspection, one discovers that even club goods—for example, help to people affected by a natural disaster, free health service and medicines for inhabitants of a shantytown, or school kits for poor children—may indeed be delivered through a clientelistic filter, and more often than not that not that is the case. Simeon Nichter addresses a dimension of this in his chapter on health care in northeast Brazil in this volume.

Other important questions, such as the question of commitment, dealing with swing versus core voters, the counterfactuals, and voter's coordination dilemmas, are addressed by Magaloni in her concluding chapter.

The Latin American Cases: Strategies of the Poor, Manipulation of the Elites

The first perspective, more structural and sociological, and the second, more decisional and political, different but not mutually exclusive, underlie, as it will be seen, the chapters of this volume.

In their comparative study of Argentina and Chile, Ernesto Calvo and Maria Victoria Murillo focus on the interaction between the distributive expectations of the voters and the parties. They begin by emphasizing—as Herbert Kitschelt had done earlier—that clientelistic parties influence how voters access all benefits, not just excludable goods, and they also examine how ideological distance from parties and proximity to party activists affect the distributive expectations of voters. As expected, ideological distance has a strong predictive effect in the case of Chile. In Argentina, by contrast, ideological distance has no significant predictive value, while proximity to party networks does. In short, they show how voters weigh the portfolio of goods offered by the parties, both excludable and nonexcludable, and how ideological affinity and party networks intervene in the definition of voters' expectations.

Both Luna and Mardones and Calvo and Murillo privilege the analysis from the point of view of the political parties. Luna and Mardones examine how the presence or absence of party machines and the strength of the state affect the likelihood of a clientelistic capture of social policies. In their analysis of Chile, quite a counterpoint to Argentina and Mexico, they show that in the absence of party machines—coupled with strong state capacity—social policies are more likely to fall into the realm of what can be considered distributive policies, either massive or selective, depending on the strength of the state as a constraining factor. In short, they demonstrate that in the absence of machine parties, like in Chile, social policies have political targeting but not a clientelistic rationale.

The chapters by Kent Eaton and Christopher Chambers-Ju and by Martin Tanaka and Carlos Meléndez explore two peculiar cases. The former demonstrates a particular subclass of clientelism, patronage, in the teachers' union FECODE. Eaton and Chambers-Ju prove that successive waves of institutional reforms have been unable to do away with the practice, which seems to metastasize from one institutional context to another, reconstituting itself after successive institutional reforms in the 1980s and 1990s attempted to eliminate or at least reduce them.

Hence, the assumption that collective actors would do away with clientelism proved wrong. In fact, when the locus of power was displaced from politicians to labor leaders, FECODE became the platform for labor "caciques" to establish their own clientelistic networks, and traditional patrons, formerly politicians, were replaced by labor leaders. Furthermore, the beneficiaries in this case were teachers, who can be considered middle or lower-middle class, whereas in the typical clientelistic setting the beneficiaries usually tend to be the informal and marginal population.

Interestingly, the authors also convincingly show that the idea that decentralization would do away with clientelism is wrong. Indeed, when substantial decentralization measures were introduced in the constitution and its amendments, national patrons were replaced by local ones, and the clientelistic networks remained intact if not stronger.

Likewise, when the electoral system was changed in the opposite direction to elect senators on a single national constituency rather than in smaller districts, the result was that candidates simply worked with local clientelistic networks as much as necessary. In short, what the Colombian case illustrates is that politicians, or labor leaders turned politicians, are unlikely to relinquish whatever voting power they have over a given electorate in the absence of strong negative or positive inducements to do so.

Tanaka and Melendez examine the anomalous case of Peru, where political parties failed to develop clientelistic apparatuses. Existing parties are neither programmatic, clientelistic, nor identity parties. As such, they fail to perform an intermediating role. Instead, this work is done by a network of relatively autonomous and competing brokers with allegiance neither to the parties that "hire" them nor to the people they purportedly serve. These brokers act as consultants and link local demands with the central bureaucracy, connecting local notables with popular organizations in an ever-changing set of alliances oriented to access local powers and engage in alliances of convenience around election time. The result is vertical and horizontal fragmentation, and the prevalence of a subclass of clientelism, pork-barrel politics, as brokers tend to mediate between entire geographical units rather than individual clients.

Javier Auyero, on the one hand, argues in his chapter that clientelistic networks thrive in a "gray zone" characterized by a "double life" of domination and veiling—and sometimes collective violence—where the needs of political machines, on the one hand, but, equally important, the daily survival imperative of the dispossessed, on the other, converge. His contribution tackles the indispensable examination of the phenomenon from the bottom up, a conceptual approach that is evidence of the rich contribution of ethnographic studies. His study highlights the agency capacity of the poor to get the most out of these policies.

Along similar lines, Nichter explores the strategies pursued by the poor in Brazil as they navigate the complicated process of local politics in order to situate themselves in the best possible position to benefit from the privileges and handouts of social policies at the subnational level. Thus, clientelism continues to be pervasive in small municipalities of less than 100,000 inhabitants, where the dispossessed develop a strategy of not declaring their political preferences as a hedge against the misfortune of picking a loser. Given that the provision of public services, especially health care, is heavily mediated by political networks, voters protect themselves by withholding their preferences. This differs quite starkly from the absence of a heavy clientelistic bias for the Bolsa Familia cash transfer program. In this case, program selection and targeting criteria are determined at the federal level and follow a very elaborate set of rules. However, the program is not flawless, because the information a recipient must provide includes their voter registration and precinct numbers.

Moreover, in addition to the usual "political" conditionalities, his study unveils a neglected dimension of gender violence, be it psychological, physical, or sexual. In short, in patriarchal societies we may be witnessing a transformation of traditional clientelistic relations into gender-based relations of domination and violence. The selection process has improved, but the implementation phase remains deeply troublesome.

Africa and East/Southeast Asia: Regime Types and State Bureaucracies

The cases of Africa examined by Nicolas Van de Walle in chapter 10 of this volume illustrate the evolution of clientelism in different regime types. During much of the postcolonial period in Africa, regimes were predominantly authoritarian. In highly presidential settings, clientelism was dominated by the executive branch and favored a "highly circumscribed socio-political elite." Clientelistic resources did not descend very far down the social pyramid. Instead, they were used to promote cross-ethnic elite accommodation, as presidents sought to build a viable coalition of national elites to support their rule.

As democratization processes began in the late 1980s, the locus of clientelism moved horizontally from the presidency to the parties and legislatures, and vertically from the better off to the poorer segments of the population. With the introduction of institutional devices such as the Constituency Development Funds in Gambia, Kenya, Uganda, Tanzania, Malawi, and Zambia comes a "codification of clientelism" that seems to suggest that clientelistic practices have come to stay. Van de Walle suggests that "clientelism should be understood as an inevitable and omnipresent feature of the modern state" and even more so in very poor countries at least "as long as the instruments of the new kind of politics, political parties, are weak and poorly organized."

The impact of the state bureaucracies and parties is quite salient in East and Southeast Asia in terms of the particular combinations that they assume. Thus Paul Hutchcroft, in chapter 8, shows how patterns of patronage vary across three countries based on their distinct institutional contexts: Japan (strong bureaucracy, strong parties), Thailand (strong bureaucracy, weak parties), and the Philippines (weak bureaucracy, weak parties). His focus is territorial politics, specifically the relative of importance of patronage in linking capital and countryside; only the Philippines, with its particularly weak institutional context, is labeled a "patronage-based state." On a conceptual level, Hutchcroft urges the untangling of two overlapping yet distinct concepts: patronage and clientelism. Whereas the former is a material resource, the latter is a personal relationship of power. Although this runs counter to the use of the term "clientelism" found in many other chapters of this volume, Hutchcroft asserts the need to achieve greater analytical precision between the two terms. He differentiates impersonal patronage from personalistic/clientelistic patronage and broadly surveys the mix of these two major types of patronage in Japan, Thailand, and the Philippines.

India, or Clientelism in a Caste Mold

In India, explains Kanchan Chandra, the pervasiveness of clientelism has transposed all barriers. The poor population, especially in rural areas, is especially vulnerable to clientelistic politics due to the difficulty of accessing state services, from hospital beds to medicines, land, electricity, water, roads, and security, both private and club goods. Even basic civic needs, such as a birth or death certificate or a caste certificate, are mediated by the favor of politicians. Additionally, given that some 70% of formal jobs are in the public sector, and 95% are in the lower ranks of the bureaucracy requiring little qualification, access to employment has also become a favor dispensed using clientelistic/patronage criteria.

Two distinctive elements set the Indian case apart. First, the basis upon which clientelism operates is ethnic. What appears to be rigidity, however, is countervailed by constant attempts at manufacturing new identities based on tribe, caste, region, language, or religion. Second, the links between politicians and clients are implied rather than direct. Clients read the clues sent by politicians and vote accordingly, and both receive their rewards. In this sense the relationship is more akin to a market transaction than to the tight networks of interpersonal relationships observed in most Latin American countries.

Structural Variables and Clientelism: Eastern and Central Europe and Russia

A classic set of questions is that of the relationship between more "advanced" socioeconomic settings and more "backward" or rural ones. Linda Cook's analysis of post-communist regimes highlights this interesting contrast. In post-communist regimes, classical clientelism is present in the less-developed, poorer, rural, and ethnically distinct regions such as Albania, Romania, Bulgaria, and rural Russia. In the more developed and urbanized regions, however, the extensive welfare system inherited from communism, a strong bureaucracy, higher levels of education, the predominance of the middle class, and the weak roots of the new parties that emerged after the collapse of communism configure a set of conditions inimical to the development of clientelism. Interestingly, as in Chile, the strong state bureaucracies in more developed countries reduce the spread of clientelistic ties.

In these settings, however, a particular intra-elite "exploitation" game that consists of the appropriation of resources for political or personal gains has emerged. Furthermore, this region also has witnessed the emergence of the "brokers for themselves" phenomenon, especially in the health sector. This consists of an extensive practice of requesting informal payments for the performance of certain services both by doctors and hospital administrators. Surveys indicated that through these shadow payments, surgeons may increase their income between 500 and 1000%, unit heads by 300 to 400%, other doctors and specialists by 200 to 300%, and nurses by between 20 and 200%. Can this reality be characterized as one of increasing private and atomized clientelism or outright atomized petty corruption?

Summing Up

The cases examined in this volume point to a number of important findings. In Latin America, the key variable to determine the presence and extent of clientelistic practices is the existence of machine parties. That is the case of Argentina, for example. In the absence of machine parties and the presence of a strong state, the outcome is distributive policies, as is the case in Chile. In the absence of machine parties but combined with weak states, the outcome is outsourced clientelism, as in Peru. In countries where machine and non-machine parties coexist with strong states, the outcome is distributive policies in some areas and clientelistic policies in others, depending on the issue area and the level of government (national or subnational) involved in the policy, as in Brazil. Gender plays a larger role in countries with machine parties (Argentina and Mexico) or weak states (Ecuador).

In Africa, different variables are at play. The most important predictor is regime type. Authoritarian regime types tend to produce narrow clientelistic networks that settle differences among ethnic groups. In democratic regimes, and to the extent that power shifts to parliaments, MPs begin to play a larger role, especially because of the availability of constituency development funds. Parties are weak, and thus clientelism tends to be rather personalistic.

In Asia and Southeast Asia, countries that by and large inherited strong monarchical legacies, the important variables are the state bureaucracies and the parties. When the state bureaucracies and the parties are strong, like in Japan, parties play an intermediary role and pork barrel prevails over clientelism. When bureaucracies are strong but parties are weak, clientelism is mostly administered by the state and also pork barrel prevails over clientelism. When both are weak, like in the Philippines, local clientelistic networks predominate.

In India, clientelism, patronage, and pork barrel are all strong and managed by the parties but on the basis of caste criteria; thus, the people attempt to manufacture new groups that would be eligible to receive benefits.

Clientelism, Quality of Democracy, and Democratic Stability

At the outset of this essay, we defined clientelism as particularly deleterious to the quality of democracy. This claims stands on firm ground. The evidence highlighted in the studies in this volume shows that by and large clientelism operates as the mechanism by which political elites hijack the political citizenry of the dispossessed in exchange for a low-quality social citizenship. As a comprehensive study by the Inter-American Development Bank has shown, even when clientelism is rooted more on the exchange of club than excludable goods, its impact on the overall quality of public policies is perverse.[12]

And yet there is another side to this coin. Kanchan Chandra strongly argues in her chapter that it is precisely the clientelistic nature of the Indian political system that makes it so stable and elicits such strong legitimacy. She even warns that the rapid process of modernization and privatization of the last few decades may erode the strong support for democracy that exists in India.

Similarly, Van de Walle argues in chapter 10 that "political clientelism should be understood as an inevitable and omnipresent feature of the modern state." The debate in academia raises this point often. For example, Steven Levitsky warns, somberly but wisely, that in "many middle and lower income countries the disappearance of clientelism would weaken, quite considerably, established political parties and, at least in the medium term, the result would be greater fragmentation, higher levels of volatility, and a greater likelihood of outsider politics and populism. This could well end up being worse for the quality of democracy."[13]

Along the same lines, Francis Fukuyama argued at the conference that "patron-client relations or patronage in general is a natural form of human association to which everyone defaults without having to be instructed. . . . [I]n the beginning everything was patrimonial, everything was clientelistic."[14]

Is it then, as Kitschelt argues, that in "democracies, from India to much of Latin America, clientelistic politics has constituted the functional equivalent of the welfare state, appeasing the have nots to abide by political orders that tremendously advantage the haves"?[15]

Fortunately, reality is not a coin, and thus one is not forced to choose heads or tails. In fact, without disputing the historical account about the evolution of societies and states—and while it is true that clientelistic networks and practices may play a stabilizing and even a democratizing role in certain lower- and middle-income countries at the early stages of the political development of democracy, as some of the contributors point out—it is also true that in the medium and long run they adversely affect the quality of democracy, for clientelism cannot substitute for citizenship.

However, the question is whether countries can simply "grow out of it" or whether other factors, such as the strength of the state, economic development, and the like, will end up wiping clientelism out and replacing it with more developed distributive schemes. The available evidence seems to suggest that in the absence of an effective strategy to combat political clientelism, countries grow deeper into it rather that out of it. They are, if we were to use a game-theoretical analogy, sub-optimal outcomes in a prisoner's dilemma situation; and as such, they do contain the seeds of their own undoing. After all, haven't current populist regimes in Latin America such as Ecuador, Venezuela, and Nicaragua emerged in countries with preexisting heavy partisan clientelistic networks?

Policy Implications for Governments, Challenges for Civil Society

Given the fact that social policies are, will be, and should remain at the forefront of the public policy agenda for the time to come, how can we best ensure that they are protected from the distortions that clientelism brings about? This volume ends with some tentative reflections about how best to address that challenge. Referring again to the prisoner's dilemma analogy, what kind of cooperative game can be triggered to produce a Pareto-optimal outcome, in which all players obtain the best socially feasible outcome?

Beatriz Magaloni makes a number of suggestions for policy makers. Development, certainly, is in the long run the surest bet, but other strategies of more immediate impact are possible. These include portfolio diversification, better institutional design, the strengthening of veto powers to check politicians, and the Ulyssean resource of tying the hands of political elites until the Sirens' island is left behind. I would add that strengthening the state and avoiding excessive decentralization are also important factors. The first argument is clearly implied in both Luna and Mardones's and Cook's contributions. As for the second, as Nichter shows clearly for the case of Brazil, programs run by the federal government involve far less clientelism than locally run ones. Similarly, Eaton and Chambers-Ju demonstrate how shallow the promise of decentralization is when the question is to evaluate concrete results. In the case of Japan, as Hutchcroft argues, the strong state/strong parties combination produces substantial amount of "meso-particularism," not an optimum outcome but less detrimental than clientelism, or "micro-particularism."

Yet the solution cannot be left in the hands of the political system alone. Civil society has an important role to play. After all, tackling the challenge of ensuring the social citizenship of the dispossessed without simultaneously sacrificing their political citizenship by reducing them to clients is a challenge that demands the concerted effort of reformist politicians and effective civil society organizations.

NOTES

1. For an earlier and illuminating precedent, see Jonathan Fox, "The Difficult Transition from Clientelism to Citizenship: Lessons from Mexico," *World Politics* 46, no. 2 (1974): 151–84.

2. Steven Levitsky, *Transforming Labor-Based Parties in Latin America: Argentine Peronism in Comparative Perspective* (New York: Cambridge University Press, 2003); Steven Levitsky and Gretchen Helmke, *Informal Institutions and Democracy: Lessons from Latin America* (Baltimore: Johns Hopkins University Press, 2006); Susan C. Stokes, "Perverse Accountability: A Formal Model of Machine Politics with Evidence from Argentina," *American Political Science Review* 99, no. 3 (2005): 315–25; Karen Remmer, "The Political Economy of Patronage: Expenditure Patterns in the Argentine Provinces, 1983–2003," *Journal of Politics* 69, no. 2 (2007): 363–77.

3. Herbert Kitschelt and Steven Wilkinson, *Patrons, Clients, and Policies: Patterns of Democratic Accountability and Political Competition* (New York: Cambridge University Press, 2007).

4. Susan C. Stokes, "Political Clientelism," in *The Oxford Handbook of Political Science,* ed. Robert E. Goodin (New York: Oxford University Press, 2009), 648–72.

5. James C. Scott, "Corruption, Machine Politics, and Political Change," *American Political Science Review* 63, no. 4 (1969): 1142–58, and "Patron-Client Politics and Political Change in Southeast Asia," *American Political Science Review* 66, no. 1 (1972): 91–113; Steffen Schmidt, J. Scott, J. C. Lande, and L. Gasti, *Friends, Followers, and Factions: A Reader in Political Clientelism* (Berkeley: University of California Press, 1977); S. N. Eisenstadt and Rene Lemarchand, *Political Clientelism, Patronage, and Development* (Beverly Hills, CA: Sage Publications, 1981); Ernest Gellner and John Waterbury, *Patrons and Clients in Mediterranean Societies* (Hanover, NH: Center for Mediterranean Studies of the American Universities Field Staff, 1977).

6. Scott, "Patron-Client Politics," 92, 108.

7. Martin Shefter, "Party and Patronage: Germany, England, and Italy," *Politics and Society* 7 (1977): 403–51.

8. Ibid., 410.

9. Stokes, "Perverse Accountability," 315–25; Simeon Nichter, "Vote Buying or Turnout Buying? Machine Politics and the Secret Vote," *American Political Science Review* 102 (2008): 19–31; Ernesto Calvo and María Victoria Murillo, "Who Delivers? Partisan Clients in Argentina Electoral Markets," *American Journal of Political Science,* 48, no. 4 (2004): 742–57; and Leonard Wantchekon, "Clientelism and Voting Behavior: Evidence from a Field Experiment in Benin," *World Politics* 55 (2003): 399–422.

10. Stokes, "Political Clientelism," 648–49.

11. Kitschelt and Wilkinson, *Patrons, Clients, and Policies*, 2.

12. *The Politics of Policies: Economic and Social Progress in Latin America, 2006 Report* (Washington, DC: IADB, 2006).

13. Personal communication to the author, November 8, 2011.

14. Personal communication to the author, November 8, 2011.

15. Kitschelt, "Linkages between Citizens and Politicians in Democratic Polities," *Comparative Political Studies* 33 (2000): 873.

PART ONE

LESSONS IN CLIENTELISM
FROM LATIN AMERICA

CHAPTER ONE

Partisan Linkages and Social Policy Delivery in Argentina and Chile

ERNESTO CALVO AND MARÍA VICTORIA MURILLO

Widespread democratization since the 1970s has generated a reassessment of the literature on party-voter linkages, with a special emphasis on whether distributive ties should be characterized as programmatic or clientelistic (see the introduction to this volume). As the delivery of private and public goods for electoral gain has become the subject of scholarly scrutiny, researchers have sought a better integration of the programmatic and clientelistic incentives that determine the strategies of parties and the behavior of voters.[1] The early literature on distributive politics saw programmatic and clientelistic parties as analytically and historically distinct. Consequently, scholars proposed competing theories to explain the electoral strategies of distinctly programmatic or clientelistic parties. Distinct theories, in turn, demanded different characterizations of programmatic and clientelistic voters.

Drawing heavily from Responsible Party models of U.S. politics, scholars characterized programmatic linkages as a policy tie where parties deliver public goods to ideologically committed voters. These voters relied on informational shortcuts (cues) to make voting decisions and develop policy expectations consistent with the electoral platforms of programmatic parties.[2] As it was eloquently described by Miller and Stokes:

> Under a system of party government the voters' response to the local legislative candidates is based on the candidates' identification with party programs. These programs are the substance of their appeals to the constituency, which will act on the basis of its information about the proposals and legislative record of the parties. Since the party programs are of dominant importance, the candidates are deprived of any independent basis of support. They will not be able to build in their home districts an electoral redoubt from which to challenge the leadership of their parties.[3]

By contrast, a separate literature described clientelistic linkages in starkly different terms, explaining the non-programmatic distribution of particularistic benefits to a restricted menu of voters on sociohistorical grounds. As described by Kitschelt and Wilkinson:

> In a clientelistic relationship, in contrast, the politician's delivery of a good is *contingent upon* the actions of specific members of the electorate. . . . What makes clientelistic exchange distinctive is not simply the fact that the benefits are targeted. Rather, it is the fact that politicians target the benefits *only* to individuals or identifiable small groups who have already delivered or who promise to deliver their electoral support to the partisan benefactor."[4]

The publication of Cox and McCubbins's *Electoral Politics as a Redistributive Game*[5] began to bridge the gulf between the clientelistic and programmatic party literatures. For the next twenty years, an increasing number of scholars recognized the programmatic and non-programmatic behavior of parties as complementary strategies.[6] Rather than a distinguishing trait of party systems, programmatic and non-programmatic distributive incentives became theoretically and empirically intertwined. However, we have yet to see an equally integrated model that explains the distributive preferences of voters.

In this chapter we fill this gap in the literature, showing that voters develop programmatic and non-programmatic expectations in regard to the delivery of private, club, and public goods. We demonstrate the distinct role of partisan networks and ideological attachments to explain the distributive expectations of voters by emphasizing how access to publicly provided benefits shapes voters' distributive expectations.

We argue that, just as parties offer voters a portfolio of benefits that include programmatic policies and non-programmatic goods, voters develop distributive expectations in regard to the delivery of public policies and goods. We describe distinct mechanisms that explain the programmatic and non-programmatic components of voters' attitudes. We provide evidence that clientelistic linkages are mediated by partisan networks that screen *deserving* voters. By contrast, programmatic linkages result from ideological attachments that may be orthogonal to partisan distribution networks.

To support our argument, we center our empirical analyses on two well-known case studies: Argentina and Chile. While researchers tend to characterize Chilean parties as programmatic and Argentine parties as clientelistic, this chapter shows that voters in these countries have distributive expectations that include both determinants of distributive expectations. Finally, we explain how partisan networks and ideological affinity differ in voters of both countries.

First, we describe the formation of party-voter linkages in Latin America, which are characterized by partisan networks that connect voters to party members as well as by policy affinity traits. In the following section, we explain how these existing partisan linkages shape the distributive expectations of voters in Latin America. We then analyze party-voter linkages in Argentina and Chile and conclude by discussing the policy implications of our analysis.

Partisan Linkages and Social Policy Delivery in the New Latin American Democracies

The literature on Latin American political parties has always emphasized their non-ideological character and weak institutionalization.[7] After the return of democracy and its coincidence with dramatic shifts in models of economic development, recent contributions have focused on the increasing reliance of Latin American political parties on clientelism and patronage for electoral gain. Throughout the 1990s, the combination of intense electoral competition and tighter fiscal environments made political parties increasingly dependent on the distribution of handouts—clientelism—and public jobs—patronage. According to this literature, the convergence toward market reforms in the 1990s limited the ability of political parties to legislate more universal redistributive policies, thereby increasing the pressure to deliver private goods to particular constituencies in order to muster political support.[8] In a context of state retrenchment, populist parties became ever more reliant on the access and distribution of particularistic benefits.

The expanding literature on clientelism in the region has benefited from an emphasis on the strategies of political parties and governments in using private goods distribution to foster political support. This literature provides important insights on the design of programs,[9] the portfolio of goods being distributed,[10] the shift from programmatic to clientelistic strategies,[11] the impact of differential access to fiscal resources,[12] and the mobilization strategies that underlie the choice of different targets of distribution.[13] Our research, by contrast, focuses on the demand side by looking at voters' distributive expectations and how they are shaped by prior experiences in the distribution of publicly financed benefits. In so doing, we assume that voter-party linkages are not spot exchanges of vote buying as described in Stokes,[14] but based on longer-term interactions with political organizations and public officials. These interactions shape voters' perceptions in regard to the political venues to access publicly funded benefits and their assessment of political parties.

In our view, voters are self-interested social actors, embedded in a complex web of political networks, who update their preferences based on information about the likelihood of receiving public and private benefits from parties. We distinguish *distributive preferences* from *distributive expectations*, with *preferences* being explained by voters' social and economic traits such as income, education, or skills, and *expectations* being explained by the perceived likelihood that parties will deliver goods and the mechanism shaping their *access* to such benefits. Such expectations, we argue, have a crucial role in defining voters' electoral behavior and thereby the programmatic and non-programmatic linkages connecting voters to parties.

Whereas most of the prior literature on voter-party linkages has focused on the delivery of different types of goods—public or private—for distinguishing programmatic from clientelistic parties, our classification probes the question of how voters access benefits. For example, while conditional cash transfers are now prominent in much of Latin America,[15] access to benefits could result from voters being proximate to party brokers or from bureaucratically defined rules that identify a target population. Access to unemployment insurance could be mediated by party brokers in one country and by bureaucratic agencies in another. Public sector posts could be filled by open searches under civil service rules or at the discretion of senior party figures. In other words, the same public or private goods may serve diverse political goals in different political environments depending on how policy access is defined in the letter of the law and, more importantly, in its implementation.

Differences in the role of party organizations for delivering publicly funded resources, in turn, are shaped by institutional constraints on policy implementation. This distinction is crucial to assess, whether or not the distributive expectations of voters are associated with specific delivery mechanisms. Consequently, while we do not ignore differences in the excludability of goods, our focus is on whether policies are implemented in a manner in which benefits depend on a voter's proximity to party members or are independent of such a connection.

Voters' Distributive Expectations and Political Linkages

Voters' distributive expectations result from their prior interactions with political networks, as described in the ethnographic literature,[16] and from retrospective assessments of policy implementation that determine eligibility to publicly provided benefits. Consequently, party-voter linkages vary both across countries (depending on institutional constraints on policy implementation) and across parties (depending on organizational capacity to deliver benefits through networks or to credibly commit to programmatic redistribution using ideological cues).

Based on prior distributive experiences, voters assign importance or weight to their connections to members of different parties as a critical mechanism for accessing benefits. Voters also assign varying levels of significance to their ideological distance from candidates of different parties. Consequently, voter-specific distributive expectations result from the relative proximity of voters to partisan networks and their relative policy distance. Consequently, whereas preferences for redistribution may be explained by socioeconomic traits such as income, class, or education, partisan networks and policy positioning play a key role in shaping the distributive expectations of voters.

We assume that voters perceive political parties as providers of benefits that are independently delivered through public policy and partisan networks. Differences in the import voters attach to each of these mechanisms in accessing publicly funded goods, we argue, allows us to distinguish between programmatic and clientelistic linkages. The emphasis on access to excludable private goods is of critical importance since the same benefit can be delivered through general criteria (either universal or group-based) or through personal connections between voters and members of parties. However, the weight that voters attach to their proximity to party members and/or their ideological affinity to platforms varies greatly, given that voters neither share the same connection to all parties nor obtain identical returns from clientelistic or programmatic distribution.

The distributive expectations of voters are characterized by three main components. First, voters have different tastes for distribution, which are largely explained by socioeconomic traits that determine the marginal value of the benefit received. A second component is the weight that individual voters attach to the probability of receiving benefits based on their ideological proximity to parties—independent of party membership. In this case, targeted distribution is the result of policies that voters perceive as beneficial to their group category. Finally, the third component is the importance that each individual voter attaches to his or her connection to party members in developing expectations for accessing benefits conditional on patterns of policy implementation that allow parties discretion in the delivery of publicly provided benefits.

It is important to note that proximity to party members is not simply need-based. Even if a voter is eager to receive goods from a party, he or she may be far removed from party members that are in position to provide access to those goods. Additionally, in contrast to ideological affinity, connection to political networks is a function of the size of an individual's personal network, of each party's organizational capacity, and of the ties that connect voters to members of each party. Because networks evolve slowly over time and require considerable effort to absorb new entrants, voters may more easily take on new ideological or programmatic positions than expand the number of ties to party members within a political network. Hence, in weighing parties' distributive promises, voters internalize the impact of institutional and organizational constraints that shape the delivery of publicly funded benefits.

Voters' distributive expectations depend on the additive combination of goods delivered, through ideological and network proximity, by parties who control different agencies and levels of government and by differences in labor market endowments (e.g., income, education, skills, etc.). Voters with similar distributive preferences and skills can still draw different benefits from these partisan networks. Whereas a low-skilled worker would perceive significant benefits from receiving a public sector job, access to such job depends critically on his or her proximity to party members in a position to deliver employment. By contrast, citizens are likely to benefit from more progressive tax policies, regardless of their connections to party members.

Voters' perceptions of the distributive benefits of partisan networks, in turn, are shaped by the organizational capacity of parties to deliver excludable goods as well as by institutional constraints on their ability to access public resources and utilize partisan networks for distribution. Subject to clearly differentiable budget constraints, not all parties will be in the same position to provide voters with equivalent combinations of goods delivered through networks and through nondiscretionary criteria. Because political parties face budgetary constraints related to the access and distribution of excludable benefits, the supply of clientelistic resources affects parties differently and is independent from programmatic decisions to implement general redistributive policies. Therefore, whereas political parties with dense organizational networks can choose between clientelistic and programmatic linkages, those lacking such networks are restricted to the latter.

Voters' experiences with each mechanism for accessing benefits shape the nature of their linkages to parties. If they perceive networks as the crucial means for accessing benefits, they will place more value on their proximity to party members in forming their distributive expectations. By contrast, if electoral platforms cue voters to policies that parties will likely implement, voters may rely on ideological proximity when defining their distributive expectations. Whereas the former process will foster clientelistic linkages between parties and voters, the latter will contribute to building programmatic linkages associated to ideological cues. In short, because political systems vary in terms of the institutional constraints they impose on the partisan distribution of excludable goods, and parties differ in organizational capacity to access and deliver resources, we expect variation in party-voter linkages across and within countries. In the following section we use this framework to explain variation in the distributive expectations of Argentine and Chilean voters, which in turn shapes the different types of linkages we observe in those countries.

Clientelistic and Programmatic Views of Partisan Politics in Argentina and Chile

Current research considers Chile and Argentina as characterized predominantly by distinct programmatic and clientelistic parties, respectively.[17] Similar on many factors theorized to affect voter-party linkages, both countries have democratized recently—Argentina in 1983 and Chile 1990—and have well-established mass parties that rely on clearly identifiable party labels and on their power over candidate nominations.[18] Both countries have a presidential executive, multiparty environments, similar levels of economic development, and ethnic, religious, and cultural legacies.

The party systems that emerged after their transitions to democracy were based on political parties and coalitions already in place prior to the repressive military regimes that ruled each country. However, current research views the Argentine party system as characterized by non-ideological and patronage-prone catchall parties: the Peronists (Partido Justicialista, or PJ) and the Radicals (Unión Cívica Radical, or UCR).[19] The two main parties have alternated in the Executive since the return of democracy in 1983. The Radicals won the 1983 and the 1999 presidential elections (the latter in a coalition with a center-left party), and the Peronists won the 1989, 1995, 2003, and 2007 elections. However, unified government—when the party of the president also controls both chambers of Congress—has only occurred under some Peronist presidents, because the Radicals have never been able to win control of the Senate. Moreover, Argentina is a federal country, and the Peronists have controlled a majority of governorships and municipalities since the return of democracy, thereby gaining more access to fiscal resources for distribution because most social policies are implemented at the provincial or municipal level.[20]

In spite of proportional representation (PR), electoral rules enacted by authoritarian rulers to minimize the electoral might of Peronists, most votes in Argentina concentrated in very few parties since democratization. The sum of the vote of the two main parties, the PJ and the UCR, ranged from 88.5% in 1983 to 67.6% in 1995.[21] In 1997, the electoral growth of a center-left party called FREPASO (Front for a Country in Solidarity) brought the Radicals to join it in an electoral coalition to win the 1999 presidential election. The collapse of a UCR-led coalition government in 2001, however, led to a substantive growth in electoral volatility, as both the UCR and the FREPASO were shunned by voters, thus reestablishing the historical dominance of the Peronists.[22] As the UCR struggled to produce credible presidential candidates, new parties emerged in an attempt to attract the non-Peronist vote. However, the UCR remains the most significant alternative to the PJ at the provincial level.

In contrast to Argentina's party system, the Chilean parties have historically been described as programmatic.[23] Before the 1973 military coup, the polity was divided into three ideological blocs (the right, the center, and the left). In 1988, two electoral coalitions of clear ideological orientation emerged during the campaign for a plebiscite on the transition to democracy. The electoral stability of these two coalitions has been reinforced since the transition to democracy by its binomial electoral system. This electoral system requires the winner to double the votes of the runner up to gain the two seats assigned to the district.[24] It thus generates an over-representation of the loser and favors the election of one legislator from each of the two main electoral coalitions that dominated Chilean politics since the transition to democracy. The center-left coalition is called Concertacion de Partidos por la Democracia (Coalition of Parties for Democracy) and includes three main parties: the Socialist Party (PS), the Christian Democratic Party (DC), and the Party for Democracy (PPD)—which split from the Socialist Party—along with other minor political parties. The Concertacion won four successive presidential elections and held the executive seat between 1990 and 2010. During this period, it had the majority in the lower chamber and gained control of the Senate after a constitutional reform removed the nonelected senators established by the outgoing military regime in 2005.

The center-right coalition is called Alianza por Chile (Alliance for Chile) and includes two parties: the National Renovation (RN), which is the heir of the traditional conservative party, and the Independent Democratic Union (UDI), which was founded by personnel of the military regime.[25] With the exception of the 2005 election, RN and UDI have always coordinated their presidential candidates and legislative electoral campaigns because the binominal electoral system favors the representation of a legislator from each coalition in a majority of districts. This coalition won the 2009 presidential election and currently holds the Presidency.

In addition to the differences between party system and the political organization —federal in Argentina and unitary in Chile—there is crucial variation in institutional constraints on the delivery of social policy that further shape the perceptions of voters about the importance of ideology and networks in guiding their distributive expectations. Chilean parties face tighter regulation and greater difficulties than their Argentine counterparts in allocating publicly funded goods through their political networks. Whereas in Argentina the resources of social programs are allocated to voters through political networks, in Chile, social policy distribution is conducted by bureaucratic agencies.[26] Differences in the role of networks imply that two workfare programs with similar designs on paper, such as *Chile Solidario* in Chile and *Jefes y Jefas de Hogar* in Argentina, both of which are implemented and administered at the municipal level, have very different delivery practices. We assume these different procedures reinforce perceptions about the role of networks in access to publicly provided benefits only in Argentina.

In addition to social policy, the Argentine public sector is more politicized than is the Chilean one.[27] Party brokers depend on patronage to sustain their political machines,[28] and public employees are required to engage in political activities—especially the large number of temporary employees appointed by current mayors without guaranteed tenure.[29] Hence, public sector jobs in Argentina are dependent on political contacts, thereby shaping voters' perceptions that the likelihood of obtaining a public sector job is related to their connection to party organizations and especially with active political participation.[30] By contrast, the several civil service reforms reduced the capacity of Chilean parties to use patronage for sustaining their organizations, while the system of party quotas within the governing coalition reduced the discretion of any one party in appointments.[31] Civil service rules, thus, should make voters perceive that access to public sector jobs is less likely to be mediated by networks in Chile than in Argentina.[32] An advisor to Socialist President Michelle Bachelet explained this policy in a personal interview with the authors:

> [Patronage] is a survival strategy that brings [political] bread today and [political] hunger tomorrow. President [Bachelet] in current surveys has an honesty index of 91%. There are more people in Chile that think that the president is honest than people that think their grandmother is honest. And that gives you great political benefits, much more than to hire your cousin, nephew, brother-in-law. If the crooks knew how good a business is to be honest, they would be honest just because of how crooked they are.[33]

As a result, Chilean politicians rely more on privately financed goods and services to persuade voters. As described by a PPD representative who is also a doctor:

> We go and provide medical services to people: "Please, come in; let me know what hurts." And we have a system of pharmacies that gives them medicine. I buy the medicine, or friends who are doctors give them to me. And the veterinarians take the parasites out of pets, the lawyers provide legal advice, and teachers play with the kids, they paint their faces, and a guy from the radio provides entertainment and karaoke. All of it on Saturday morning in my headquarters.[34]

Similarly, a UDI representative described his work with constituents in the following way:

> We made a law . . . at the proposal of UDI representatives, that allows the sale or gift of glasses for farsightedness without a medical prescription as a transitory

solution . . . we adopted this program that allows us to have daily contact, almost the obligation to be in permanent contact with the voter . . . [and we deliver the glasses] . . . in their homes, in the sports clubs, in the neighborhood associations, in the parks. I have a mobile office that offers the program.[35]

Institutional constraints lead us to expect variation in the development of clientelistic and programmatic linkages across both countries since party networks have more ability to shape access to publicly funded resources in Argentina than in Chile. Yet variation in the capacity of voters to use ideology to identify the distributive goals of parties and in the organizational structure and ability of parties to distribute publicly funded resources should generate patterns of variation within countries.

Ideology and Party Organization in Argentina and Chile

Given the differences in the institutional constraints for using political networks for the distribution of publicly funded benefits, we need to assess the ability of voters to either use ideology or rely on their proximity to political organizations to inform their distributive expectations. We expect clientelistic linkages to be strongest when voters have prior experience with strong political machines used to distribute publicly funded benefits, especially when ideology cannot serve as a cue for programmatic distribution so that proximity to such networks has greater weight in defining distributive expectations.

Using an original survey of 2,800 voters conducted in Argentina and Chile in early 2007, we show that Chilean voters could readily identify the ideological orientation of parties in a dominant left-right dimension. As shown in figure 1.1, a majority of Chileans identify the PS on the left side of the political spectrum, with 70% of respondents characterizing the party as outright left (40.3%) or center-left (30%). Seventy-six percent of respondents identify the DC in the center and locate the PPD as center-left, between the PS and the DC. Respondents also clearly identify the RN and UDI by their ideological placement on the right of the political spectrum. Thus in Chile, ideology is a useful cue for voters in defining their distributive expectations. Moreover, the post-transition Chilean party system displays remarkable ideological stability and low electoral volatility, and in every election since 1990 the two coalitions have gathered more than three-quarters of the vote.

By contrast, Argentina's two main political parties were established as catchall parties appealing to broad multiclass coalitions and thereby chose not to define themselves ideologically. The Radical Civic Union (UCR), established in the 1890s, and the Partido Justicialista (PJ), created by Juan Perón in the 1940s, lack clear

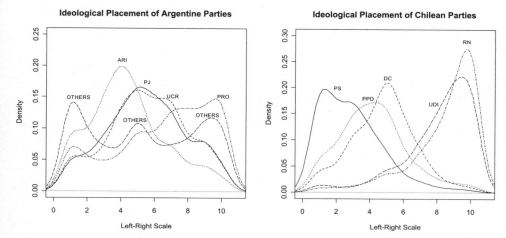

Figure 1.1. Reported Ideological Location of Largest Political Parties in Chile and Argentina

ideological niches—although the PJ possesses more extensive labor-based roots, and the Radicals a stronger appeal to the middle class.[36] Our survey results reflect the difficulties voters have in locating the parties ideologically. The ideological mode of the PJ, with its centrist position, only includes 21% of respondents; this increases to 47% if we combine the categories of center, center-left, and center-right. Similarly, the UCR mode includes only 18.4% of respondents, increasing to 45% if we include the categories of center, center-left, and center-right. The survey also reported a high number of nonresponses to the ideology questions: 36% of those surveyed did not respond for the PJ, and 40% for the UCR. Two of the new parties that formed in response to the 2001 economic crisis were the Alliance for a Republic of Equality (ARI) and Republican Proposal (PRO), with better defined ideological profiles and clear programmatic goals that catered to voters on the center-left and center-right, respectively (see fig. 1.1). However, electoral support for these new parties is limited to metropolitan areas.

In sum, the weak ideological identifications of the two major parties in Argentina make it difficult for voters to use ideology as a distributive cue, whereas Chilean voters (and voters for two minor Argentine parties) can more clearly identify the policy goals of parties and coalitions. These differences in the impact of ideological cues should affect voters' capacity to form expectations about policy redistribution to groups of citizens through general criteria.

Regarding the strength of party organization, Kitschelt and Wilkinson articulate the conventional wisdom: "Because programmatic party competition does not necessitate direct individual or indirect social-network-based monitoring of voters' electoral conduct, it is cheaper to construct organizational machines than in the clientelistic case. After all, programmatic parties need fewer personnel to manage exchange relations."[37] Using the same survey, we applied a measurement technique to assess the scope and structure of networks—both personal and political—so that we are able to estimate the size of networks of party activists, party candidates, and the number of voters who received gifts, favors, or handouts from each party in both countries.[38] Using such data, we find that, contrary to Kitschelt and Wilkinson, the number of political activists is similar across the two countries despite the different weight of ideological cues in defining political parties' future behavior. Political activists comprise up to 1.4% of the population in Argentina and 1.2% in Chile. Hence, a strong party organization may be a necessary, but not sufficient, condition for defining clientelistic linkages.

In spite of these similarities, there are also cross-country differences in party organization. All Chilean political parties have relatively similar contingents of activists. The Socialist Party has the largest network of activists, which includes around 45,000 people or 0.356% of the Chilean population. The PS is not much larger than its competitors: the Christian Democrats (0.299%), the PPD (0.2%), the UDI (0.2%), and the smaller RN (0.147%). By contrast, in Argentina, the contingent of PJ activists is much larger than that of their competitors. The PJ has approximately 291,000 activists, representing 0.766% of the Argentine population, almost twice the number of activists of the UCR (approximately 160,000 or 0.42% of the population). Both activist contingents are dramatically larger than those of the young PRO and ARI, which include 0.029 and 0.056% of the Argentine population, respectively. The role of the Peronist network in delivering benefits to voters has been widely documented,[39] but the following quotation from a personal interview with a PJ activist in the province of Buenos Aires provides a good illustration of how experience often shapes voters' perceptions:

> We call it "multiplicative work": each of us has acquaintances in the street where we live, friends. We tell each of them to get out, to speak, to publicize our political work. Thanks to this "multiplicative work" we are known around here, because we do not control any media outlet. Groundwork [trabajo de base], wherever we are needed we go. They call us from some community and say: "We have a problem, the street needs repairing, the water, the septic tanks, we call the municipality and they are taking two, three days."[40]

Differences in the size of activists' networks in Argentina reflect the Peronists' post-2001 electoral dominance and the fragility of new entrants in the political system as well as the impact of historical legacies in the development of the PJ and UCR networks. That is, despite the electoral weakening of the UCR, the slow evolution of networks has endowed both parties with a greater capacity than their rivals to deliver benefits through political networks. As described by a Radical representative (and former presidential candidate): *"[The UCR] is a party that keeps its organization . . . it is a network that was developed in more than a hundred years, it cannot collapse overnight. It can have ups and downs, it can go forward or backward, but it does not disappear overnight."*[41]

Hence, networks are slow to build, and the predominance of Peronism in building its political organization reflects its impact on voters, who have firsthand experience with its capacity to deliver. According to our calculations, the number of voters who received handouts from the PJ in 2007 includes 0.48% of the population (185,000 people approximately), and is more than twice as large as that of the UCR—with 0.19% or around 72,500 voters—and much larger than those of other parties. This predominance is explained by the combined effect of larger political networks and access to fiscal resources due to the Peronist predominance in governorships and municipalities across the country.[42]

Although networks provide capacity for delivering handouts, they do not imply that parties will choose to employ their organizational capacity in that way. This is confirmed by the differences in the range of distribution of handouts in Chile, where the Socialists have the largest network of activists, but not of handout distribution, which in their case reaches 0.11% of the population or 17,250 citizens approximately. By contrast, the UDI has a smaller network of activists than the Socialists but provides handouts to the largest number of people (0.155% of the population or 23,400 people), which still remains less than the proportion of the population reached by the Argentine Radicals. This is remarkable, given the clear ideological location of the UDI on the right of the political spectrum (see the single peaked distribution on fig. 1.1) and confirms Luna's account of an electoral strategy that combines ideological appeal from well-off voters and clientelism—financed by private funds—for poorer voters.[43]

In short, whereas the proportion of activists in the population is similar across both countries, the differences in the way their parties work seem to be associated with the advantage of the Peronist (and to a lesser extend the Radicals) in terms of the reach of their organization and its capacity to deliver publicly funded benefits. Put differently, political networks seem to constitute a necessary but insufficient condition for the construction of clientelistic linkages between parties and voters. As a result, whereas in Argentina the larger size of the PJ activists' network correlates with the largest number of handout recipients, in Chile the Socialists have the largest activists' network, but the UDI has the largest number of handout recipients. Moreover, Chilean political parties are more balanced in their level of organizational capacity than are Argentine ones, thereby reducing the incentives for any of them to increase discretion—and therefore clientelism—in the delivery of public policy, since none of them will clearly benefit.

Distributive Expectations and Social Policy in Argentina and Chile

The combination of institutional constraints on policy delivery, party organization, and ideological identification by voters leads us to expect that voters would be more likely in Chile than in Argentina to use ideology (and their ideological distance from each political party) to define their distributive expectations. However, in Argentina we expect that voters for the two new and more ideological parties could use ideology in forming their distributive expectations, even when we do not expect this to be the case for supporters of the PJ and the UCR. Moreover, in thinking about the impact of party organizations, political networks should not have a strong effect on voters' distributive expectations in Chile, but connections with party organizations should be important in defining the distributive expectations of voters regarding the Argentine PJ and UCR. We have associated these differences not only to the easier time that voters have in identifying parties' ideology in Chile and to more even nature of party organization in Chile but also to institutional differences reducing the capacity of parties to rely on networks to distribute publicly financed private goods. To assess this last effect, we use two programs that look similar on paper—the Argentine *Jefes y Jefas de Hogar* and the Chilean *Chile Solidario*—but which we expect to shape voters' expectations of receiving handouts from parties only in Argentina.

Analyses from two 2007 surveys conducted in Argentina and Chile provide statistical evidence of the determinants of distributive expectations in these two countries.[44] In these surveys, we asked respondents to report, on a scale from 0 to 10, "How likely would it be that, after winning the election, [*Party j*] would provide you with [food, clothing, money, or other material benefits] or [a public job]?"[45] We then used a number of covariates to find out what determines the distributive expectations of voters.

Findings show that in Chile, a one-unit increase in ideological proximity between voters and activists from the Concertacion resulted roughly in a ≈3% increase in the expectations of receiving handouts. However, ideological proximity failed to explain expectations of handout distribution for the UDI and RN. The effect of ideological proximity on public sector employment was statistically significant for all five Chilean parties, with a one-unit increase in ideological proximity leading to a roughly ≈2% to ≈4% increase in the expectations of being offered a public sector job.

While ideological proximity had a statistically significant effect in the expectation of perceiving goods in Chile, linkages to the party organization (assessed by the number of activists that voters were connected to in a sustained relationship) had no statistically significant effect on the expectation of receiving handouts and just a small effect for public sector employment by the PS and the DC. Our findings thus confirm that ideological cues had a stronger impact than party organization in shaping the distributive expectations of Chilean voters, even for non-policy-provided benefits. We also found no effect of voters' connections to the network of recipients of *Chile Solidario* on the expectation of receiving handouts. This finding confirms our expectations about institutional constraints since connections to recipients of *Chile Solidario* are a proxy for voters' experience on how the state distributes a cash transfer program that could shape their views about parties' distributive intentions. Moreover, we complement the findings of Luna on the UDI by showing that it distributes not only to poor voters but also to voters who are ideologically distant from the party and not well connected to its activists. These findings confirm interviews with UDI politicians in which they claim the provision of goods and services is a mechanism to attract voters, who can then be persuaded by the party ideas.

In Argentina, by contrast, ideological proximity between voters and parties had no statistically significant effect on the expectation of receiving handouts or a public sector employment from the Peronists or the Radicals. Conversely, the connections between voters and PJ and UCR activists does shape the expectations of receiving handouts, with a one standard deviation increase in proximity to the network of activists resulting in a ≈7% increase in the expectation of receiving handouts from the Peronists and a ≈5% increase in the expectation of receiving handouts from the Radicals. The effect was even stronger for public sector job offers, resulting in a 9.5% increase for the Peronists and 6.5% increase for the Radicals.[46] Moreover, in defining expectations of getting a public job, voters' connections to both the network of party activists and that of party candidates shapes their expectations in a positive way.

The more connections to party activists and candidates, the more voters are likely to expect a public job if this party wins the election. These findings correspond with the literature on Argentine politics that suggests that public jobs are more likely to be distributed among party activists or volunteers, who then can participate in political activities, whereas handouts are distributed to voters and participants in meetings.[47] Moreover, voters who are more connected to the network of recipients of *Jefes y Jefas de Hogar* (meaning they know more recipients than the average population controlling for the size of their personal network) have higher expectations of receiving handouts from the Peronist and the Radical parties. These findings confirm our expectation that voters' experiences with the politicized pattern of distribution associated with this social policy shaped their distributive expectations for access to benefits from the PJ and the UCR. Since the PJ and the UCR are the main political parties in power at the municipal level—where this social program is administered—this finding indicates that the implementation of social policy and the role of political networks in the delivery of publicly financed benefits is crucial in shaping voters distributive expectations in Argentina.

In short, we find that clientelistic linkages are more pervasive in Argentina, while programmatic linkages are predominant in Chile, which is in line with the findings of Luna and Mardones in this volume. However, we use a different mechanism to examine this cross-national variation, one that relies on the capacity of voters to use ideological cues to predict the distributive goals of a party as well as on institutional constraints rather than state bureaucratic capacity. These institutional constraints could also be associated with the effect of having a legislative opposition in control of policy design. Gryzmala Busse makes the argument that legislative opposition is crucial to shape institutional design and generates incentives that constrain state politicization.[48] Ana De la O applies a similar argument for the design of social policies based on conditional cash transfer programs in Latin America.[49] However, the fact that both the Peronists and the Radicals in Argentina seem reliant on the particularistic distribution of benefits through their networks speaks to the minimal impact of legislative opposition on institutional design, regardless of the bureaucratic capacity of the state, which varies widely across municipalities. Moreover, Weitz-Shapiro has shown that even when comparing the implementation of the same policy across municipalities, Argentine mayors have significant discretion, which they choose to limit by delegating to bureaucrats only when they are facing local legislatures with strong opposition representation in electoral constituencies with middle class voters.[50] In any case, the effect of institutional constraints on social policy delivery is crucial in shaping the distributive expectations of voters. However, the capacity to take advantage of the discretion provided by institutions requires political organization, and the variation within Argentina between the Peronist and Radicals on the one hand and the new ideological political parties on the other is a testament to such an effect.

Lesson for Social Policy Design

In this chapter we build on an emerging literature which recognizes that parties offer voters a portfolio of benefits that include non-excludable public policies and excludable goods, rather than single-mindedly specializing in one of those types of benefits. We describe how voters weigh the different goods offered by parties and highlight the role of ideological affinity and partisan networks for explaining the distributive expectations of voters.

When institutional constraints limit the use of political networks and when parties provide clear ideological cues to signal policies to voters, programmatic linkages serve a more important function in shaping the distributive expectations of voters. By contrast, when there are few institutional constraints to delivering goods through partisan networks or when party labels are uninformative—for example, when party labels fail to signal future policy implementation—non-programmatic linkages play a more prominent role in shaping the distributive expectations of voters. Furthermore, as successful clientelistic and programmatic strategies reinforce existing party-voter linkages, the development of stable distributive expectations through clientelistic and programmatic strategies facilitates the sustainability of stable electoral support.

Understanding how distributive expectations are formed and maintained also provides insight into an important question raised by the participants of the conference that inspired the creation of this volume: How and why would parties decide to abandon their clientelistic (programmatic) strategies in favor of more programmatic (clientelistic) goals? Existing literature on market reforms in Latin America suggests that state retrenchment reduces the ability of political parties such as the PJ to deliver programmatic policies and generates incentives to devote more organizational resources to the delivery of non-programmatic goods.[51]

Our research shows that changes in the portfolio of goods offered by parties also result in a change in the developing expectations of voters, decreasing the importance that voters attach to ideological proximity (and responsiveness to policy in general) and increasing the organizational importance of local partisan networks. The specialization toward voters that are sensitized to non-programmatic distribution and the demands imposed by the parties' distribution networks make a rapid shift to more programmatic strategies difficult. However, our research also shows that party systems in both Chile and Argentina do not sing to a single tune. Voters for parties with broad distribution networks that deliver non-programmatic benefits also care about programmatic policies. Consequently, partisan realignments and exogenous shocks that increase the value of the party label should favor distributive portfolios with smaller non-programmatic content.

Our research also contributes to the understanding of the transition from predominantly clientelistic to more programmatic linkages at the country level. The shift from *Pronasol* to *Progresa/Oportunidades* identified by Luna and Mardones in this volume suggests that either changes in state capacity or the loss of congressional support may explain the need to seek broader support from voters and parties that are sensitized to programmatic distribution or afraid of their competitive disadvantage in using political networks for social policy delivery.[52] Indeed, political compromise was crucial in restricting the partisan content of programs such as *Chile Solidario,* in contrast with more politicized initiatives such as *Jefes y Jefas de Hogar* in Argentina.

Another avenue to produce a change in equilibrium can be caused by electoral realignment. When a more programmatic party, such as the Brazilian Workers Party (PT) or the Uruguayan Broad Front (FA), expands electorally and gains access to the executive seat, it has incentives to weaken local patronage machines with well-targeted social policies, as Nichter's chapter in this volume describes in relation to Brazil's Bolsa Familia program. Zucco has shown that in the case of Brazil, these policies were rewarded with more electoral support for the PT presidential candidate.[53] Similar realignments were observed in Argentina, with the UCR experiencing sustained electoral decline due to the failure to hold on to ideologically aware center-left voters after the collapse of the coalition with the FREPASO in 2001.[54]

In short, political parties may have a predominant linkage with voters, but they combine different types of linkages with heterogeneous voters who form their distributive expectations based on their experience of access to publicly funded benefits. Successful changes in electoral strategies need to be triggered by the end of their success; that is, by voters' either demanding or rewarding policies that do not require proximity to the party networks to gain access to publicly provided benefits.

NOTES

1. P. Keefer and R. Vlaicu, "Democracy, Credibility, and Clientelism," *Journal of Law Economics & Organization* 24 (2008): 371–406; H. Kitschelt, "Linkages Between Citizens and Politicians in Democratic Polities," *Comparative Political Studies* 33 (2000): 845–79; Herbert Kitschelt and Steven Wilkinson, *Patrons, Clients, and Policies: Patterns of Democratic Accountability and Political Competition* (Cambridge: Cambridge University Press, 2007); Beatriz Magaloni, Alberto Diaz-Cayeros, and Federico Estevez, "Clientelism and Portfolio Diversification: A Model of Electoral Investment with Applications to Mexico," in *Patrons, Clients, and Policies,* ed. Kitschelt and Wilkinson.

2. Melvin Hinich and Michael Munger, *Ideology and the Theory of Political Choice,* Michigan Studies in Political Analysis (Ann Arbor: University of Michigan Press, 1994).

3. Warren Miller and Donald Stokes, "Party Government and the Salience of Congress," *Public Opinion Quarterly* 26 (1962): 531–46, quote at 533.

4. Kitschelt and Wilkinson, *Patrons, Clients, and Policies,* 10.

5. Gary Cox and Mathew McCubbins, "Electoral Politics as a Redistributive Game," *Journal of Politics* 48 (1986): 370–89.

6. Alberto Diaz-Cayeros, "Electoral Risk and Redistributive Politics in Mexico and the United States," *Studies in Comparative International Development 43* (2008): 129–50; Avinash Dixit and John Londregan, "The Determinants of Success of Special Interests in Redistributive Politics," *Journal of Politics 58* (1996): 1132–55; Assar Lindbeck and Jorgen Weibull, "Balanced-Budget Redistribution and the Outcome of Political Competition," *Public Choice 52* (1987): 273–97; and Susan Stokes and Thad Dunning, "How Does the Internal Structure of Political Parties Shape their Distributive Strategies?" (unpublished paper, 2010).

7. Joe Foewaker, Todd Landman, and Neil Harvey, *Governing Latin America* (Cambridge: Polity Press, 2003); and Scott Mainwaring and Timothy Scully, *Building Democratic Institutions: Party Systems in Latin America* (Stanford, CA: Stanford University Press, 1995). Douglas Chalmers, *The New Politics of Inequality in Latin America: Rethinking Participation and Representation,* Oxford Studies in Democratization (Oxford: Oxford University Press, 1997).

8. Kenneth Roberts, "Neoliberalism and the Transformation of Populism in Latin America: The Peruvian Case," *World Politics 48* (1995): 82–116; Steven Levitsky, *Transforming Labor-based Parties in Latin America: Argentine Peronism in Comparative Perspective* (Cambridge: Cambridge University Press, 2003).

9. Ana De La O, *The Politics of Conditional Cash Transfers* (New Haven, CT: Yale University Press, 2011).

10. Magaloni, Diaz-Cayeros, and Estevez, "Clientelism and Portfolio Diversification."

11. Levitsky, *Transforming Labor-Based Parties in Latin America.*

12. Ernesto Calvo and M. Victoria Murillo, "Who Delivers? Partisan Clients in the Argentine Electoral Market," *American Journal of Political Science 48* (2004): 742–57.

13. Simeon Nichter, "Vote Buying or Turnout Buying? Machine Politics and the Secret Ballot," *American Political Science Review 102* (2008): 19–31; and S. C. Stokes, "Perverse Accountability: A Formal Model of Machine Politics with Evidence from Argentina," *American Political Science Review 99* (2005): 315–25.

14. S. C. Stokes, "Perverse Accountability," 315–25.

15. Alberto Diaz-Cayeros and Beatriz Magaloni, "Aiding Latin America's Poor," *Journal of Democracy 20* (2009): 36–49.

16. See Auyero, this volume.

17. Herbert Kitschelt, Kirk A. Hawkins, Juan Pablo Luna, Guillermo Rosas, and Elizabeth J. Zechmeister, *Latin American Party Systems,* Cambridge Studies in Comparative Politics (Cambridge: Cambridge University Press, 2010).

18. Mark P. Jones, "Political Parties and Party Systems in Latin America" (paper presented at the "Symposium on the Prospects for Democracy in Latin America," University of North Texas, Denton, TX, April 5–6, 2007).

19. Jamer W. McGuire, *Peronism without Perón: Unions, Parties, and Democracy in Argentina* (Stanford, CA: Stanford University Press, 1997); Levitsky, *Transforming Labor-Based Parties in Latin America;* and Calvo and Murillo, "Who Delivers? Partisan Clients in the Argentine Electoral Market."

20. Calvo and Murillo, "Who Delivers?" 742–57.

21. Mark P. Jones, "Evaluating Argentina's Presidential Democracy: 1983–1995," in *Presidentialism and Democracy in Latin America,* ed. S. Mainwaring and M. S. Shugart (Cambridge: Cambridge University Press, 1997), and Ernesto Cabrera, "La Cuestión de la Propor-

cionalidad y las Elecciones Legislativas en la República Argentina," in *El Federalismo Electoral Argentino,* ed. E. F. Calvo and J. M. h. Abal Medina (Buenos Aires: EUDEBA, 2001).

22. Ernesto Calvo and Marcelo Escolar, *La nueva politica de partidos en la Argentina: Crisis politica, realineamientos partidarios y reforma electoral, Coleccion Democracia, partidos y elecciones* (Buenos Aires: Prometeo, 2005).

23. Peter Siavelis, "Coalitions, Voters and Party System Transformation in Post-Authoritarian Chile," *Government and Opposition* 37 (2002): 76–105; Manuel Alcántara, "La ideología de los partidos políticos chilenos, 1994–2002: Rasgos constantes y peculiaridades," *Revista de Ciencia Política* 23 (2003): 68–87; Samuel Valenzuela, *Orígenes y transformaciones del sistema de partidos en Chile,* Vol. 58 (Santiago: Estudios Públicos, 1995); and Patricio Navia, *Las grandes alamedas: el Chile post Pinochet* (Santiago: Tercera-Mondadori, 2004).

24. The binominal electoral system assigns two seats per electoral district with a d'Hont divisor method and open list voting. As a result, the most voted list receives the first seat and the runner up, the second seat unless the winner obtains more than two thirds of the votes in the two member district. It thereby generates a strong minority bias and was designed to give a boost to the right-wing parties by military rules.

25. Carlos Huneus, *El Régimen de Pinochet* (Santiago: Editorial Sudamericana Chilena, 2000).

26. Agustina Giraudi, "The Distributive Politics of Emergency Employment Programs in Argentina (1993–2002)," *Latin American Research Review* 42 (2007): 33–55; and Juan Pablo Lunes and Rodrigo Mardones, "Distributive Politics in a Non-Machine Party System: The Allocation of Targeted Social Funds and Subsidies in Chile (2000–2008)" (unpublished paper, 2009). Cited with authors' permission.

27. Merilee Grindle (forthcoming), *Jobs for the Boys* (New York: Cambridge University Press).

28. Maria O'Donnell, *El aparato: los intendentes del Conurbano y las cajas negras de la política* (Buenos Aires: Aguilar, 2005); and Mariela Szwarcberg, "Counting Heads and Votes: Authoritarian and Democratic Strategies of Electoral Mobilization in Argentina" (paper presented at annual meeting of the MPSA National Conference, Chicago, 2008).

29. Virginia Oliveros, "Public Employment, Political Competition and Clientelism: Evidence from Survey Data in Argentina" (paper presented at the annual meeting of the Southern Political Science Association, New Orleans, January 5, 2011).

30. Szwarcberg, "Counting Heads and Votes"; and Ozge Kemahlioglu, "When the Agent Becomes the Boss: The Politics of Public Employment in Argentina and Turkey" (PhD diss., Colombia University, 2006).

31. The Chilean civil service is among the less politicized in the region, according to a comparative study by Merilee Grindle. The process of de-politicization was facilitated by a 1994 and 2003 reform including total quality management, process simplification, citizen-rights charters, awards for innovation, information offices, and a variety of programs for improving management. According to Grindle, "recruitment processes were devised that gave presidents, ministers, and other high-level officials ultimate control over appointments, but which mandated processes of review of candidates as a way of 'rationalizing' patronage appointments at middle and upper levels" (Grindle, *Jobs for the Boys,* 349). The process was complemented by a system of party quotas within incumbent coalitions to coordinate electoral competition (by rewarding losing candidates) with government positions and to sustain

the coalitional balance within each bureaucratic agency. See John Carey and Peter Siavelis, "Insurance for Good Losers and the Survival of Chile's Concertación," *Latin American Politics and Society* 47, no. 2 (2005): 1–22; and Alfredo Rehren, *Clientelismo polâitico y reforma del estado en Chile* (Santiago: Centro de Estudios Pâublicos, 2000).

32. Catalina Bau Adeo, "Experiencias exitosas en la profesionalizacion de la funcion publica en America Latina. El caso Chile," in *Foro Iberoamericano: Revitalizacion de la administracion publica. Estrategias para la Implantacion de la Carta Iberoamericana de la Funcion Publica* (Mexico City, 2005); and Rehren, *Clientelismo polâitico y reforma del estado en Chile.*

33. Socialist President Michelle Bachelet explained this policy in a personal interview with the authors (July 14, 2009).

34. PPD representative who is a medical doctor (personal interview with authors, March 2009).

35. UDI representative (personal interview with authors, March 2009).

36. Calvo and Murillo, "Who Delivers?"

37. Kitschelt and Wilkinson, *Patrons, Clients, and Policies,* 9.

38. For a description of methodology, see Ernesto Calvo and M. Victoria Murillo, "When Parties Meet Voters: Partisan Networks and Distributive Expectations in Argentina and Chile,*" Comparative Political Studies,* forthcoming 2013.

39. Javier Auyero, *Poor People's Politics: Peronist Survival Networks and the Legacy of Evita* (Durham, NC: Duke University Press, 2001); and Levitsky, *Transforming Labor-Based Parties in Latin America.*

40. Personal interview with a PJ activist in the province of Buenos Aires (August 2009).

41. Radical representative and former presidential candidate (personal interview with authors on July 20, 2009).

42. Calvo and Murillo, "Who Delivers?"

43. Juan Pablo Luna, "Segmented Party Voter Linkages in Latin America: The Case of the UDI," *Journal of Latin American Studies* 42 (2010): 325–56.

44. Calvo and Murillo, "When Parties Meet Voters."

45. Using the responses to these questions as dependent variables, we run ordered beta regression models for each party and estimate whether ideological distance and proximity to party members explains the perceived propensity to receive goods, jobs, or public works.

46. Full results are in Calvo and Murillo, "When Parties Meet Voters."

47. Szwarcberg, "Counting Heads and Votes"; and Oliveros, "Public Employment, Political Competition and Clientelism."

48. A. Gryzmala Buss, *Rebuilding Leviathan: Party Competition and State Exploitation in Post-Communist States* (New York: Cambridge University Press, 2007).

49. De La O, *Politics of Conditional Cash Transfers.*

50. Rebecca Weitz-Shapiro, "Choosing Clientelism: Political Competition, Poverty and Social Welfare Policy in Argentina" (PhD diss., Columbia University, 2008).

51. Levitsky, *Transforming Labor-Based Parties in Latin America;* Edward Gibson and Ernesto Calvo, "Federalism and Low-Maintenance Constituencies: Territorial Dimensios of Economic Reform in Argentina," *Studies in Comparative International Development* 35 (2005): 32–55; and Edward Gibson, "The Populist Road to Market Reform: Policy and Electoral Coalitions in Mexico and Argentina," *World Politics* 49 (1997): 339–70.

52. De La O, *Politics of Conditional Cash Transfers.*

53. Cesar Zucco, *Poor Voters vs. Poor Places: Persisting Patterns and Recent Changes in Brazilian Electoral Patterns* (Princeton, NJ: Princeton University, 2010).

54. Juan Carlos Torre, "Los huérfanos de la política de partidos Sobre los alcances y la naturaleza de la crisis de representación partidaria," *Desarrollo Economico* 42 (2003): 647–65.

CHAPTER TWO

Chile's Education Transfers, 2001–2009

JUAN PABLO LUNA AND RODRIGO MARDONES

The political targeting of social policy in Chile diverges from the standard predictions in the literature on distributive politics and clientelism. In this case, political distortions of social policy allocations are marginal. We attribute this result to the absence of a political-machine party in the system and to the presence of a strong and bureaucratically capable state.[1]

Those two conditions (i.e., the absence of a machine party and the presence of a strong state), we argue, explain the patterns of marginal political targeting we observe in Chile. Incumbents operating in this type of context face a set of opportunities and constraints: (1) they have more autonomy than machine-party leaders to design political investment strategies, but due to their inability to implement clientelistic monitoring, they are less certain about the returns on their investments; and (2) they have less discretionary funds available than incumbents implementing less well-designed/bureaucratically monitored programs, but they also have access to better quality information for fine-tuning investments of the scarce resources that are available for political targeting.

What would be an adequate investment strategy for incumbents confronting this set of opportunities and constraints? Following the financial analogy of Magaloni et al. (2007), we claim that incumbents working within this scenario should pursue an insurance investment strategy[2] that is best undertaken by implementing a highly diversified portfolio that yields minimal risks (and payoffs).

The evidence we present in this chapter is consistent with this prediction and reveals two intriguing points. First, even in the context of efficient socioeconomic targeting and "cleanly" designed programs, political targeting is also present. Second, in such contexts, political investment rationales partially diverge from those observed both in machine-party cases and in those without the bureaucratic capacity to enforce technical criteria in social policy allocation.[3]

Along with marginal electoral targeting, we identify investment strategies that distort the allocation of social policy resources to pursue non-strictly electoral goals (e.g., to build congressional coalitions). Regarding electoral targeting, we argue that the Concertación in Chile did not target core constituencies for electoral payoffs (Magaloni et al. 2007) or turnout (Nichter 2008). Instead, political incumbents in Chile targeted non-core voters to boost absolute levels of turnout and to "fight" a more economically powerful opposition.

On this basis we claim that our analysis has important implications for other cases. Our results suggest that the political and institutional context in which social policy is implemented can shape political biases in ways that contradict insights derived from current theory. Specifically, the theoretical modeling of incumbents' investment rationales currently draws—too heavily in our view—on insights from two bodies of literature. The first set analyzes clientelism and vote-buying by political machines in pursuit of contingent exchanges with voters, usually on election day (Calvo and Murillo 2004; Nichter 2008; Stokes 2005; Wantchekon 2003). The second set analyzes the political economy of geographically targeted investments and pork, and draws more directly on studies of distributive politics in the United States (Cox and McCubbins 2001; Dixit and Londregan 1996).

The previously mentioned theoretical literatures do offer critical insights. For instance, we explicitly follow the proposal of Magaloni et al. (2007) to understand political targeting as an investment strategy that could be deployed through a diversified portfolio. By engaging both literatures critically, however, we seek to expose their limitations in generating useful results applicable to a broader set of cases. In particular, we maintain that incumbents do not always pursue immediate electoral objectives through contingent exchanges with either core or swing voters. In some contexts they may pursue other important but less theoretically salient goals, at least some of which are not tied to generating immediate electoral returns.

The presence of a party-machine, rare in contemporary Latin America, is a crucial factor that shapes current modeling of incumbents' incentives for disbursing social policy in pursuit of political goals. Furthermore, as we will claim, the party system interacts with the characteristics of the social policy program, and perhaps more broadly with state capacity, in shaping incumbents' investment rationales.

Empirically, our argument is illustrated through an analysis of three targeted education-oriented social funds in Chile that have been systematically implemented since the 1980s. Chile is useful in correcting for selection bias because it fails to conform to the assumption of a governing party-machine. At the same time, it has a capable state that is able to design and implement "clean" social programs, making it an unlikely place to observe political targeting strategies by incumbents. Available accounts of conditional-cash-transfers designed in the same period (Borges and Hunter 2009; De la O 2010; Zucco forthcoming) suggest that this new generation of programs has been implemented "cleanly," without gross political manipulation, and in accordance with technocratic allocation criteria. Thus, the insights we derive from our case study of Chile could be useful for analyzing cases in which these new programs are implemented in the absence of governing party-machines.

In the next two sections we provide a theoretical rationale backed by evidence for treating Chile as a non-party-machine / strong bureaucratic capacity case. The subsequent section elaborates on the implications of that specific context (the absence of an electoral machine and the technocratic implementation of targeted education policy) for incumbent strategizing, arguing that political investment rationales can diverge from predictions offered in the literature on clientelism and distributive politics. We then justify our selection of educational social programs and discuss data and model specifications. After this we present our empirical results, which deviate from the standard predictions found in the literature. We then conclude and draw implications for future research.

Chile: A Non-Party-Machine System

For the twenty years leading up to March 2010, Chile's national government was led by the Concertación, a center-left coalition of four political parties of unequal electoral size that shared access to government positions. At the congressional level, the Christian Democratic Party (PDC) was able to retain the largest electoral plurality during the period, while the Radical Party (PRSD) remained the smaller coalition partner, followed by the Party for Democracy (PPD), and the Socialist Party (PS). In terms of leadership, however, the presidents who held office during the period between 2001 and 2009 covered by our data were both members of the PS.

Despite their sustained electoral success over an extended period, the partisan apparatuses of the Concertación block do not fully conform to the ideal machine-party type. Therefore, even if partisan activist networks are traceable and similar in size to those seen in Argentina, as reported in Calvo and Murillo (2009), the relative size of partisan networks is more even than in the latter machine-ridden system, where the Peronist party network—usually identified as the main provider of targeted benefits to its constituency—is overwhelmingly larger than its competitors. We also suggest that the strategic role of the Concertación activist networks is functionally different from that of a machine-party system such as the one in Argentina. On this basis, we will further claim that this difference in functioning makes it problematic to extrapolate incumbents' strategic considerations from a machine-party context to one in which incumbents lack access to this type of political organization.

In previous works we have argued that local Chilean partisan organizations are more evenly distributed across party lines, less vertically integrated into national party structures, and lack direct access to central state officials (Luna 2008; Luna and Mardones 2010). Here we provide some additional evidence for the portrayal of Chile as a non-machine-party context, drawing on LAPOP's most recent wave of regional surveys (2010).

Assuming that partisan machines operate on the basis of party activists and sympathizers, the percentage of party sympathizers—and especially of campaign activists —in a given country could provide a rough proxy for comparing the scope of partisan machines. According to LAPOP results, of the 23 countries surveyed in 2010, Chile has the least number of people who sympathize with a political party (11% compared to the regional average of 35%).

Meanwhile, the percentage of those sampled that claims to have worked for a candidate or political campaign in the last electoral round is negligible (2.9% compared to a regional average of 11%). Additionally, 94% of Chilean respondents say they have not received a clientelistic offer in recent electoral campaigns. The regional percentage stands at 88%, and it is even lower in Mexico (83%) and Argentina (82%), two cases often described as prototypical instances of machine-politics.

Around 20% of Chilean citizens recall having seen people "from a political party" handing out goods in their neighborhood during the most recent electoral campaign. However, when asked about the goods distributed, respondents overwhelmingly describe campaign merchandise (key-chains, shopping bags, t-shirts, pens, and coffee mugs) instead of more traditional clientelistic handouts, and more than 70% of them identified opposition parties as the source of these goods (the UDI with 26%, RN with 16%, and Alianza parties with 11%) along with one presidential candidate: Sebastián Piñera (with 16%). In the previous election, according to Chile's 2006 LAPOP Survey, aggregate figures were similar, with the UDI (66%), RN (5%), and Alianza (9%) accounting for more than 80% of such instances.

In sum, at least until December 2010, it appears to be the Chilean opposition, not the incumbents, that more often engages in particularistic campaigns that entail the targeted distribution of material benefits. It is also worth noting that an important feature of governing political-machines is that they provide incumbents with ways to monitor their clients' electoral behavior (Stokes 2005) and in doing so facilitate the coercive arrangements that sustain the clientelistic pact.

In terms of monitoring capacity, unfortunately we lack comparative data for different governments in the region. Still, the data gathered for Chile (also in the LAPOP 2010 Survey) suggests that partisan networks do not often fulfill monitoring functions. While 17% of respondents believe that the government can eventually sort out their vote, the great majority of respondents (83%) think that the government is unable to monitor electoral behavior. In a follow-up question on the nature of monitoring technologies, more than half of those who believed that monitoring was possible (9%), affirmed that it could be achieved via public opinion surveys. Thus, even if monitoring is marginally present, technically its does not rely on partisan networks; indeed, a qualitative exploration of the 2009 congressional campaign reveals that Chilean marketing firms are increasingly supplying political candidates with block-level maps of electoral behavior to improve the design of electoral strategies (Recart 2010).

A similar picture was obtained from a qualitative survey we conducted with 25 social organizations in seven poor municipalities in Santiago, roughly half of which received government and municipal funds and approximately half of which competed for those funds but failed to obtain them. Our interviews did not provide consistent evidence of partisan networks engaging in brokerage or monitoring activities in allocating these funds when they were targeted to small neighborhood organizations rather than individuals.

Bureaucratic Capacity for Implementing Targeted Social Policies in Chile

Chile often has been praised for its relatively high state capacity and low levels of corruption (see, e.g., Inter-American Development Bank 2005). In this regard, the country is usually portrayed as a model of social reform and social policy implementation.

In terms of state capacity for implementing social policy, over time the country has developed a series of social indicators that have improved targeting in different ways; these include the National Household Socioeconomic Survey (CASEN), applied every two or three years since 1985 and considered statistically representative at the district level (*comuna*), and the National System of Municipal Indicators (SINIM), which is updated annually with data from several national agencies and the municipalities themselves. These information-generating tools have facilitated fiscal and citizen oversight of policy.

On this last point, public officials seem very conscious of the potential risks of political targeting. For instance, key informants we interviewed about the links between local administrators and the central government systematically instructed us to look at the smaller funds available (less than $4000 US), because central oversight agencies focus their monitoring efforts on large funds and projects, which are often found to be relatively well-targeted. If this common perception is true, we might not find evidence of political targeting in Chile, because the smaller funds are those lacking the type of systematic information that our empirical tests are based upon.

Cases in which targeting deviated from technocratic criteria to favor political campaigns (such as the Employment Generation Program [PGE] scandal in 2005 and the Chiledeportes scandal in 2006) received widespread media exposure and led to charges against the politicians involved. Arguably, these few highly visible cases might have provided further incentives to constrain political targeting and enhance the transparency of fund allocations. In short, at least in comparison to other Latin American countries, in Chile the state bureaucracy has the technical capacity to implement social targeting in a "clean" way. Indeed, the country is widely perceived as a case in which gross political distortions are not likely to be observed.

Greater bureaucratic capacity reduces the amount of discretionary spending available to incumbents, thus limiting the space for gross political distortions in the implementation of targeted social policies. At the same time, however, high bureaucratic capacity provides technical information that might be useful to incumbents still seeking to pursue political objectives through the implementation of political targeting. In particular, technical capacity provides useful information for devising and fine-tuning more complex and discreet political distortions.

Incumbent Incentives in Non-Machine / High Bureaucratic Capacity Contexts

The distribution of scarce resources that fosters, whenever possible, the advancement of an incumbent's own political goals is essential to political life. However, since the institutional room for politically targeting these resources varies across cases, incumbents' rationales for investing those goods may also vary substantially.

Imagine an incumbent without a party-machine at her disposal who is implementing a targeted social policy program that allows for small distortions in its socioeconomic eligibility criteria. The absence of the machine makes clientelistic monitoring impossible and turns electoral investments riskier. At the same time, the absence of a machine provides the incumbent with more freedom to seek investment strategies beyond the electoral constituency and brokers.

While it is true that a well-designed social policy program has inherent constraints on the amount of discretionary resources available, high-quality information and bureaucratic oversight capacity are a convenient counterweight to such discretionary spending constraints and could provide valuable information for designing and fine-tuning political investment strategies.

As in financial markets, in non-machine systems diversified political investment portfolios can be deployed to tame uncertainty and reduce investment risk. In a nutshell, in non-machine settings it makes sense for the government to allocate targeted social funds outside the core constituency and beyond strictly electoral objectives. In these settings, the greater the risk of such investments and the more autonomy provided by the absence of a machine, the more likely we are to find a diversified portfolio investment strategy.

Thus, incumbents pursuing this type of strategy should implement a complex portfolio to allocate marginal discretionary spending in the pursuit of multiple political objectives. This type of portfolio, which works only on the margins of technocratic allocation, makes political discretion less pervasive, giving incumbents that succeed in profiting from it the best of both worlds because they are able to extract modest, but potentially useful, political returns without visibly distorting objective socioeconomic eligibility criteria to favor certain beneficiaries. However, these marginal, highly diversified investment strategies could also turn out to be relatively ineffective in advancing the political objectives of incumbents.

The menu of possible investment strategies available to incumbents situated in a non-machine/strong state context, we believe, offers more than just a binary choice between a core constituent and a swing-voter strategy. Indeed, we maintain that analyses of such strategies should consider the pursuit not only of immediate electoral returns but also of different political objectives that are strategically important to the incumbent.

Let us examine the implications of our theoretical argument about the nature of political investment in social transfers in non-machine/strong state scenarios. First, in this type of strategic scenario we would expect to observe relatively efficient socioeconomic targeting; second, we also would expect to see marginal, though still significant, political distortions in the allocation of social programs; and third, we should also observe multiple electoral and non-electoral investment rationales combined into a diversified portfolio for the political allocation of social funds. Lastly, such strategies might not produce sizable electoral returns, because they are marginal and because strictly electoral objectives are only one type of goal that incumbents might pursue through the allocation of targeted social policies.

Beyond these broad expectations, our analytical approach does not allow for precise theoretical predictions on the nature of the specific investment rationales that could be observed. Indeed, we expect such strategies to be contingent on the political-institutional context in which a given incumbent operates, because this context will determine the incumbent's precise needs and objectives as well as the political instruments that could be used to fulfill them through marginal distortions in the allocation of social funds.

The empirical information we offer below describes political targeting in Chile, a case that approximates the theoretical scenario examined in this chapter, in order to illustrate the plausibility of our analytical framework. The implications of this analysis go beyond the Chilean case, however, since the non-machine / high bureaucratic capacity scenario is a plausible one for several other developing countries as well.

On the one hand, party-machines with decentralized electoral enforcement capacities are the exception, not the rule. On the other, technical expertise, as well as foreign assistance programs—the conditions imposed by multilateral donors—could contribute to better-designed social programs even in the context of low state capacity.

Data, Methods, and Results

Social funds and benefits for the poor have been made available in Chile through many different programs, some through a direct link between beneficiaries and the central government and others through regional prefects (*intendentes*) appointed by the president or decentralized institutional venues (municipalities). Still others depend on local capacity to design projects that capture central government funding. Since data on specific targeted social funds in the public domain is available for the period from 2001 to 2009 only through the National System of Municipal Indicators (SINIM), our selection of funds was limited to this source.[4]

The fact that political targeting might be restricted overall to small and non-reported funds has obvious implications for our analysis because it increases the risk of producing a non-finding. Moreover, even if we do encounter evidence of political targeting, we will not be able to provide a reliable estimate of the proportion of funds politically targeted in the country because we lack data on many other existing social programs. At best, our data allows us to estimate a lower limit for political distortions in the allocation of targeted social funds.

Admitting these limitations, we present evidence of three different types of funds—which constitute our three dependent variables—operating in a single sector: education. Despite this truncated program sample, we seek to show how, even within the same social policy sector, different investment rationales are present.

Chile, having carried out major educational reforms, presents an interesting case.[5] The most comprehensive reform took place in the 1980s under the dictatorship, when the responsibility for public education was transferred to municipalities, which, along with private providers, began to receive a per-child state-issued voucher (Cox 2005; Gauri 1998). Under democratic governments, education policy and reform has been at the forefront of Chilean social policy, with an emphasis on correcting the unequal performance of municipal and private schools.

Chile is a classic case of neoliberal reform under dictatorship, a situation that deeply framed the country's education system, prospects, and evolution over the last 20 years of democratic rule by four consecutive governments from the center-left Concertación coalition. The country was not included as a case study in either Grindle (2004) or Kaufmann and Nelson (2004), two well-known volumes of comparative education reform in Latin America. However, there are a few policy oriented case studies that describe the political process of education reform in Chile (Delannoy 2000; Espínola and De Moura Castro 1999; Gauri 1998). Most literature has focused either on the politics of education reform or on identifying variables affecting school performance and school choice, but none has looked at education policy as an arena for clientelistic or distributive politics. The fact that both scholars and development officials consider education policy a key tool for overcoming underdevelopment makes this policy sector a good place to begin looking at the political use of funds.

As our first dependent variable we will examine discretionary central government education transfers to municipalities. We have excluded education vouchers transferred from the central government from our consideration since this system (*subvención escolar*) provides a fixed amount for each child enrolled in a municipal school. This leaves central government education transfers from other sources that are not based on formulas and therefore can be considered discretionary; examples include monies allocated to build or improve infrastructure and for specific educational programs.[6]

The second dependent variable we analyze here is the allocation of the presidential scholarship program (Beca Presidente de la República). Through this fund, socioeconomically disadvantaged gifted students (from primary, secondary, and higher education levels) receive scholarships directly from the central government, although potential beneficiaries must apply annually through their municipality. Because of this configuration, beneficiaries might not know if the municipality or the central government provides the scholarships, allowing politicians from both levels of government to claim credit.

For the education transfers the dependent variable is measured as the annual per capita amount allocated to municipalities. In contrast, for the presidential scholarship we took the number of scholarships awarded to children attending secondary school in each district as a percentage of all school-aged children.[7]

The third fund we study as a dependent variable is the indigenous scholarship (Beca Indígena), which is allocated to gifted indigenous students who demonstrate financial need. These scholarships are awarded based on three criteria: socioeconomic vulnerability, academic performance, and membership in one of Chile's indigenous groups.[8] As with the presidential scholarship, students must apply for this central government award through their municipalities, which may also confuse recipients about the real source of the benefit. For the indigenous scholarship fund, we took the number of scholarships that were allocated to indigenous children attending primary and secondary school in each district as a percentage of all indigenous people living in that district.[9]

Our independent variables are grouped into two subsets. First, we characterize each mayoralty and congressional district in terms of the socioeconomic, demographic, and territorial variables that drive socioeconomic allocation criteria. We also relied on the SINIM for this information. Among the nonpolitical variables, we included a proxy to represent the relative affluence of municipalities, since poor ones benefit from higher social policy spending. For this purpose we used the degree of dependence on the Municipal Common Fund (FCM) as the first independent variable, calculated as the percentage of total municipal income provided by this national redistributive rule-based financial mechanism.[10] Greater municipal dependence on the FCM (measured as a percentage) is treated as a proxy for municipal fiscal poverty. Although we initially considered using the percentage of residents living under the poverty line as a better proxy for social conditions in municipalities, that indicator is highly correlated to our variable on the FCM. Moreover, poverty data for households is collected once every two or three years through a national survey (CASEN), which is representative at the municipal level, making the poverty indicator less appealing within our nine-year time span.[11] We considered a dummy variable for whether or not each municipality is an official regional or provincial capital, since municipalities that are regional or provincial capitals may receive more funds per capita or as a percentage of population—reflecting centralism—or may receive less funds, indicating that they have relatively higher social indicators, which would require the central government to target municipalities that are not regional or provincial capitals.[12] We also introduced a control for "year," based on the assumption that social policy resources are annually increasing due to Chile's positive GDP growth between 2001 and 2009 and the fiscally expansive education policy pursued by the Concertación governments.[13]

The second group of independent variables was built upon data from three municipal elections (2000, 2004, and 2008) provided by the Ministry of the Interior.[14]

For one subset of independent political variables we computed party dummies, identifying the partisan affiliation of mayors. Taking the PS as the baseline party (the party of the two presidents that held office during the period under study), we included dummies for the remaining five largest parties in our model (UDI, RN, PDC, PRSD, and PPD), as well as a residual category that grouped together independent mayors and those from smaller parties. In a second subset of independent political variables we include three indicators related to elections. We considered abstention rates in the previous municipal race, the competitiveness of the mayoral race—measured as the percentage difference between the winner and his or her closest competitor—and the presence of "electoral cycles," including dummy variables for each presidential, congressional, and municipal campaign year.[15]

We considered two types of statistical models. First, we ran pooled OLS models to predict each of our three educational funds. Across these funds we defined a simple model predicting allocations to municipalities by drawing on our socioeconomic proxy, our controls, and our political variables. The models are basically the same, differing only in the dependent variable. In the second statistical model we ran a series of seemingly unrelated regressions (SUR) using the same independent variables set in our OLS models. If, as theoretically claimed, incumbents are pursuing a unified portfolio investment strategy, statistically this would lead to the presence of correlated residuals for different types of funds across the specified models. In other words, in a portfolio investment strategy, allocations in one fund are not independent of allocations in others. So if residuals across models are found to be independent, this would substantively imply that the criteria for allocating the funds are not partially contingent upon other components of the portfolio.

For the three educational funds we estimated an SUR model. The Breusch-Pagan test of independence reported significance levels below 4%, indicating low correlations among errors in the scholarship models with respect to the transfers on education model; it also reported relatively high correlation among the scholarship models related to each other (25.2%). For this reason, in table 2.1 we reported an OLS estimation for transfers and education, and SUR specification models for the presidential and indigenous scholarships. The SUR specification suggests some strategic coordination among scholarships, while the transfers to education are beyond the reach of such a strategy.

From a substantive point of view, our results suggest that the three educational funds are overall effectively targeted to the poor. Our independent variables covering these socioeconomic factors perform remarkably well, obtaining significant and correctly signed results in virtually all analyzed targeted social funds. The negative

TABLE 2.I.
Allocation of targeted educational funds from the Chilean central government
to municipalities (2001–2009)

	Discretionary transfers to municipal education (OLS estimation)[1]	SUR estimation[2]	
		Presidential scholarship program	Indigenous scholarship program
Dependence on Municipal Common Fund	229.08 (130.40)*	0.01 (0.00)***	0.06 (0.01)***
Year	11,408.17 (1,005.94)***	–0.07 (.012)***	0.65 (0.05)***
Regional or provincial capital	–28,646.76 (11,658.97)**	–0.28 (0.09)***	–0.80 (0.39)**
UDI	4,543.32 (813,739.63)	0.06 (0.12)	–0.91 (0.50)*
RN	136.61 (11,006.22)	0.08 (0.12)	0.13 (0.49)
PDC	–2,349.76 (9,512.62)	0.07 (0.11)	–1.07 (0.45)**
PRSD	–8,977.33 (19,196.23)	0.19 (0.17)	0.48 (0.73)
PPD	–8,473.00 (11,240.40)	0.17 (0.13)	–1.51 (0.56)***
Other party	2,657.96 (10,331.39)	0.21 (0.11)*	–0.20 (0.47)
Abstention	5,460.15 (1,384.57)***	–0.00 (0.01)	0.00 (0.02)
Competitiveness	697.81 (204.85)***	0.00 (0.002)	–0.00 (0.01)
Electoral year	6,206.33 (3,346.20)*	0.29 (0.06)***	0.07 (0.25)
Constant	–2.29e+07 (2,018,939)***	132.28 (24.65)***	–1,300.28 (103.88)***
No. of observations	2,991	2,793	2,793
R-squared	0.1613	0.04	0.10

Note: Dummy variables for parties includes Socialist Party as base dummy.
[1]Robust standard errors in parenthesis
[2]Seemingly Unrelated Regression (SUR) with a 0.2443 correlation of residuals. Standard errors in parentheses.
***significant at 1%, **significant at 5%, *significant at 10%

value of the coefficient on the dummy variable capturing the provincial and regional capital is statistically significant in all three models, confirming that less affluent municipalities are receiving more funds.

Regarding the political variables, the results differ among programs, as expected. For the education transfers, the party variables are not significant. However, the other three political variables related to elections (competitiveness, electoral year, and abstention) are significant. Districts where competitiveness between the elected mayor and his/her closest competitor is high also tend to receive more transfers from the central government. Second, in an election year (presidential, congressional, or municipal) districts tend to receive more funding, beyond the political affiliation of the mayor. Third, districts where abstention is high tend to receive more education transfers. Municipalities with higher abstention rates received more funds than those that *ceteris paribus* turn out to vote in higher numbers. A plausible rival hypothesis, however, is that abstention rates may be correlated to socioeconomic factors, which coincide with technocratic criteria included in the social targeting of these funds and subsidies. However, according to our data set, municipalities falling within the poorest decile (among which rural localities figure prominently) exhibit 10% more abstention and invalid voting (an average of 30.7%, with a standard deviation of 15.5) than the average obtained for all municipalities included in the analysis (22.7% sd 7.9). Thus, it is evident from the standard deviation observed for the poorest 10% of municipalities in our sample, which is almost double that of our complete set of observations, that poorer municipalities display greater abstention rates on average but also greater levels of intra-group heterogeneity. In short, though abstention is marginally correlated to socioeconomic factors, poor communities differ widely in their electoral abstention rates. Our findings suggest that, *ceteris paribus,* the Chilean government invested more educational transfers in low-turnout municipalities.

For the indigenous and presidential scholarships, however, the opposite is true. Some party variables appear significant, while political variables related to elections tend to be non-significant, except for electoral year, in the case of the presidential scholarship. Indeed, for this scholarship, between 2001 and 2009 the socialist central governments tended to favor with statistical significance municipalities governed by mayors from parties other than those belonging to the ruling coalition (Concertación) or to the right wing opposition (Alianza). In the case of the indigenous scholarship, the socialist central governments appear to have been punishing mayors belonging to the UDI (Alianza) and two coalition partners, the PDC and PPD.

On this basis we can assess our initial set of hypotheses. Regarding the first, we did find evidence of efficient socioeconomic targeting. Even in this best-case scenario—and with respect to our second hypothesis—we also identified significant systematic political distortions in the allocation of the specific funds for which we had data, which experienced politicians expected to be "clean." The fact that public information was readily available for these funds (and not for others) made us pessimistic about finding evidence of politically distorted allocations. Overall, our findings seem to support the second hypothesis. Regarding our third hypothesis, we observed evidence of political targeting strongly influenced by the partisan machine-assumption, which defies conventional wisdom. *Ceteris paribus*, we found that—at least for discretionary education transfers—the Concertación invested more resources in municipalities where citizens vote significantly less than in others with similar socioeconomic conditions. We also reported evidence of disproportional investment in favor of mayors outside of the traditional Concertación/Alianza divide. This may suggest an attempt to extend the reach of the Concertación to independent mayors and the extra-parliamentary left (Communist Party and other), while punishing the PDC and the PPD, two PS coalition partners that obtained more seats in the Chamber of Deputies. Indeed, the PS obtained just 12.5% of seats in the lower house, while the PDC and PPD won 16.7% and 17.5% respectively. Our third hypothesis also predicted the presence of a strategic investment portfolio that combined different allocation rationales. The results obtained suggest that in the case of the two scholarships, the different investment rationales examined below might be strategically combined into an investment portfolio, since patterns observed for one scholarship correlate with those observed for the other. We will provide evidence for our fourth hypotheses after describing the investment rationales we have identified.

Investment Rationales

The bundle of evidence presented above runs contrary to expectations derived from theoretical analyses of machine-ridden systems in which incumbents are expected to favor the partisan machine in ways that are proportionally related to each member's capacity to deliver votes to the incumbent; for example, spending should favor actual voters, especially core constituents, as well as large coalition partners, including mayoral parties or factions. Our evidence also suggests that the core versus swing voter distinction found in distributive politics literature fails to adequately account for the different political investment rationales that incumbents can deploy when allocating targeted social policies in the region.

   This section briefly describes the context and a possible rationale for the different investment strategies empirically observed in the targeting of education funds in Chile as an instance of a non-machine / strong state context. To clarify, we make no claim that these particular investment strategies are transferable to other cases with non-machine / strong state configurations. Neither do these investment strategies necessarily exhaust the possible political allocation criteria of Chile's governing Concertación coalition in the period between 2001 and 2009. What our evidence does illustrate, however, are the limitations of previous theoretical and empirical models in analyzing the political rationales for targeted social fund allocations and the varieties of "political targeting" that may exist even in the context of a "clean" political system that only allows for marginal political distortions.

Turnout Boosting

In a machine-ridden system, greater investment in poor districts with high voter turnout is expected because it increases incumbents' electoral payoff. Why, then, would the Concertación invest more resources in municipalities that *ceteris paribus* have lower turnout rates? Over the last two decades, electoral turnout and valid voting have steadily decreased in Chile (Altman 2004), but our regression results for discretionary education transfers show that municipalities with higher electoral abstention rates receive more resources. This is intriguing: Why should an incumbent invest in non-voters when he or she can target resources to a core constituency or swing voters, thereby obtaining greater payoffs by systematically trying to shape the electoral decisions of consistent voters, particularly where the electorate is shrinking?

According to Escobar-Lemmon (2003, 688), voter turnout is the best available proxy for citizen distrust in government, political parties, candidates, and the political system. Thus it is a turnout boost,[16] independent of partisan content, and might be sought by politicians to enhance legitimacy. This would be particularly attractive for a governing coalition like the Concertación, which remained in power for a long time in the context of growing voter apathy and decreasing electoral participation (see Luna and Mardones 2010). Eventually, alienated and socially marginalized citizens who receive government assistance packages might turn out to vote in the next election, and if they do, they could be expected to at least marginally support the government that provided previously absent social benefits. Therefore, while unfeasible in a machine-ridden system, a turnout-boosting strategy might be pursued in a non-machine system in an attempt to marginally increase support for the governing coalition while potentially increasing political legitimacy. This is particularly relevant in the Chilean context, where decreasing turnout has been systematically identified as a symptom of democratic decay.

Coalition Expansion

Which municipalities should the government target with more funds, given its command of scarce resources and the presence within the governing coalition of four partners with asymmetrical electoral shares and access to government positions? In machine-ridden systems, mayors from electorally stronger parties would likely receive more resources, which would subsequently favor the machine's core constituents. This appears to be true in Chile in the case of the indigenous scholarship. Although major coalition parties compete at the presidential level and share access to top national offices, small parties outside the coalition lack viable national-level figures. Their electoral continuity depends on securing lower national offices and a few local strongholds. As a result, they might receive more politically targeted social funds than coalitional partners that enjoy national visibility and greater representation in national government posts. Effectively, bigger parties—especially the party that promoted a successful presidential candidate—would be relatively penalized in favor of minor coalitional partners or even in favor of extra-parliamentary forces such as communist and independent mayors that could expand the Concertación's support base.

This rationale is consistent with our observations in Chile and with the history of its party system. Until 1973, the Chilean party system was vertically integrated with a flow of state goods from the center to the periphery, channeled through hierarchical lobby structures organized along partisan lines (Borzutzky 2002; Valenzuela 1977). In Valenzuela's account, national and local authorities were mutually dependent—the former providing goods, projects, and petty favours, and the latter delivering national election votes. While decentralized and hierarchical territorial networks equate the pre-1973 system with that of a machine-ridden system, continuous electoral turnover (combined with strong ideological identities) prevented the consolidation of a dominant machine—like the PJ in Argentina or the PRI in Mexico—once democracy was restored in Chile.

In post-1990 Chile, the balance of power between the central and local governments leaned slightly in favor of municipalities, still within the context of a highly centralized unitary country. This was the combined effect of central state retrenchment and moderate decentralizing reforms (Mardones 2007). Paradoxically, these reforms gave central government officials greater autonomy from their partisan bases and territorial organizations. Moreover, while decentralization weakened national partisan structures in other Latin American party systems (for example, Colombia after its 1991 constitutional reforms, and Peru following its 1993 reforms), massive partisan denationalization has not yet occurred in Chile.

The electoral strength of mainstream parties (organized around two electoral pacts, the Concertación and the Alianza) has hitherto been explained as a result of the institutional power granted by the electoral system to national party executives, who remained powerful by exerting control over congressional candidacies (Siavelis 2002). Without ignoring the electoral system's role in keeping nationalized partisan structures in place, we propose a complementary explanation that is applicable to at least the governing coalition.

The Concertación was in power from 1990 to 2010. As the original grievances that consolidated this coalition diminished and programmatic tensions increased within this electoral pact (particularly in the early years of the Lagos administration), the distribution of social funds to coalition partners could have been used politically as a "coalition maintaining" mechanism. Therefore, even if electorally innocuous (or at least less effective than in systems with pervasive machines), the distribution of targeted social funds to coalition partners might have helped keep the Concertación in place. So far, we have found no evidence that supports this hypothesis. There is, however, evidence that the Concertación has tried to expand its electoral base through different mechanisms and reform efforts, such as allowing Chileans living abroad to vote, boosting the electoral participation of youth, and allowing the Communist Party representation in Congress. Our regression results for the presidential scholarship support the latter.

Opposition Fighting

In non-machine-ridden systems, incumbent parties do not usually enjoy monopolistic access to clientelism or massive distributive politics. In Chile, the opposition frequently attempts to make electoral inroads by distributing social assistance and campaign giveaways to working class sectors. This is especially common for the UDI, a rightist party that enjoys substantial access to private sector funding. Electoral results suggest that such attempts have been at least partially successful, and support for the UDI has steadily grown, especially among the poorest segments of the Chilean electorate (Altman 2004; Luna 2010). In 2001, the UDI became Chile's most-voted-for party in congressional elections and it successfully preserved its electoral constituency in 2005 and 2009. It would thus be in the interest of the governing Concertación to counteract the UDI electoral strategy, especially in working class sectors where most social transfers are disbursed.

Indeed, the Concertación government's "social protection" agenda, which included multiple targeted social funds, may be partly an attempt to counteract the opposition's electoral success among popular sectors. That social policy agenda was implemented more broadly after the presidential election of 2000, which was the closest race in the post-1990 period and saw the UDI leader, Joaquín Lavín, almost defeat the Concertación candidate, Ricardo Lagos. While the timing of this policy change might also reflect a partisan effect on social policy as an SP leader rose to the presidency, the influence of the UDI scare on Concertación cannot be dismissed. In effect, facing an opposition party making significant inroads among poor and electorally pivotal segments gave the governing coalition a strong incentive to under-disburse discretional social funds to UDI-headed municipal governments, especially for programs where municipal governments could claim more credit than the executive. We found evidence of this strategy in the case of the indigenous scholarship.

Electoral Effects of Targeted Education Funds

We have claimed that the Concertación in Chile pursued, on the margins of efficient socioeconomic targeting, a risk-coping portfolio-investment strategy that combines electoral and non-electoral objectives. The marginality and diversification of such an investment strategy is expected to produce low or insignificant electoral returns. Although the funds we analyzed in this work are not part of a CCT program, we use the results of a question included in the LAPOP 2010 round and applied in nine countries on the presence of at least one CCT beneficiary at the interviewee's household to comparatively assess the relative traction of CCT programs for predicting electoral behavior.

Table 2.2 displays the results obtained for Chile when predicting each of three dichotomous dependent variables: electoral turnout in the last election (= 1), vote for the incumbent's presidential candidacy (= 1), and sympathy for one of the political parties in the incumbent's pact (1 = Concertación). Our model includes a dummy variable that reports the presence (1) or absence (0) of a CCT beneficiary in the household, along with a series of socioeconomic controls (gender, age, education, and income decile). We also incorporated a series of political attitudes as controls (left-right self-placement, political interest, and attributing electoral monitoring capacity to the incumbent), as well as a dummy variable to indicate if someone in the respondent's family is employed by the municipality.

Our results clearly indicate that being a CCT recipient does not significantly shape the electoral behavior of Chilean citizens. Indeed, in two of the models, the coefficient (though not significant) indicates that CCT recipients have a relatively higher chance of having voted for the opposition.

In table 2.3, we replicate the baseline model (excluding two questions that were not applied in every case: attribution of monitoring capacity to the incumbent

TABLE 2.2.

Effects of targeted social benefits on declared electoral behavior and partisanship in Chile

	Turnout	Voted for the incumbent's presidential candidacy	Sympathizes with a party of the incumbent coalition
CCT (1 = beneficiary in the household)	0.19 (0.21)	−0.13 (0.27)	−0.38 (0.34)
Left-right self-placement	−0.00 (.03)	−0.29 (0.04)***	−0.36 (0.06)***
Gender (1 = male)	0.10 (0.14)	0.03 (0.19)	−0.56 (0.26)*
Age	1.35 (0.10)***	0.02 (0.13)	0.22 (0.16)
Income decile	0.06 (0.03)	−0.02 (0.04)	−0.09 (0.06)
Education	−0.01 (0.02)	−0.06 (0.02)*	0.07 (0.04)
Interest in politics	−0.32 (0.08)***	0.14 (0.10)	−0.71 (0.14)***
Attributes monitoring capacity to the government	0.12 (0.17)	−0.20 (0.23)	0.18 (0.31)
Has a job in the municipality	0.53 (0.27)*	0.02 (0.32)	0.42 (0.37)
Constant	−1.90 (0.64)	1.50 (0.83)	−0.11 (1.10)
N	1215	638	1209
Pseudo R square	0.19	0.10	0.17

Source: LAPOP 2010

Note: Robust standard errors in parenthesis

***significant at 1%, **significant at 5%, *significant at 10%

and a family member employed by the municipality) for the nine cases in which the CCT question was applied. For simplicity's sake, the table reports the obtained coefficient, standard error, and significance level for the CCT dummy. Chile is the only case in which the CCT dummy fails to produce a significant result in at least one of the three observed dependent variables.

In brief, this evidence is consistent with our fourth hypothesis regarding the electoral effects of the type of strategy that incumbents operating in a non-machine / strong state context might pursue. As with financial investments, allocating a small amount of resources in a highly diversified portfolio—which is more oriented to

TABLE 2.3.

Effects of targeted social benefits on declared electoral behavior and partisanship in selected Latin American countries

	Turnout	Voted for the incumbent's presidential candidacy	Sympathizes with a party of the incumbent coalition
Mexico	−0.32 (0.18)	0.49 (0.16)**	0.30 (0.27)
Colombia	0.10 (0.15)	0.32 (0.15)*	−0.16 (0.20)
Ecuador	0.04 (0.21)	0.42 (0.12)***	0.18 (0.17)
Bolivia	0.11 (0.15)	0.21 (0.10)*	0.06 (0.12)
Uruguay	0.08 (0.27)	0.23 (0.16)	0.38 (0.17)*
Brazil	0.30 (0.17)	0.41 (0.13)**	0.10 (0.15)
Venezuela	0.06 (0.21)	0.36 (0.19)	0.87 (0.22)***
Argentina	−0.45 (0.19)*	−0.23 (0.21)	0.90 (0.40)*
Chile	**−0.07 (0.21)**	**0.16 (0.23)**	**0.36 (0.33)**

Source: LAPOP 2010

Note: Robust standard errors in parenthesis. Generic control variables: left-right self-placement, gender, age, income decile, education, and interest in politics.

***significant at 1%, **significant at 5%, *significant at 10%

insurance (non-electoral goals) than to (electoral) profit—is likely to yield fewer returns.

Concluding Remarks and Future Considerations

Although the investment rationales we identified above might be specific to the Chilean education policy sector and should not exhaust the incumbent investment portfolio, our analysis yields some comparative implications. From a substantive point of view, we believe the literatures on clientelism and distributive politics fall short in guiding contemporary empirical analyses of targeted social funds in Latin America. While the former assumes the presence of a machine party in deriving investment rationales, the latter only distinguishes between "core" and "swing" investments. Since machine parties are not present in the majority of Latin American countries, incumbents might pursue non-electoral objectives or the mobilization of other electoral groups (such as non-voters) that are neither "core" nor "swing."

In response to these shortcomings, we claim that the nature of partisan organizations, and in particular the presence (or absence) of a strong partisan machine, should be considered a fundamental variable in shaping the types of political targeting available to incumbents. The design of social policy programs, in terms of their capacity to allocate resources according to targeting criteria and to oversee social policy implementation, should also be considered.

In the absence of a partisan machine, incumbents can further diversify their political investment options by implementing redistributive tactics, even to non-voters or non-members of their coalition (independents and communist mayors), that are clearly irrational in the context of a machine-ridden system. Moreover, non-electoral investment strategies (for example, coalition expansion) might also be part of the portfolio.

To be clear, the absence of a machine party complicates the monitoring of clientelistic transactions. While according to some definitions of clientelism (e.g., Stokes 2005) monitoring is a necessary condition for observing clientelism, to others (e.g., Auyero, this volume) clientelism can still exist without the stringent monitoring provided by party machines. We do not delve into this definitional matter here. We argue that the absence of a party machine—a widespread condition in Latin America—constrains monitoring, and shapes the incentives of incumbent politicians for investing social policy funds in significant ways. Therefore, investment rationales derived from very influential analyses of party machines (the PJ and the PRI are the favorite Latin American cases for such analyses) fall short in describing the investment portfolio that non-machine incumbents might implement.

Our argument also considers the role of social policy design and implementation, which are related to state capacity. Where a well-designed program is present, the scope for political targeting is reduced, but more and better information is available to fine-tune a complex investment portfolio, which is needed to offset the greater investment risk created by the absence of a party machine. Interestingly, while complex investment portfolios that work only on the margins of technocratic allocation make political discretion less visible (and pervasive) in the allocation of social funds, they provide opportunities for seeking seemingly contradictory objectives and achieving even more fine-tuning. In summary, our argument discourages the automatic translation of investment rationales (frequently inspired by the literature on machine-ridden party systems and distributive politics in the U.S.) across party-system and program-design contexts.

We advocate the need for a multiprogram and multisector methodological approach for understanding the nature of political distortions in targeted social funds. The vast majority of available studies either focus on one case and one type of transfer or lump together very different types of programs into a single discretionary spending indicator. As Bonvechi and Lodola (2009, 2–5) point out, this leads either to incompleteness (looking at one program) or clustering (seeing all available information on targeted disbursements as an aggregate). In both scenarios, significant cross-program variance within cases is obscured, leading once again to biased generalizations. Theoretically, clustering and incompleteness also obscure the role that different institutional formats might play in creating distinct opportunities for political targeting within a national politico-institutional scenario.[17]

Regarding the Chilean case, this chapter has only scratched the surface of the political dynamics driving targeted education funds. Although we have chosen education—a policy sector that is a central ingredient in the development recipe— further research should engage in more refined quantitative analysis that would cover more social sectors and programs, draw on government and independent sources, and reach back to earlier periods. So far, however, the lack of data has made this impossible. It therefore would be useful to engage in process tracing and qualitative analysis of selected programs to better understand and empirically test the investment rationales elaborated above.

Two possible avenues for further research appear promising to us. First, in our program sample we included educational funds with different institutional architectures. Holding the party system constant by looking only at one case, we observed significant variance across programs in terms of the scope and nature of their political targeting. We therefore hypothesize that within a given systemic scenario, different institutional architectures can significantly shape the room for political targeting and the types of political goals that incumbents can pursue while implementing a given social policy package. For instance, different programs provide distinct credit-claiming opportunities for local- and national-level politicians. Therefore, they might also have a selective affinity with different types of investment rationales. Further research is needed to explore this set of hypotheses.

Second, more in-depth analysis is needed of the political logic driving the emergence of the investment portfolio we described. This should be accomplished through qualitative process tracing to sort out whether or not the portfolio investment strategy described resulted from a centrally devised plan or came about by default, as a consequence of the decentralized administration of particular social policy funds—and their distinct institutional architecture—by different political factions of the incumbent coalition.

ACKNOWLEDGMENTS

The authors received funding for this chapter from Chilean public research funds through FONDECYT (research project 1110565), the Millennium Nucleus for the Study of Stateness and Democracy in Latin America (NS 100014), and the Centro de Estudios de Políticas y Prácticas en Educación (CEPPE) (CONICYT CIE01-4).

NOTES

1. We refer to a strong state as one that combines high levels of bureaucratic capacity and a professionalized/depoliticized bureaucracy. We acknowledge nonetheless that both conditions are not absolutely collinear and can vary significantly in the context of other cases.

2. The recent literature on clientelism also describes individual strategies as part of a portfolio investment strategy (see, e.g., Gans-Morse et al. 2009; Magaloni et al. 2007; and Nichter 2008). This chapter draws on this terminology but applies it in more general terms to include noncontingent exchanges and investments having motives other than the immediate pursuit of electoral payoffs.

3. We have identified only one article on the subject that focuses on Chile. Using pooled regressions with data between 1999 and 2002, Chumacero and Paredes (2002, 21) conclude that Chilean mayors belonging to the governing coalition were systematically favored with a higher number of beneficiaries in a central government emergency employment program (between 0.1% and 0.4% more than mayors from the opposition), controlling for unemployment rate, poverty rate, and median per capita income by district. This conclusion provides evidence of a "core" constituency investment strategy. However, we suggest that this is one of several strategies of the central government's political investment portfolio of targeted social funds.

4. See http://www.sinim.cl/

5. A number of the 93 bills related to education were passed in the Chilean Congress since the restoration of democracy in 1990 until the end of 2010. Some important laws among these are: Law 19,247 (9/15/1993), which enacted a system of shared funding (State-parents) for municipal and private schools that receive per pupil public vouchers; Law 19,532 (11/17/1997), which extended the number of hours that children spend at school; Law 19,876 (5/22/2003), a constitutional reform that made high school education mandatory; Law 19,938 (10/3/2004), which introduced the teaching of human rights issues at schools; Law 19,961 (8/14/2004), which established a teacher evaluation system; and Law 20,370 (9/12/2009), the last comprehensive reform of the Chilean educational system (Ley General de Educación).

6. We built our first dependent variable and named it Discretionary Transfers to Education, DTEDUC. For this purpose we took the following indicators with the original SINIM nomenclature and performed some basic calculations: Total Income Received for Education (IEDU16) minus Voucher Transfers from the Ministry of Education to Municipal Schools (IEDU18), minus Municipal Own Income Allocated to Education (IEDU20). Because SINIM figures are in thousands of Chilean pesos for each year, we multiplied the resulting figure by 1000 and then divided it by the total number of school-aged children in each district (IPEEC).

This procedure accounts for discretionary transfers that are controlled by educational demand in each district. Therefore, DTEDUC = ([IEDU16 − IEDU18 − IEDU20] × 1000) / IPEEC.

7. The SINIM variable for number of scholarships is MTSBP, while the number of school-aged children is IPEEC. The formula used for the number of presidential scholarships as percentage of school-aged children: (MTSBP / IPEEC) × 100.

8. The last national census (2002) includes the question: "Do you belong to any of the following native or indigenous peoples: Alacalufe (Kawaskar), Atacameño, Aymara, Colla, Mapuche, Quechua, Rapanui, Yámana (Yagán), none of the above?" According the results of the census, 4.6% of the total Chilean population declared themselves as indigenous.

9. In this case there is no official account of the number of indigenous children per district, and no official estimation of indigenous population per district (*comuna*) per year other than for 2008. For this reason, our yearly data (2001 to 2009) on the number of indigenous scholarships allocated to each district (MEPBI) was divided by the 2008 indigenous population by district (ITPCI = 2008). Thus, the formula for the number of indigenous scholarships as a percentage of indigenous population is: (MEPBI / ITPCI = 2008) × 100.

10. The official SINIM code for this indicator is IADM3. The FCM was created in 1979 under the military dictatorship to redistribute resources from rich to poor municipalities. Without taxation authority, Chilean municipal income comes from three main sources: the FCM, transfers from the central government, and own revenue. The latter includes income from property taxes (defined and collected by the central government), user fees for several municipal services such as garbage collection and disposal, and fees for vehicle and other permits required for different commercial activities.

11. We also controlled for the rural versus urban character of each district, as well as for the percentage of municipal employees that hold professional degrees, as indicators of bureaucratic capacity. However, none of these variables obtained significant results and were therefore removed from the final model specification.

12. Administratively, Chile is divided into 15 regions, 54 provinces, and 345 local municipal districts (*comunas*). Regional and provincial governors are delegates of the President of Chile, whereas mayors at the district level are elected by citizens to head each municipality. Each region and province has a *comuna* that is the regional and provincial capital.

13. We tested for non-linearity in the dependent variables under the assumption that the programs might present decreasing marginal utilities in richer municipalities; however, we did not find any evidence of non-linearity. To deal with heteroskedasticity we ran the proper tests for robust standard errors on all models.

14. See http://www.elecciones.gov.cl/

15. We initially included a dummy variable for mayors re-elected in the last municipal election, since arguably re-election goes along with more technical and political expertise to effectively lobby the central government for more targeted social funds; however, we consistently had no significant finding.

16. Note that we do not refer to "turnout buying," as proposed by Nichter (2008), who draws on machine party literature when referring to a contingent transaction on Election Day.

17. Although a thorough analysis of how different institutional social transfer architectures create incentives for different political investment strategies (i.e., by providing different credit-claiming possibilities to local versus national leaders, or introducing harsher social

conditionalities) exceeds the scope of this paper, we find systematic differences across the programs we analyze here. We have criticized previous works for mechanically translating assumptions on incumbent investment rationales across contexts (from machine-party systems to non-machine ones). We do not wish to engage in the same type of fallacy, even at the cost of theoretical elegance and parsimony at this stage.

REFERENCES

Altman, David. 2004. "Redibujando El Mapa Electoral Chileno: Incidencia De Factores Socioeconómicos Y Género En Las Urnas." *Revista de Ciencia Política* 24 (2): 49–66.

Bonvecchi, Alejandro, and Germán Lodola. 2009. "The Dual Logic of Intergovernmental Transfers: Territorial Coalition-Building in Argentina." Paper presented at the Congress of the Latin American Studies Association, June 11–14, Rio de Janeiro, Brazil.

Borges, Natasha, and Wendy Hunter. 2009. "Democracy and Social Policy in Brazil: Advancing Basic Needs, Preserving Privileged Interests." *Latin American Politics & Society*.

Borzutzky, Silvia. 2002. *Vital Connections: Politics, Social Security, and Inequality in Chile.* South Bend, IN: University of Notre Dame Press.

Calvo, Ernesto, and Maria Victoria Murillo. 2004. "Who Delivers? Partisan Clients in the Argentine Electoral Market." *American Journal of Political Science* 98 (4): 742–57.

———. 2009. "Patronage Networks, Ideological Proximity, and Vote Choice." Paper presented at the Annual Meeting of the American Political Science Association, September 3–6, Toronto, Canada.

Cox, Cristián. 2005. "Las políticas educacionales de Chile en las dos últimas decadas del siglo XX." In *Politicas Educacionales en el Cambio de Siglo: La Reforma del Sistema Escolar de Chile,* ed. C. Cox. Santiago: Editorial Universitaria.

Cox, Gary W., and Mathew D. McCubbins. 2001. "The Institutional Determinants of Economic Policy Outcomes." In *Presidents, Parliaments, and Policy,* ed. S. Haggard and M. D. McCubbins. New York: Cambridge University Press.

Chumacero, Rómulo, and Ricardo Paredes. 2002. "Does Centralization Imply Better Targeting? Evaluating Emergency Employment Programs in Chile." In *Documentos de Trabajo*: Departamento de Ingeniería Industrial y de Sistemas, Pontificia Universidad Católica de Chile.

Delannoy, Françoise. 2000. "Education Reforms in Chile, 1980–98." In *Country Studies. Education Reform and Management Publication Series.* The World Bank.

De la O, Ana. 2010. "The Politics of Conditional Cash Transfers." Presented at Redistribution, Public Goods, and Political Market Failures, Yale University, April 9–10, New Haven, CT.

Dixit, Avinash, and John B. Londregan. 1996. "The Determinants of Success of Special Interests in Redistributive Politics." *Journal of Politics* 58 (4): 1132–55.

Escobar-Lemmon, Maria. 2003. "Political Support for Decentralization: An Analysis of the Colombian and Venezuelan Legislatures." *American Journal of Political Science* 47 (4): 683–97.

Espínola, Viola, and Claudio De Moura Castro, eds. 1999. *Economía Política de la Reforma Educacional en Chile. La Reforma Vista por sus Protagonistas.* Washington, DC: Inter-American Development Bank.

Gans-Morse, Jordan, Sebastian Mazzuca, and Simeon Nichter, "Who Gets Bought? Vote

Buying, Turnout Buying, and Other Strategies." 2009. *Weatherhead Center for International Affairs*. Working Paper 09-0006.

Gauri, Varun. 1998. *School Choice in Chile: Two Decades of Education Reform*. Pittsburgh: University of Pittsburgh Press.

Gobierno de Chile, Instituto Nacional de Estadísticas (INE) / Programa Orígenes (MIDE PLAN / BID). 2005. Estadísticas Sociales de los Pueblos Indígenas en Chile Censo 2002. Santiago de Chile.

Grindle, Marilee S. 2004. *Despite the Odds: The Contentious Politics of Education Reform*. Princeton, NJ: Princeton University Press.

Inter-American Development Bank. 2005. *The Politics of Policies: Economic and Social Progress in Latin America, 2006 Report*. Washington, DC: Inter-American Development Bank / David Rockefeller Center for Latin American Studies, Harvard University.

Kaufman, Robert R., and Joan M. Nelson, eds. 2004. *Crucial Needs, Weak Incentives: Social Sector Reform, Democratization, and Globalization in Latin America*. Washington, DC: Woodrow Wilson Center Press / The Johns Hopkins University Press.

Luna, Juan Pablo. 2008. "Partidos Políticos y Sociedad en Chile: Trayectoria Histórica y Mutaciones Recientes." In *Reforma de Los Partidos Políticos en Chile*, ed. A. Fontaine, C. Larroulet, J. Navarrete, and I. Walker. Santiago: PNUD / CEP / Libertad y Desarrollo / Proyectamerica / CIEPLAN.

———. 2010. "Segmented Party Voter Linkages in Latin America: The Case of the Udi." *Journal of Latin American Studies* 42 (2): 325–56.

Luna, Juan Pablo, and Rodrigo Mardones. 2010. "Chile: Are the Parties Over?" *Journal of Democracy*, 21 (3): 107–21.

Magaloni, Beatriz, Alberto Diaz-Cayeros, and Federico Estévez. 2007. "Clientelism and Portfolio Diversification: A Model of Electoral Investment with Applications to Mexico." In *Patrons, Clients, and Policies: Patterns of Democratic Accountability*, ed. H. Kitschelt and S. I. Wilkinson. New York: Cambridge University Press.

Mardones, Rodrigo 2007. "The Congressional Politics of Decentralization: The Case of Chile." *Comparative Political Studies* 40 (3): 333–58.

Nichter, Simeon. 2008. "Vote Buying or Turnout Buying? Machine Politics and the Secret Ballot." *American Political Science Review* 102 (1): 19–31.

Recart, Gonzalo. 2010. "Geosegmentación y política en chile: Monitoreo sin máquina." Seminario de Tesis de Licenciatura, Instituto de Ciencia Política, Pontificia Universidad Católica de Chile.

Siavelis, Peter. 2002. "The Hidden Logic of Candidate Selection for Chilean Parliamentary Elections." *Comparative Politics* 34 (4): 419–38.

Stokes, Susan. 2005. "Perverse Accountability: A Formal Model of Machine Politics with Evidence from Argentina." *American Political Science Review* 99 (3): 315–27.

Valenzuela, Arturo. 1977. *Political Brokers in Chile: Local Government in a Centralized Polity*. Durham, NC: Duke University Press.

Wantchekon, Leonard. 2003. "Clientelism and Voting Behavior: Evidence from a Field Experiment in Benin." *World Politics* 55 (3): 399–422.

Zucco, Cesar. Forthcoming. "When Pay Outs Pay Off: Conditional Cash-Transfers and Voting Behavior in Brazil 2002–2010." *American Journal of Political Science*.

CHAPTER THREE

The Future of Peru's Brokered Democracy

MARTIN TANAKA AND CARLOS MELÉNDEZ

Analyses of political representation in Peru tend to refer to the weakness of political parties and civil society organizations, of a "democracy without parties," which would go hand in hand with the scant legitimacy of the country's democratic institutions. The limits of conventional mechanisms of representation may be relatively clear, but what is less clear is the way links between citizens and their political authorities are built, however volatile and unstable they may be. Despite everything, the parties have candidates who win votes and are elected to the extent that they convince voters and manage to act collectively (at least during electoral campaigns), and politicians operate by trying to express the wishes and interests of sectors of society, combining their demands, interacting with political authorities and other representatives nationally, regionally, and locally.

A number of studies (e.g., Kitschelt 2007) suggest that representative ties may or may not be based on rational calculation: the former may assume the outline of an agreement with political programs or clientelistic exchange, while the latter may assume the form of identification with a party or with charismatic figures. Many observers have noted the general weakening of programmatic links and traditional party identities in Latin America, as well as the growing importance of clientelistic networks for maintaining parties, which increasingly depend on personalistic leaders. The existing literature has rightly pointed out the limits of these forms of representation as top-down, not pluralist, and barely democratic structures. Nevertheless, despite all their limitations, clientelistic links produce a sophisticated and complex form of representation, and this becomes apparent in an analysis of Peru.

It is clear that in Peru citizens do not vote because they are persuaded by political programs—traditional party identities are nonexistent—but clientelistic relationships are also absent, and hence identification with charismatic leaders is highly volatile and unstable. Clientelistic relations require relatively complex, stable, and lasting organization. These conditions barely exist in Peru, where political elites face legitimacy issues and society grapples with major problems of independent collective action. Although there are no representative links in the strict sense, there are connections between politics and society, and varied and specific forms of mediation between both spheres. They relate parties without politicians, politicians without parties, and brokers. Brokers are agents who have their own interests and compete with each other in articulating community groups at the social level with the small core parties and the politicians around them, playing a valuable role as intermediaries without which politics would not function.

This kind of relationship between society and politics in Peru clarifies the reasons that the country has highly volatile elections, parties, and political organizations— which are hardly more than names on a ballot—and an extremely weak civil society. But at the same time, there are links—albeit circumstantial, momentary, and unstable —between the political and social domains and between national, regional, and local levels, which can become intense and take the form of demonstrations and protests that often follow noninstitutional, confrontational, and violent forms of action. Such fragmented connections have not interrupted the institutional continuity that began with the 1993 Constitution (as has happened in other Andean countries in recent years), despite its minimal legitimacy.

One of the consequences of this argument is that opening spaces for participation and direct democracy in the political system, intended to foster its legitimacy, will not necessarily have the outcomes expected by its proponents. This is because there are no established players to use those opportunities, only a series of mediators or brokers with their own particularistic goals. For this reason, parties and representative institutions should be strengthened, both on a regional and nationwide basis.

Peru in the Regional Context

Analyses of representative links in Latin America tend to highlight the growing problems of legitimacy of the political systems all over the region. Cracks are beginning to appear in countries like Chile and Colombia, which traditionally have more structured political parties and party systems. Countries with weak systems but traditionally strong political parties, like Argentina, are witnessing the fragmentation of their parties, and in recent years party systems are collapsing in increasing numbers.[1] In this context, while programmatic links appear to remain in some countries (Hawkins et al. 2008), they have eroded, and personalistic leadership is beginning to proliferate, offering populist measures (De la Torre and Peruzzotti, eds. 2008), coupled with clientelistic practices as a means of building political legitimacy. In recent years, the entire region has seen economic growth stimulated by an increase in the price of raw materials exports, which have enabled countries to significantly increase their revenues; this situation, in barely institutionalized political contexts with questionable legitimacy, has entailed the implementation of social policies with a strongly clientelistic bias.

Recent years have seen a growing and important discussion focused on this topic, of which this book is a testimony. In countries with strong political leadership, like the Kirchners in Argentina, Chavez in Venezuela, Correa in Ecuador, Morales in Bolivia, or Lula in Brazil—all left-wingers—the implementation of social policies has been the foundation of attempts to construct a new politically legitimate base. There has also been much discussion over the construction of the clientelistic apparatus, especially where there is less political competition and pluralism. The countries with traditionally strong parties, such as the PRI in Mexico, the liberal and conservative parties in Colombia, or the Peronist Party in Argentina, debate whether the maintenance of clientelistic networks is the key to their survival, despite their legitimacy problems.[2]

Against this backdrop, Peru appears to be an anomaly. In Peru, traditional party identities have practically disappeared, political programs have been replaced by extreme pragmatism, and politics has become personalized and defined in terms of *caudillos,* or individual leaders, but it is still volatile and unstable. At the same time, the weakness of the *caudillos* and their parties, and the fact that they are barely rooted throughout the country,[3] leads to a lack of the necessary mechanisms for implementing clientelistic practices. These include having effective political mediators in all the country with roots in local areas, the ability to mediate the distribution of goods and services given in exchange for political support, and the capacity to monitor compliance or to sanction failure to comply with the deal.[4]

Why have politicians in Peru not attempted to build a clientelistic network in recent years? This occurred in other countries also without strong political parties such as Ecuador (Basabe 2009), and is a way to build political legitimacy. It is surprising that neither the governments of Alejandro Toledo (2001–2006) nor Alan Garcia (2006–2011) have adopted such practices, given the abundance of fiscal revenue levied in recent years. It is especially surprising in the case of Garcia, whose first government implemented populist policies with a strong clientelistic component,[5] and because the APRA is possibly the only party capable of doing so. It is even more surprising in view of the fact that in the recent past those in power have made some successful attempts, in terms of political benefits, at building clientelistic structures, despite lacking a real party apparatus. This occurred under the rule of Fujimori (1990–2000). During those years, the government took conscious advantage of social programs for the very poor to build political power bases and thereby reverse adverse elections results.[6]

Tanaka (2008) has suggested that Garcia's second government preferred not to implement clientelistic networks or major social polices because of the markedly conservative alliance that enabled him to win the second round of the 2006 elections, and because he needed to "clean up his image" and wipe away the populist and clientelistic record of his first government. Garcia won the second round of the 2006 elections against Ollanta Humala because of support from conservative sectors, after earning only 24.3% in the first round of voting. These sectors provided their support, despite their considerable distrust of Garcia after the actions of his first government, and agreed to vote for him only to prevent a Humala victory. Garcia realized that with a very weak party the viability of his government depended on his alliance with conservatives, and he made it an objective of his second government to erase the memory of his 1985–1990 term, which was irresponsibly populist and dragged the country into hyperinflation. Implementing effective redistribution policies would have involved a logic of political action and political alliances very different from those at President Garcia's disposal.

Peru has implemented social policies similar to those of other countries, like conditional cash transfers, but in a very small scale. In Peru the program is called *Juntos*. This kind of initiative has been crucial to the construction of political legitimacy in most of the countries in the region, but in Peru it has been modest. In Peru, *Juntos* reaches 17% of the poor, while the *Plan Familias* in Argentina reaches 27% *Chile Solidario* 47%, Colombia's *Familias en Acción* 39%, *Oportunidades* in Mexico 72%, *Bolsa Familia* in Brazil 84%, and Ecuador's *Bono de Desarrollo Humano* 100%, according to 2008 figures (Johannsen 2009).[7] Garcia and Toledo were presidents with approval ratings among the lowest in Latin America. Toledo had very low approval ratings during most of his term, with an average of little over 10% from late 2003 until the end of 2005, according to nationwide *Apoyo* surveys. Garcia's government approval rating averaged 25% between 2009 and 2010. According to the Mitofsky survey in October 2010, Garcia was the worst-rated president in Latin America in the fifty-first month of his government, together with Fernando Lugo of Paraguay, in his twenty-fifth month. By the end of their governments, neither *Peru Posible* nor the APRA managed to field presidential candidates, and the number of seats they had in parliament fell to a minimum (only two and four members of Congress, respectively).

If there are no representative parties capable of awakening strong identification or clientelistic networks or apparatuses, if politics have become filled with "antipolitical" content that hampers the development of programmatic bases, if personalistic leaders cannot build up a strong base, then the question is: how is politics conducted in Peru? How are society and politics related? This chapter looks at how these spheres are linked through parties without politicians, politicians without parties, and brokers. The next question is: how did such a strange situation emerge in Peru? We propose that it is the consequence of the gradual destruction of the various mechanisms that relate society and politics that were attempted in Peru in recent decades. Peru witnessed the destruction of an oligarchic model of representation in the 1960s; failed to build corporatist links in the 1970s under Velasco; experienced the collapse of party representation mechanisms on the basis of associations, unions, and social movements in the 1980s; and endured the failed attempt to build clientelistic networks under Fujimori in the 1990s.[8]

Peru: Destructuring without Restructuring

Until the 1960s, Peru was not particularly dissimilar to other Andean countries, in which the rural population was ruled by *hacendados,* land-owners, and local bosses. Cotler (1968 and 1969) described this type of relationship as "a triangle with no base."[9] The rural population had no autonomous organization and was linked to power in a position of subordination, divided under the local elites, who in turn had connections with national power brokers. In the more modern and urban spheres, organizations like the APRA and the Socialist Party prospered as representatives of the working class; although they remained cramped by the military dictatorships, which persecuted them and implemented clientelistic policies in order to get political legitimacy, although not in a particularly systematic fashion (Collier 1978).

The traditional rural order in Peru ended with the land reform of the military government of General Velasco, who ruled from 1968 to 1975; the great *haciendas* were expropriated and passed to those who worked on them. While the land reform in Peru did not largely affect the redistribution of income (it did not affect most of the land laborers, who belonged to peasant communities not to the *haciendas;* see Webb and Figueroa 1975), it did destroy the power of the *hacendados* and the local bosses connected with them. This helps to understand the differences between Peru and countries like Colombia, Ecuador, and Bolivia (as well as Brazil and Mexico), where there are still powerful local landowners who structure the political dynamic in rural areas. The military government aimed to create new relationships between politics and society—alternatives to the old oligarchies and the representative democracy espoused by parties between 1963 and 1968 under corporatist schemes. The proposal was the "fully participatory social democracy," consisting of the "direct representation" of organized workers. The National System of Social Mobilization

(SINAMOS), an entity that encouraged the people to organize in trade unions and associations, played an important role in this scheme. During the military government period between 1968 and 1979, more trade unions were formally created than during the entire period between 1936 and 1968. It is important to mention that during these years the left wing grew rapidly, underpinned by these mobilizations and the encouragement of participation, and was able to wrest from the APRA—at that time perceived as a conservative party—its representation of unions and community organizations, something which would become evident in the following years (see Cotler 1977, 1971; Stepan 1978).

However, Velasco's reforms came to a halt in the "second phase" of the military government, which opened the way to a transition to democracy and established an inclusive system during the "third wave" of democratization. In the 1980s a highly corporative form of representation emerged, in part as a consequence of the Velasco reforms, and the parties connected with citizens through the unions and associations developed during the military government. The left-wing parties, for example, grew and developed in close connection with the organizations of popular sectors (the leaders of these organizations were generally also party militants and leaders, and would follow party orders). Business associations also had close relations with political organizations, particularly with the *Partido Popular Cristiano* (People's Christian Party). In that decade, power and political influence lay in the ability to represent, express, or mediate with the state the interests and demands of social and interest groups, which intensified their demands and entrenched them in positions of strength in order to better negotiate politically and produced a dynamic that can be characterized as *movimientista*.[10]

The 1980s culminated in growing political polarization, terrorist action, hyperinflation, and the arrival of an outsider who consolidated power. His message and practice were anti-establishment, and he set in motion a neo-liberal program that is still in force today. Violence, the economic crisis, and later market-driven adjustment and structural reform programs weakened Peru's civil society organizations, and they lost their critical role in political life and became practically irrelevant.[11] Fujimori destroyed the party system and tried to build a system of representation with no institutional channels in which the clientelistic use of social policies was a key card. It laid the basis for political legitimacy in which public spending was concentrated in areas where Fujimori received less electoral support (for example, the referendum to approve the 1993 Constitution), and as a result he obtained greater support in rural areas and shanty towns.[12]

In spite of this, Fujimori's government did not manage to firmly entrench his system. It collapsed shortly after the disputed 2000 presidential and congressional elections, and since then democracy has returned to Peru.[13] Fujimori's government did not create a real party or well-articulated clientelistic networks, but used the state to offset the absence of militants and political agents; once he had lost the state, the movement led by Fujimori was reduced to whatever support his personal image could create. The fall of Fujimori opened the way to democracy and the reemergence of the country's "traditional" parties (Kenney 2003; Meléndez 2009). However, Peruvian politics has changed substantially, and relations between society and politics are not based on landlords and local bosses, corporatist schemes, a *movimientista* dynamic, or clientelistic structures. Political actors in general have styles and practices that emerged in the 1990s; parties are personalistic, pragmatic, internally fractious, and highly volatile, with no links to specific organizations or social sectors (Tanaka 2010a).

As has been said, it is clear how politics *do not work* in Peru, and how *there is no* representative party system, linked to civil society, nor representative organizations linked to different social and interest groups. Nevertheless, some community groups do organize, mobilize, and articulate demands. They are able to move beyond their local area and connect to the political sphere on a national level. To understand this phenomenon, it is necessary to make a detailed analysis of the specific mechanisms through which these connections are created.[14]

This chapter maintains that on the ruins of past social and political structures—and the frustrated attempts to build alternatives—operate a number of parties without politicians, politicians without parties, and brokers who act as indispensable intermediaries between communities and community organizations, and public authorities and political players whose leaders are usually based in Lima or in large cities and have no national coverage or local bases. The importance of these mediators—with their own agendas, in competition with each other, and differing from both their party structures and their social groups—explains why Peru is facing increasing numbers of protests and certain forms of regional and local leadership during a period of fragmentation, volatility, and undisciplined political and social organizations.[15]

Parties without Politicians and Politicians without Parties: Short-term Agreements and Personalistic Movements

How does the mediation between politics and society actually work in Peru? It resembles a fractured chain that links politics with society. At one end there are political elites based in Lima, in the case of the "national" parties, or in regional capitals in the case of regional movements, which generally have no leaders, militants, cadres, or local branches able to cover the entire area they purport to represent. The national parties and regional movements are characterized by personalism, improvisation, and electoral volatility, and do not have the necessary political staff to run candidates to elections, fill national or subnational executive positions, or represent social interests. Clearly, there are major differences of degree: the APRA, or the *Partido Popular Cristiano,* with its long tradition, or *Perú Posible,* which previously held power, operate differently than *Solidaridad Nacional* or *Renovación Nacional.* Similarly, matters in some regions are more fragmented and volatile than in others.

Peru has some of the lowest levels of political institutionalization in the region, in addition to the highest volatility, and the lowest levels of congressional re-election in the world.[16] During the April 2011 elections only 18% of members of Congress were re-elected, only 30% of congressional candidates possessed some kind of political experience, and 24% of candidates had been politically active in a different organization or party—a percentage that rises to 33.3% in the case of the current alliance in government, *Gana Perú.* Another sign of the existence of "parties without politicians" is that in the current Congress, 45% (59 out of 130) of legislators are "independent" or "invited" members of their parties.

This suggests that the current parties do not possess large numbers of their own political members; this dearth is covered by *politicians without parties.* These are people with their own political capital, who have political careers outside the parties (or rather, across various parties), both at the national and subnational level, and are known for their volatility.[17] Their independent political capital lies in enjoying certain recognition for their involvement in a previous political movement or government administration. These politicians usually ran as a candidate in previous elections, served as an elected authority, or held a government position. Some also possess private sector or civil society experience, for example, a former leadership role in a business, a union, a university, the media, or a development agency.

In order to participate in active political life, they can choose to strictly advocate for a particular party and develop a political career inside it (something seen less and less, given the weakening of the identity and programmatic profile of the parties and the increasing electoral volatility), to work with multiple parties to maximize their personal electoral and political chances, or to create their own party or movement. Each decision carries a significant amount of risk, and the art of these politicians without parties is sustaining a long and successful career. For example, the former president of the Cajamarca region from 2006 to 2010, Jesús Coronel, has been involved in politics since the 1980s, when he joined the *Izquierda Unida* (United Left), and ran for provincial mayor of Cajamarca. For many years Coronel was a secondary figure in the politics of Cajamarca, which for much of the 1980s and

1990s was home to clashes between two important local leaders, Luis Guerrero and Francisco Arroyo. After the disappearance of *Izquierda Unida,* Coronel ran unsuccessfully for Congress in 2000 for the *Frente Independiente Moralizador* (FIM) and for the regional presidency in 2002 for *Unidad Nacional.* He fell far short of being elected on both occasions.

Coronel started his career in *Izquierda Unida,* a political front that entered a serious crisis in 1989 and disappeared in the 1990s. At that time, the FIM, center right, looked like a political group opposed to Fujimori, and it led the fight against corruption. He subsequently stood for *Unidad Nacional* (National Unity), a political alliance dominated by the right-wing *Partido Popular Cristiano.* Clearly, Coronel ignored ideological differences and joined the coalition because it strengthened his electoral chances and also maintained his credibility as a candidate. After the 2002 campaign, Coronel decided to "stop knocking on the doors" of the national parties and prepared for the 2006 municipal and regional elections. Previously, he established a personalistic regional movement, *Fuerza Social* (Social Strength) to bolster his candidacy for the regional presidency. He allied with promising provincial figures (former candidates, elected authorities, and also local politicians without parties). Coronel offered the "franchise" of *Fuerza Social* for those standing to be provincial mayors and allowed his allies to elect their candidates for councilors. In exchange, he expected they provide support for his regional campaign. Coronel seemed a good leader to endorse because he was well known from his previous campaigns. With deals in place, and carrying the mantel of independence, autonomy, and freedom as the result of being the "owner" of a regional movement, Coronel finally won the regional presidency, beating a discredited APRA candidate (who led an inefficient 2002 to 2006 provincial and regional administration) and the *Movimiento Nueva Izquierda* (New Left Movement), which managed to create political capital from the role its community leaders played in the unrest against mining activities in the region.

Nevertheless, *Fuerza Social* was not an organized movement with local roots and militants. It was the sum of efforts based on short-term and narrow agreements in which the promise of sharing the administration did not provide the necessary level of cohesion within an individualistic and volatile political system. For example, Coronel's administration was embroiled in a contretemps with his vice-president, Aníbal Balcazar, who was dismissed from *Fuerza Social* in September 2007 because he "betrayed its party principles, being found to have sought the dismissal of the regional president." In April 2008, Balcazar was reported for corruption, arrested, imprisoned, brought before authorities, and suspended from duty by an administrative sanction until January 2010. At that point, Coronel had to decide whether to resign as regional president, to stand for re-election, or to remain in his post. Since it was unlikely he would win, and likely that Balcazar would complete his term of office, Coronel remained in his post. Not surprisingly, the *Fuerza Social* candidate for the presidency of the Cajamarca regional government was Coronel's wife, Beltina Gonzales, a jarring reminder that regional movements are personality-based.

During the 2010 municipal and regional elections and the 2011 general elections, the *Fuerza Social* group in Cajamarca joined an alliance with a national social-democratic party of a similar name (*Partido Descentralista Fuerza Social*). The alliance performed poorly; on the regional level it only managed to present candidates as part of alliances and did not win any campaigns. At the municipal level, it ran candidates in 2.1% of the disputed provincial municipalities, and won 12.9% of votes nationwide, and emerged victorious in the Lima city council election. However, excluding Lima voters, the alliance only won 0.2% of the vote. In Cajamarca, the *Fuerza Social* candidate was defeated, and earned 12.8% of the vote, far behind the 30.8% won by the winner, Gregorio Santos, of the *Movimiento de Afirmación Social* (Social Affirmation Movement), who ran in 2006 as a candidate of the *Movimiento Nueva Izquierda*.[18]

Another kind of career for the politician without a party is that in which their political capital is drawn from their links with community organizations and with groups that can be mobilized and are needed for political action. These actors have connections with the world of brokers that mediate between the social and political spheres, as will be shown below. Jaime Zea, for example, was a political cadre of the former *Izquierda Unida* who emerged as part of the team of the former mayor of the Lima district of Villa El Salvador, Michael Azcueta. Zea made his political career as a community leader in the lower-class district of the city. At 23, he was elected councilor, precisely when Azcueta was elected mayor (from 1984 to 1986) and was re-elected with him (from 1987 to 1989). After two terms in the district, Azcueta decided to run for mayor of the municipality of Lima as part of the *Izquierda Unida* list and lost. Ricardo Belmont, a radio and TV host and member of the *Obras* movement, won the election and initiated the era of the crisis of the traditional parties, the emergence of outsiders, and the boom of "independent" candidates. However, the left won again in Villa el Salvador, and José Rodriguez was elected in 1989. The period between 1989 and 1993 featured a political crisis in the municipality, which was previously known for its community and participatory traditions.[19] Political violence factored into the crisis; the terrorist organization Shining Path killed the deputy mayor of the municipality, María Elena Moyano, in 1992 and then her successor, Rolando Galindo, at the beginning of 1993, when he was a candidate for mayor. Another candidate, Alejandro Pantigoso, was assassinated along with his wife. Shining Path later conducted failed assassination attempts against former mayor Michel Azcueta and the deputy mayor of the municipality, César Soplín.[20]

Jorge Vazquez, a member of the *Obras* movement, succeeded Rodriguez in 1993, which momentarily ended three periods of leftist hegemony (that occurred between 1983 and 1993). However, Vazquez was unable to complete his term of office because of problems with the law and the threat of dismissal. He was replaced by deputy mayor César Soplín, who was also dismissed because of corruption charges. In 1996, Michel Azcueta returned for a third term as mayor of Villa El Salvador, this time on the ticket of *Somos Lima*—a movement led by the mayor of Lima, Alberto Andrade. Zea joined him on the council. Martin Pumar, another of Azcueta's associates, took over from Azcueta from 1999 until 2002, won local elections under the banner of the Andrade party renamed *Somos Perú,* and consolidated a generational change in the council administration. Zea joined him and for the first time held the post of deputy mayor. *Somos Perú,* as an independent movement, did not grow out of the Marxist Left—on the contrary, it was quite liberal—but converted itself into an important opposition group fighting against the authoritarianism of Fujimori's government. Many leftists without a party ended in *Somos Perú.* In Villa El Salvador, Azcueta and his associates were asked to set up a local group opposed to Fujimori's clientelism. Azcueta's political leadership and experience in local government under the banner of *Somos Perú* was a strong and effective combination for the elections.

By 2002, however, *Somos Perú* was no longer an attractive movement, a victim of Peruvian electoral volatility. The long-standing friendship and association of Martin Pumar and Jaime Zea cooled during their term in local government, and they decided to seek election independently. Pumar ran under a new national party, *Mi Perú,* with no success, and Zea accepted the invitation of Lourdes Flores to join *Unidad Nacional* (National Unity), a right-wing political alliance. Zea benefited from the triumph of *Unidad Nacional* in the municipality of Lima, with Luis Castañeda, and was elected district mayor for the first time, with 24% of the vote. (It is interesting to note that the deputy mayor under Zea, Efraín Sánchez, ran on Fujimori's list *Vamos Vecinos* in the 1998 elections.)

An electoral map of Lima shows the growth of *Unidad Nacional* in the capital, based on strong support in lower-class areas, which were former strongholds of the Left and Fujimori. However, this is not a consequence of having a party with an organization and structure, but instead—as shown by the case of Zea—a consequence of a good process of selecting candidates, often "invited independents," to join the ranks of a movement without politicians. As might be expected, this does not presuppose any particular degree of political commitment. *Unidad Nacional,* regardless of its local government administration, "does not exist" in the district, and Zea, who was in effect "invited," did nothing to change this situation. During the local government elections of 2006, Zea once again contacted Lourdes Flores and suggested that he could seek re-election within that political alliance. However, disputes within *Unidad Nacional* led to the decision that candidates for the Lima districts would be selected by the mayor of Lima, Luis Castañeda, and the leader of the *Solidaridad Nacional* party, who was seeking re-election and did not have Zea in his plans. Zea, mayor and candidate for re-election, was left with no movement and waiting for a good offer.

The offer came when the recently created party *Restauración Nacional* (National Restoration), which has connections with evangelical churches, invited Zea to join its ranks almost unconditionally. In November 2006, Zea was re-elected, winning 20.2% of the vote in the district, slightly above those obtained by the candidate running for *Unidad Nacional,* Zea's former political party, who got 19.3%. Michel Azcueta finished third, as the head of a local independent movement, *Confianza Perú,* which earned 18.6% of the vote. In the October 2010 local government elections Zea ran for a third term, this time as a Unidad Nacional candidate, in response to an invitation from Lourdes Flores, who ran for provincial mayor of Lima. Susana Villaran, of *Fuerza Social,* emerged victorious with 38.4% of the vote, and was followed by Flores with 37.5%. Humberto Lay, candidate for *Restauración Nacional,* finished in third place with 8.6%. In Villa El Salvador, Zea lost the local government, finishing in third place, with 12.2% of the votes.

This is how Zea—a community leader who grew up adhering to the principles and canons of the Peruvian Left—ended up as a politician without party, joining groups ideologically opposed to his formative socialist principles: *Unidad Nacional* is a center-right alliance, and *Restauración Nacional* is an evangelical party. In all his considerable political experience, he did not form a political movement of his own, but rather, a group of associates connected to grass-roots organizations—since he was with Azcueta in his time—who migrate from political forces depending on the context and conditions. But throughout his career, Zea has been a successful politician, a recognized leader, and always held a local government position (councilor, deputy mayor, or mayor), which shows that he has worked effectively. This is why it is relatively simple for him to change his political affiliations—it is very likely that political organizations without enough party members will "invite" a successful politician who has an excellent chance of winning elections—and explains why he does not invest resources in creating an independent organization, as Coronel did in Cajamarca.[21]

Brokers and Mediation between the Social and Political Spheres

So far we have been chiefly concerned with the political arena. But to discuss its connections with the grassroots level, we need to look to brokers. The problems of representation in Peru are not simply the result of limitations of political actors; social actors also have serious difficulties defining their interests, formulating demands, acting collectively, and putting into practice a repertoire of actions that would help satisfy their demands. Here external actors take action, giving form to the groups' appeals, organizing activities for exerting pressure, negotiating with the authorities on the basis of the law, jurisprudence, and the "technical" aspects of the issues at stake. They may be NGOs, churches, or other civil society organizations. When they intervene, they tend to give the demands more complex form associated with their own agendas. However, there are also individualistic social mediators who play the same roles but follow pragmatic and short-term considerations.

Just as there are politicians without parties, there are grassroots leaders without organizations. Just as the former based their political capital on prior experience in politics, public administration, the private sector, or civil society, the latter base their social capital on prior experience in political militancy and trade union activity, access to informal political and social networks, their capacity for mobilizing, lobbying, and protesting, and their management of useful negotiating tools and information. In other circumstances these people would be union leaders or party militants, but given the crisis in the parties and community organizations, they become brokers: they offset the social groups' lack of autonomous collective action and play a role as intermediaries with elected authorities and political elites. They aim to use these actions as a stepping-stone to a career and become politicians without a party.

Brokers come in many shapes and forms: some work solely at the local or regional level and channel their diverse demands within their "scope of action." Others specialize in some social areas of specific issues such as the management of environmental conflict and the negotiation of labor talks and are active both in Lima and the rest of the country. Others articulate between local actors with differing approaches (such as the defense fronts) or between actors who operate at different scales (national, regional, and local) within a single sector (for example, the organization of the coca-growers' movement to negotiate with the authorities). Below are the stories of a number of people who could be considered representative brokers.

It is common for local community organizations to depend on a variety of bridges and options to link their particular demands with national policy and to establish temporary alliances with players with national level contacts. Such is the case of the coca-growers' movement in the Apurimac and Ene River Valley (VRAE). Six hours by road on public transport from Huamanga, the capital of Ayacucho, the VRAE is difficult to access. It is composed of six districts in Cusco and Ayacucho, where in the 1990s the Shining Path, counter-subversion, and the coca boom all coincided. Residual Shining Path forces are still in the area, and the valley still produces a large percentage of the coca sold on the black market. In the absence of real alternatives for economic and productive development (since USAID projects and others have a very limited impact), the region's coca farmers recently managed to establish one of the most active community organizations in the region. The farmers' main agenda was to demand the right to grow coca, the rejection of forced eradication policies, and demands for "serious" alternatives.

The primary school teacher Nelson Palomino emerged as a leader of the movement and a figure in the larger cause. He used a radio program and his ability to communicate to become a reference for the coca-growers' movement in this remote area where few government entities are found. Unlike other community leaders, Palomino had no previous political experience. He won his political spurs in the midst of political violence as part of the civilian population caught in the crossfire of counter-subversion and the Shining Path. His political development took place in an authoritarian context, in the absence of the state—a context in which the struggle of the coca-growers' movement has been shaped above all by the fight to survive rather than by a political platform as in Bolivia. As a community leader, Palomino was always at the limit of the law and was very anti-establishment. In 2002, he forced his way into a local radio station that broadcast programs in support of USAID's alternative crop projects. Palomino captured the owner of the radio station and paraded him, dressed up as a woman, through the streets of San Francisco in full view of the authorities, who took no action out of fear of aggravating his supporters. The journalist was freed a few hours later, but the incident gave the police the justification they needed to issue a warrant for Palomino's arrest, which was carried out by Peruvian Special Forces.

After Palomino was captured, charged, and imprisoned, the coca-growers' movement was able to organize an important mobilization to Lima in 2003, but afterward it found itself without a national leader and a strategy. Ricardo Noriega—a Lima lawyer who had run for the presidency in 2001 as a member of an independent personalistic movement, "*Todos por la Victoria*," which won 0.3% of the vote—emerged as Palomino's defense lawyer in an attempt to earn political capital.[22] However, Noriega's participation was short-lived, and his political ambitions were hardly realistic. The coca-growers' movement needed a bridge to national politics, which is what Palomino provided because he was seen as a potential threat to the political system, a possible "radical outsider." Although Noriega hailed from Lima, he did not enjoy sufficient legitimacy to replace Palomino as an intermediary in the coca-growers' negotiations. Leaderless, the movement's organization spiraled into internal conflict and lost the binding force that had held it together.[23]

After serving a third of his sentence, Palomino was paroled in June 2006. Shortly afterward, he announced the creation of the *Kuska* ("Together" in Quechua) movement, which was to be the political branch of the coca-growers' movement, based on the model of the Bolivian MAS. *Kuska* intended to participate as a national party in the regional elections of November 2006 but failed to meet registration requirements. Finally, *Kuska* formed the *Qatun Tarpuy* alliance with the regional movement *Turpay* formed in 2002. The alliance finished second in the Ayacucho regional elections and won a few municipalities in the VRAE. One of *Tarpuy*'s top leaders was José Urquizo, who adhered to positions close to Fujimori in the 1990s. Urquizo is a typical regional politician without a party: in 1998 he ran unsuccessfully as an independent to be mayor of Ayacucho; in the 2002 Ayacucho regional elections, he was elected regional vice-president on the APRA party list; in 2006 he stood for Congress on Ollanta Humala's ticket and was elected for the Ayacucho electoral district; and in 2011 he was re-elected once more, again as a member of Humala's alliance. Recently he served also as Minister of Production (December 2011–May 2012) and then as Minister of Defense for an even shorter period (May–July 2012).[24]

Clearly, Palomino can be seen as a broker, an intermediary between community local organizations and national politics, trying to be a politician without party, like Noriega and Urquizo. They all give priority to their individual careers, not the building of institutions, and certainly not to following specific ideologies or programs. Their careers will develop depending on their effectiveness in responding to the demands and needs of their power bases, and pragmatism will remain crucial to their success.

There are also brokers who act as links between actors and demands from different local spaces by creating defense fronts for better negotiations with the central government. In this case, because of the complexity of related demands, current "free agents" with experience in party militancy or union leadership carry a lot of weight. Such is the case of Washington Román.

Román was a union leader and militant of the Communist Party in Cusco. In the late 1990s a number of unions, associations, professional colleges, and other civil society organizations in Cusco created the Regional Assembly as a pluralist front to mobilize Cusco's decentralization demands, which were under threat from Fujimori's government. It was easy for Román to move to the forefront of this assembly because of his skill as a mediator. Despite the absence of a solid organization, he was a key figure in connecting the regional protests in southern Peru and utilizing his union connections. Román details the organization of the 1999 regional strike in southern Peru:

> I went to Puno with another member of the assembly. Our only contact was a fellow unionist who had a fifteen-minute spot on a radio program. We got there early and we went straight to the radio station, and we began to call all Puno's community leaders to a meeting in the construction workers' hall. This was at about 6 in the morning. By 9 a.m., fifty people were there. We explained the strike agenda, and they agreed to support us. The next day we went to Tacna, where we did the same thing. As you know, the strike was a success.

Román turned out to be effective in mobilizing the "fight of the south" in Fujimori's downfall. His relative success put him in contact with other regional fronts, where he swiftly gained influence, given the success of the mobilization in the south. As representative of the National Regional Fronts Coordinating Committee, Román was a signatory to the *Acuerdo Nacional* (National Agreement) promoted by the government of Alejandro Toledo in 2002. He was the last to sign the agreement and was the only representative of "regional civil society." In that same year, Román ran for the regional presidency of Cusco with *Plataforma Democrática* (Democratic Platform), a political organization formed through the interaction of community leaders and NGO professionals with a strong left-wing bias. In theory, *Plataforma* had promise, with solid programs and the support of the populace, and it had won legitimacy in the fight against Fujimori. It also seemed to be a pluralist organization, since the chairman of the Cusco Chamber of Tourism was involved as a candidate for provincial mayor. However, the movement won barely 2% of the vote in the regional election.

Currently, the National Regional Front Coordinating Committee is effectively nonexistent and no longer holds a place in the National Agreement. The Regional Assembly still exists and maintains an office in the Cusco workers' union. Román retired from active politics to study journalism; he currently hosts a daily radio program broadcast at 8 a.m. He has exchanged mobilizations and demonstration slogans for the microphone and radio set, but he understands this change as one more step in his career as a community mediator and a future political leader.[25]

Some Conclusions

The argument presented here suggests that to understand the functioning of a democracy without parties in Peru it is necessary to comprehend the legacy of the collapse of the party system and recognize that no political organization has a network of activists or reliable militants able to cover the entire political battlefield. Political organizations are composed of a relatively small central core that possesses fragile contacts with core groups in other places and comprises a relatively precarious network. This is true for all Peruvian political groups, including the APRA. Political groups must mobilize their network of relations to field a minimum number of relatively loyal candidates, obtain funding, and mount a successful political campaign. The older parties have established networks of militants, activists, and former public servants as well as familiar and viable political identities (the APRA, *Accion Popular,* the *Partido Popular Cristiano,* the left-wing parties, and Toledo and Fujimori supporters). Less-established groups have a basic core of militants overlapping other networks: the military and former left-wing militants (the *Partido Nacionalista,* for example), the evangelical churches (*Restauración Nacional*); others have networks that rally around a single figure (*Solidaridad Nacional*). The national parties, apart from some sporadic core groups, do not have enough militants or sympathizers to provide the requisite number of political candidates and must therefore mobilize their networks to field large numbers of candidates for political office.

This is true both of the national parties, which have core groups in Lima and try to establish relations with core groups all over the country, and of the regional movements with core groups found in regional capitals, which try to establish relations with core groups in the region's districts and provinces. In Peru, political participation is intense and takes place not through consolidated national parties or regional movements but through politicians without a party—people who develop their political careers independently or as members of several parties, people that are products of the crisis of political parties and are signed by an extreme pragmatism. They have prior experience in politics or public administration or are prominent local figures with experience as entrepreneurs, journalists, or teachers. These politicians try to develop a political career by building a reputation as credible representatives of sectorial or regional interests. How do these politicians calculate the costs and benefits of trying to develop a career within a party, to switch among parties, or to create a party of their own? What kind of profiles could we make of these politicians, distinguishing between national parties or among regions at a subnational level? We face a very big research agenda.

Just as political activity is intense, so is community mobilization. Mobilizations occur despite the fact that political parties do not represent unions or community organizations and face serious constraints to collective action. In fact, the amount of social conflict and protest has increased since the end of the 1990s.[26] The intervention of independent agents, organizations, and brokers that assume costs and provide technology make collective action possible. However, given the fragmented and particularistic nature of these actors, the intense conflictivity does not translate into national mass demonstrations able to alter the dynamics of national politics as has happened in countries like Bolivia, for example.

In Peru, relations between society and politics do not derive from a traditional party system but from precarious and unstable links formed by intermediaries, politicians without parties, and brokers. The weak links explain the poor quality and scant legitimacy of Peru's political institutions. What can be done? In recent years, the limits of representation offered by democracy have opened the way to broader-based election mechanisms. These imply going from the election of representatives to direct participation of the population through the incorporation of participatory mechanisms in which stakeholders and community movements influence government decision making. In developed Western democracies, this type of broadening shows that the participatory mechanisms can complement the representative ones, at least in principle. However, in Peru and other Latin American countries, the relationship has not been an easy one. This is because the sequence in which the participatory mechanisms are incorporated is crucial—the assumption that they are complementary presupposes the existence of political parties, a party system, minimally consolidated state institutions, and representative community organizations. Without these institutions, the opportunity for participation can weaken representation and the validity of the state and can consolidate fractious groups with particular interests.[27]

Proposals for political reform in Peru are generally guided by the need to open the political system, provide an opportunity to new political actors, and enlist citizens' participation. This is a mistake. In practice it provides more opportunities to politicians without a party and individualistic brokers. In fact, the reform of Peru's representative system should attempt to strengthen national parties; encourage political careers within a stable party system; link national, regional, and local politics; and connect political representatives with community organizations and interests through established channels for dialogue and consensus building such as decentralized congressional hearings, municipal and regional councils, and local and regional coordination councils to bring together elected authorities and civil society representatives.

If there is no progress in political reform, politics in Peru will not be the result of political deliberation but will continue to be characterized by unstable and precarious representation mechanisms forged by pressure from technocratic policy networks, de facto powers, lobbies, demonstrations, and violent and disruptive civil unrest.

NOTES

1. On representation and legitimacy problems, see Luna 2007. On Chile, see Altman and Luna 2010; on Colombia, Bejarano et al. 2010. On Argentina, see Cavarozzi and Casullo 2002; Torre 2003; Calvo and Escolar 2005; and Leiras 2007. On the collapse of party systems, see Tanaka 2010b.

2. See Hevia 2011, and González 2011.

3. See Tanaka 2005a; Levitsky and Cameron 2003.

4. On this monitoring process, see Szwarcberg 2010.

5. See Graham 1992.

6. See Graham and Kane 1998; Roberts and Arce 1998; Schady 1999; Tanaka and Trivelli 2002.

7. On *Juntos,* see Díaz et al. 2009; Trivelli, Montenegro, and Gutiérrez 2011; Perova and Vakis 2010.

8. See Tanaka 2002.

9. Also see Fuenzalida 1970, among others.

10. See Tanaka 2005b and 1998; Gonzales and Samamé 1991.

11. For example, the affiliation to unions among white and blue collar workers went from 55.8% and 59.6% in 1981 to 10.2% and 11.2% in 2001, respectively, following Verdera 2007. On the destructuring effects of the internal armed conflict, see Comisión de la Verdad y Reconciliación (CVR) 2003.

12. See Carrión et al. 1999.

13. See Cotler and Grompone 2000; Tanaka 2005b.

14. First formulations of the following ideas can be found in Tanaka 2001; Tanaka and Meléndez 2005; and Meléndez 2005.

15. In recent years the weakening of national parties and institutional mechanisms of representation have gone together with an increase of the number of actions of social protest. See Grompone and Tanaka, eds., 2009.

16. See Jones 2007 and 2005; Mainwaring and Torcal 2005.

17. Is interesting to see the contrast between how political careers are built in Peru and other Latin American countries with stronger parties. See Siavelis and Morgenstern, eds., 2008.

18. On politics in Cajamarca, see Barrantes, Cuenca, and Morel 2012.

19. On Villa el Salvador, see Zapata 1996.

20. On political violence in Villa el Salvador, see CVR 2003, vol. V, chapter 2.16, and vol. VII, chapter 2.62; and Burt 2009.

21. About Zea, see also Rojas 2006.

22. Noriega could be considered a politician without a party: he ran again in the 2011 presidential election, this time under the party Despertar Nacional (National Awakening), and obtained 0.1% of the valid vote.

23. Some leaders of coca grower's organizations ran for Congress in the 2006 elections under the banner of Ollanta Humala's Gana Perú, for example. On the cocalero movement, see Durand 2009 and 2005.

24. About Kuska and Tarpuy, see Huber 2008.

25. On Román, see Meléndez 2012.
26. See Tanaka and Vera 2010; Grompone and Tanaka 2009.
27. See Tanaka 2010c and 2009.

REFERENCES

Altman, David, and Juan Pablo Luna. 2010. "Chile: ¿institucionalización con pies de barro?" In *Democracia en la región andina: diversidad y desafíos,* ed. Maxwell Cameron and Juan Pablo Luna, 273–314. Lima: Instituto de Estudios Peruanos.

Barrantes, Roxana, Ricardo Cuenca, and Jorge Morel. 2012. *Las posibilidades del desarrollo inclusivo: dos historias regionales.* Lima: Instituto de Estudios Peruanos.

Basabe, Santiago. 2009. "Ecuador: Reforma constitucional, nuevos actores políticos y viejas prácticas partidistas." *Revista de Ciencia Política* 29 (2): 381–406.

Bejarano, Ana María, et al. 2010. "Colombia: 'Democracia amenazada.' " In *Democracia en la región andina: diversidad y desafíos,* ed. Maxwell Cameron and Juan Pablo Luna, 101–64. Lima: Instituto de Estudios Peruanos.

Burt, Jo-Marie. 2009. *Violencia y autoritarismo en el Perú: Bajo la sombra de Sendero y la dictadura de Fujimori.* Lima: Instituto de Estudios Peruanos.

Calvo, Ernesto, and Marcelo Escolar. 2005. *La nueva política de partidos en la Argentina: Crisis política, realineamientos partidarios y reforma electoral.* Buenos Aires: Prometeo Libros.

Cavarozzi, Marcelo, and Esperanza Casullo. 2002. "Los partidos políticos en América Latina hoy: ¿consolidación o crisis?" In *El asedio a la política: los partidos latinoamericanos en la era neoliberal,* comp. Marcelo Cavarozzi and Juan Abal Medina, ed. Rosario, Homo Sapiens, 9–30.

Collier, David. 1978. *Barriadas y élites: de Odría a Velasco (1976).* Lima: Instituto de Estudios Peruanos.

Comisión de la Verdad y Reconciliación. 2003. *Informe final.* Lima: CVR.

Cotler, Julio. 1968. "La mecánica de la dominación interna y del cambio social en el Perú." In José Matos Mar et al., *Perú problema: Cinco ensayos,* 153–97. Lima: Instituto de Estudios Peruanos.

———. 1969. "Actuales pautas de cambio en la sociedad rural del Perú." In José Matos Mar et al., *Dominación y cambios en el Perú rura: la micro-región del valle de Chancay,* 60–79. Lima: Instituto de Estudios Peruanos.

———. 1971. "Crisis política y populismo militar." In Fernando Fuenzalida et al., *Perú, hoy,* 87–174. México D.F., Siglo XXI.

———. 1977. "Perú: Estado oligárquico y reformismo militar." In *América Latina: historia de medio siglo. Vol. 1: América del Sur,* ed. Pablo González Casanova, 373–423. México D.F., Siglo XXI.

Cotler, Julio, and Romeo Grompone. 2000. *El fujimorismo: Ascenso y caída de un régimen autoritario.* Lima: Instituto de Estudios Peruanos.

De la Torre, Carlos, and Enrique Peruzzotti, eds. 2008. *El retorno del pueblo: Populismo y nuevas democracias en América Latina.* Quito: FLACSO.

Díaz et al. 2009. "Análisis de la implementación del Programa 'Juntos' en las regiones de Apurímac, Huancavelica y Huánuco." Lima: CIES.

Durand, Anahí. 2005. "El movimiento cocalero y su (in)existencia en el Perú: Itinerario de desencuentros en el río Apurímac." In *Boletín del Instituto Francés de Estudios Andinos, 34* (1): 103–26.

———. 2009. "'Aquí están los cocaleros': Un acercamiento a las protestas cocaleras en el valle del río Apurímac." In *Las protestas sociales en el Perú actual: Entre el crecimiento económico y la insatisfacción social,* ed. Romeo Grompone and Martín Tanaka, 263–320. Lima: Instituto de Estudios Peruanos.

Fuenzalida, Fernando. 1970. "Poder, raza y etnia en el Perú contemporáneo." In Fernando Fuenzalida et al., *El indio y el poder en el Perú.* Lima: Instituto de Estudios Peruanos.

Gonzales de Olarte, Efraín, and Lilian Samamé. 1991. *El péndulo peruano: Políticas económicas, gobernabilidad y subdesarrollo, 1963–1990.* Lima: Instituto de Estudios Peruanos.

González, Zaira. 2011. "Rewarding Voters through Welfare Transfers in Mexico and Brazil." Unpublished paper.

Graham, Carol. 1992. *Peru's Apra: Parties, Politics, and the Elusive Quest for Democracy.* Boulder, CO: Lynne Rienner.

Graham, Carol, and Cheikh Kane. 1998. "Opportunistic Government or Sustaining Reform? Electoral Trends and Public-Expenditure Patterns in Peru, 1990–1995." *Latin American Research Review* 33(1): 67–104.

Grompone, Romeo, and Martín Tanaka. 2009. "Las nuevas relaciones entre protestas sociales y política." In *Las protestas sociales en el Perú actual: Entre el crecimiento económico y la insatisfacción social,* ed. Romeo Grompone and Martín Tanaka, 381–415. Lima: Instituto de Estudios Peruanos.

Hawkins, Kirk, et al. 2008. "Revisiting the Programmatic Structure of Latin American Party Systems." Paper presented at the Annual Meeting of the American Political Science Association, August 28–31, Boston.

Hevia, Felipe. 2011. "Relaciones sociedad-Estado, participación ciudadana y clientelismo político en programas contra la pobreza: El caso de *Bolsa Familia* en Brasil." In *América Latina Hoy,* vol. 57, p. 205–38.

Huber, Ludwig. 2008. "La representación indígena en municipalidades peruanas: Tres estudios de caso." Lima: Instituto de Estudios Peruanos.

Johannsen, Julia. 2009. "Conditional Cash Transfers in Latin America: Problems and Opportunities." Unpublished presentation, Manila, July 23–24.

Jones, Mark. 2005. "The Role of Parties and Party Systems in the Policymaking Process." Unpublished paper.

———. 2007. "Democracy in Latin America, Challenges and Solutions: Political Party and Party System Institutionalization and Women's Legislative Representation." Unpublished paper.

Kenney, Charles. 2003. "The Death and Rebirth of a Party System, Peru 1978–2001." *Comparative Political Studies* 36 (10): 1210–39.

Kitschelt, Herbert. 2007. "Party Systems." In *The Oxford Handbook of Comparative Politics,* ed. Carles Boix and Susan Stokes, 522–54. Oxford: Oxford University Press.

Leiras, Marcelo. 2007. *Todos los caballos del rey: la integración de los partidos políticos y el gobierno democrático de la Argentina, 1995–2003.* Buenos Aires: Prometeo Libros.

Levitsky, Steven, and Maxwell Cameron. 2003. "Democracy without Parties? Political Parties and Regime Change in Fujimori's Peru." *Latin American Politics and Society* 45 (3): 1–33.

Luna, Juan Pablo. 2007. "Representación política en América Latina: el estado de la cuestión y una propuesta de agenda." *Política y Gobierno* 14 (2): 391–435.

Mainwaring, Scott, and Mariano Torcal. 2005. "Party System Institutionalization and Party System Theory after the Third Wave of Democratization." Kellogg Institute for International Studies, Working Paper, no. 319.

Meléndez, Carlos. 2005. "Mediaciones y conflictos: las transformaciones de la intermediación política y los estallidos de violencia en el Perú actual." In *El Estado está de vuelta: desigualdad, diversidad y democracia,* ed. Victor Vich. Lima: Instituto de Estudios Peruanos.

———. 2009. "La insistencia de los partidos: Una aproximación sobre la permanencia de los partidos políticos tradicionales en los países andinos." In *La nueva coyuntura crítica en los países andinos,* ed. Martín Tanaka. Lima: Instituto de Estudios Peruanos–IDEA.

———. 2012. *La soledad de la política: Transformaciones estructurales, intermediación política y conflictos sociales en el Perú (2000–2012).* Lima: Mitin eds.

Perova, Elizaveta, and Renos Vakis. 2010. "El impacto potencial del programa Juntos en Perú: Evidencia de una evaluación no experimental. Lima: Juntos–Banco Mundial.

Roberts, Kenneth, and Moisés Arce. 1998. "Neoliberalism and Lower-class Voting Behavior in Peru." *Comparative Political Studies* 31 (2): 217–46.

Rojas, Rolado. 2006. "Poder local y participación ciudadana: la experiencia del presupuesto participativo en Villa el Salvador." In *Investigaciones Sociales,* año X, no. 17, p. 121–58. Lima: UNMSM-IIHS.

Schady, Norbert. 1999. "Seeking Votes: The Political Economy of Expenditures by the Peruvian Social Fund (FONCODES), 1991–1995." Washington, DC: World Bank.

Siavelis, Peter, and Scott Morgenstern, eds. 2008. *Pathways to Power: Political Recruitment and Candidate Selection in Latin America.* University Park: Pennsylvania State University Press.

Stepan, Alfred. 1978. *The State and Society: Peru in Comparative Perspective.* Princeton, NJ: Princeton University Press.

Szwarcberg, Mariela. 2010. "Who Monitors? Clientelism and Democratic Representation in Argentine Municipalities." Unpublished paper.

Tanaka, Martín. 1998. *Los espejismos de la democracia: El colapso del sistema de partidos en el Perú, 1980–1995, en perspectiva comparada.* Lima: Instituto de Estudios Peruanos.

———. 2001. *Participación popular en políticas sociales: Cuándo puede ser democrática y eficiente y cuándo todo lo contrario.* Lima: Consorcio de Investigación Económica y Social (CIES)–Instituto de Estudios Peruanos.

———. 2002. "Las relaciones entre Estado y sociedad en el Perú: Desestructuración sin reestructuración. Un ensayo bibliográfico." In *América Latina Hoy,* vol. 31, p. 189–218. Ediciones Universidad de Salamanca.

———. 2005a. *Democracia sin partidos, Perú, 2000–2005: los problemas de representación y las propuestas de reforma política.* Lima: Instituto de Estudios Peruanos.

———. 2005b. "Peru 1980–2000: Chronicle of a Death Foretold? Determinism, Political Decisions and Open Outcomes." In *The Third Wave of Democratization in Latin America:*

Advances and Setbacks, ed. Frances Hagopian and Scott Mainwaring, 261–88. Cambridge: Cambridge University Press.

———. 2008. "Del voluntarismo exacerbado al realismo sin ilusiones: El giro del APRA y de Alan García." *Nueva Sociedad* 217: 172–84.

———. 2009. "Representación, descentralización y participación ciudadana en el Perú: ¿la mejor combinacion?" In *Democracia y ciudadanía: Problemas, promesas y experiencias en la región andina,* ed. Martha Márquez, Eduardo Pastrana, and Guillermo Hoyos, 105–38. Bogotá: Pontificia Universidad Javeriana, Instituto Goethe y FESCOL.

———. 2010a. "How Does a Democracy with a Weak Party System Work? The Peruvian Case." In *Political Parties and Democracy,* Vol. 1, *The Americas,* ed. Kay Lawson and Jorge Lanzaro, 173–94. Westport, CT: Praeger.

———. 2010b. "Agencia y estructura, y el colapso de los sistemas de partidos en los países andinos." In *La iniciación de la política: El Perú político en perspectiva comparada,* ed. Carlos Meléndez and Alberto Vergara, 125–60. Lima: PUCP.

———. 2010c. "Entre la democracia elitista y los personalismos autoritarios: Reformas institucionales y gobernabilidad democrática en la región andina." In *Desafíos de la gobernabilidad democrática: Reformas político-institucionales y movimientos sociales en la región andina,* ed. Martín Tanaka and Francine Jácome. 339–64. Lima: Instituto de Estudios Peruanos.

Tanaka, Martín, and Carlos Meléndez. 2005. "¿De qué depende el éxito de las experiencias de participación ciudadana?" In *Participación ciudadana y democracia: Perspectivas críticas y análisis de experiencias locales,* ed. Patricia Zárate, 165–92. Lima: Instituto de Estudios Peruanos.

Tanaka, Martín, and Carolina Trivelli. 2002. "Las trampas de la focalización y la participación: Pobreza y políticas sociales en el Perú durante la década de Fujimori." Working Paper no. 121. Lima: Instituto de Estudios Peruanos.

Tanaka, Martín, and Sofía Vera. 2010. "Perú: la dinámica 'neodualista' de una democracia sin sistema de partidos." In *Democracia en la región andina: Diversidad y desafíos,* ed. Maxwell Cameron and Juan Pablo Luna, 197–242. Lima: Instituto de Estudios Peruanos.

Torre, Juan Carlos. 2003 "Los huérfanos de la política de partidos: Sobre los alcances y la naturaleza de la crisis de representación partidaria." *Desarrollo Económico* 42, no. 168: 619–52.

Trivelli, Carolina, Jimena Montenegro, and María Gutiérrez. 2011. "Un año ahorrando: Primeros resultados del programa piloto 'Promoción del ahorro en familias Juntos'." Lima: Instituto de Estudios Peruanos, Working Paper no. 159.

Verdera, Francisco. 2007. *La pobreza en el Perú: un análisis de sus causas y de las políticas para enfrentarla.* Lima: Instituto de Estudios Peruanos.

Webb, Richard, and Adolfo Figueroa. 1975. *Distribución del ingreso en el Perú.* Lima: Instituto de Estudios Peruanos.

Zapata, Antonio. 1996. *Sociedad y poder local: la comunidad de Villa el Salvador, 1971–1996.* Lima: DESCO.

CHAPTER FOUR

Teachers, Mayors, and the Transformation of Clientelism in Colombia

KENT EATON AND CHRISTOPHER CHAMBERS-JU

Even for Latin America, a region widely marked by patron-client relations, Colombia stands out for the pervasiveness and extensiveness of its clientelistic networks. In part this is because clientelism requires elections, and few countries in Latin America have accrued as impressive an electoral record as Colombia. In the absence of lengthy periods or repeated cycles of direct military rule, clientelism could and did become deeply embedded in the country's political life. But clientelism became entrenched not just because elections were held mostly without interruption. Until very recently, these elections were dominated by the Conservatives and the Liberals, two traditional parties that from the mid-nineteenth century cemented their hold on power through clientelism. Though these parties initially used clientelism to reinforce the rule of landowners over peasants, they continued to use clientelistic exchanges even as patron-client ties broke down in the countryside in the first half of the twentieth century.[1]

Elsewhere in Latin America, economic modernization, state expansion, and urban migration limited the scope for clientelism and created more programmatic forms of political exchange—but not in Colombia. In fact, the strength of clientelism helps explain the relative absence of macroeconomic populism in Colombia's history[2] as well as the absence of a competitive populist party in its party system.[3] Unlike countries such as Argentina, Peru, and Mexico, where the differing logics of clientelism (or *individual* exchange between a patron and client) and populism (or an exchange relation involving a *class* or *coalition*) have competed for predominance, in Colombia clientelism alone has remained paramount.

If clientelism is deeply entrenched as a political practice in Colombia, the coun-

try also stands out for the frequency and seriousness of institutional responses designed to limit or eliminate clientelism. In fact, the former seems to explain the
latter as widespread clientelistic abuses have provoked recurrent attempts to check
this political practice, both in the form of "bottom-up" civic movements that demanded an end to clientelism, and "top-down" efforts by reform-minded politicians
and bureaucrats to redesign institutions. As a result, not only is Colombia an important case of entrenched clientelism, but it is also an important case of concerted
efforts to attack clientelism via institutional change. As we describe below, these
attempts took a number of forms. Some, in a pragmatic mode, tried not to reform
clientelistic politicians but merely to limit their participation in the policy process.
Others sought deeper change and attempted to transform the very incentives that
politicians faced so that they would adopt new linkages with voters. Others focused
on cutting the access of patrons to fiscal resources in order to limit contingent and
discretionary spending by politicians. The vigorous pursuit of these various strategies over the past half century makes Colombia a critical case study of how institutional reform shapes clientelistic networks. Unfortunately for the reform cause, the
Colombian case suggests that even serious and earnest efforts at institutional reform
may yield limited results in terms of reducing clientelism.

In this chapter we evaluate the impact of major institutional reforms designed to
disrupt and eradicate clientelistic networks in Colombia. We argue that institutional
reforms yielded some important benefits: they prevented clientelism from producing macroeconomic turbulence, protected teachers from clientelistic abuses, and
freed mayors from regional party bosses. However, a more striking finding in our
analysis is the tendency of reforms to transform, rather than eradicate, practices of
clientelism. An unintended consequence of these reforms was the empowerment of
new patrons who constructed new clientelistic networks.[4] In response to repeated
reform efforts, Colombia has shifted from a system of clientelism dominated by
national party leaders, national legislators, and regional party bosses to a proliferation of new, more complex patron-client relationships. Not unlike the balloon
effect or "whack-a-mole" problem that has been used to describe Colombia's other
plague—drug trafficking—clientelism has been eliminated in certain institutional
and organizational spaces only to pop up in new venues and among new actors.
No longer primarily the purview of the two traditional parties, which have experienced a precipitous decline over the last two decades, clientelism has undergone a
process of fragmentation and multiplication. As a result, not only did institutional
reforms fail to eradicate clientelism, but they changed it in ways that are likely to
render future reform efforts even more difficult to achieve. Disputing the view that

institutional reforms have been simply insufficient, we argue that the Colombian case must be taken as one that casts doubt on the viability of a purely institutional approach to curb clientelism.

In Colombia, institutional reforms may have failed in their efforts to eliminate clientelism, but institutional analysis of the sort we offer in this chapter provides critical insights into the remarkably protean quality of clientelism. Specifically, we show that institutional changes transformed clientelism in Colombia by focusing on change over time in how two different types of actors—teachers and mayors—are inserted into patron-client relations. Throughout the twentieth century, teachers have been central to the story of clientelism in Colombia, where the national teachers' federation (Federación Colombiana de Educadores, or FECODE) emerged as an organization that initially protested against clientelistic practices but later perpetuated these practices in new forms. Thanks to electoral reforms introduced in the 1991 constitution, leaders of the teachers' union have become patrons in their own right; teachers who had been caught in the regional clientelistic networks of party bosses are now in the clientelistic networks of union leaders who have entered political office. A similar dynamic can be discerned in the case of mayors. As politicians who used to be appointed by higher-level officials, mayors participated in a wave of civic strikes demanding decentralization in the 1970s and 1980s in an attempt to escape their subservient status as clients. Subsequent to decentralizing reforms in the 1980s and 1990s, mayors have become important patrons at the local level who are now autonomous from national and regional political actors. Our sectoral (i.e., education and teachers) and territorial (i.e., municipal governments and mayors) case studies suggest that institutional reforms in Colombia have transformed clients and/or the organizations that represent them into patrons in their own right.

In terms of theory building, our contributions in this chapter are modest. Our aim is to sketch out changes in the structure of clientelistic networks in Colombia and to demonstrate how these changes were induced by institutional reforms. Because clientelism as a practice and institutional reform as a prescriptive solution vary widely by country, caution is in order when generalizing the findings of this chapter. Still, we exhort would-be reformers—in Latin America and beyond—who view institutional design as a "solution" to clientelism to carefully consider the unintended consequences of reform in the Colombian case.

This chapter proceeds as follows. It first describes the evolution of regional clientelistic networks that operated as the organizational infrastructure of Colombia's two traditional parties—or the baseline organization of clientelism in Colombia. It then describes institutional reforms designed to either contain the negative side effects of clientelism or curb the practice altogether. The next section turns to our sectoral and territorial cases. In the education sector, the position of teachers in clientelistic networks was transformed over time. Initially, teachers were the clients of party bosses; they then became the clients of politicians who used union and educational resources to pursue electoral office. Similarly, mayors at first were political appointees who served at the pleasure of regional party bosses. Decentralization made mayors autonomous from such bosses, assigning them their own responsibilities and resources and thereby enabling them to create their own clienteles. We end with a brief discussion of how our analysis of Colombia fits within theoretical debates about the relationship between formal institutions and clientelism.

Clientelism before Reform: Traditional Parties and Regional Brokers

To set up our analysis of institutional reforms as well as sectoral and territorial changes following reform, we describe traditional clientelistic practices. Contemporary forms of clientelism in Colombia must be traced back to their political origins. Scholars of Colombian political history have written extensively on traditional practices of clientelism,[5] and this overview establishes a baseline against which change and continuity can be measured.

Colombian clientelism has roots in historical forms of rural social organization. A quasi-feudal system in Colombia between rural notables and peasants dating back to the colonial period and the struggle for independence created networks of loyalty and exchange that endured well into the twentieth century. Powerful *caudillos* (political-military leaders at the command of militia forces) emerged who exercised considerable influence over regional politics. These *caudillos* lacked ties to central state actors—whose efforts to control territory faced major challenges in Colombia, given the country's mountainous geography—but instead developed connections to national party elites, and served as brokers between these elites and subnational clients.[6] Moreover, these caudillos formed networks with *gamonales* (local landowners) or *caciques* (local political bosses) that held influence at the local level and mobilized votes.[7] Regional elites operated through brokers, who included landowners, teachers, health workers, priests, and local officials.[8] Hence, social organization exhibited a hierarchical, pyramidal structure featuring clientelism as the primary mode of exchange.

The formation and evolution of Colombia's party system further reinforced clientelism as the primary mode of interest representation. Since independence, Colombia had two traditional parties that brought together various regional notables. These parties, which became known as the Liberals and Conservatives, evolved directly from heterogeneous groupings of regional elites: both parties were non-ideological, pragmatic, and internally fragmented.[9] Thus, partisanship developed in large part through personal loyalties to *gamonales* and *caciques* that were cemented through land tenancy and were reinforced by multiple outbreaks of civil violence.[10]

Both inter- and intra-party electoral competition activated clientelistic networks. Inter-party competition produced a winner-take-all spoils system during the first half of the twentieth century. While Colombia regularly held semi-competitive elections, the competitiveness of these elections varied considerably over time. Increased electoral competition seemed to intensify patronage and clientelistic appeals. For example, before *La Violencia,* during periods of one party's dominance over the other (such as the Liberal Republic of 1930–1946), each party would pack bureaucracies with party loyalists to maintain control over patronage and state resources in order to delay the ascendance of the other party. In contrast, during periods of uncompetitive elections—most importantly the consociational National Front (1958–1974), in which both parties adhered to the principles of *parity* in the division of legislative positions and *alternation* in the presidency—bureaucracies developed more technical expertise, and traditional regional bosses (at least temporarily) lost control.[11] To be sure, the National Front brought about only a brief and partial de-politicization of state-run services. The end of the National Front, deepening party fragmentation, and waning party discipline resulted in renewed clientelism.

In addition, intra-party competition among factions also engendered patronage and clientelism. Prohibitions on inter-party competition during the National Front led to considerable intra-party, or factional competition, based on personalistic and regional loyalties. Within parties, power lay with regional brokers. Regional directorates determined party lists for legislative elections, and regional notables nominated presidential candidates, who lacked their own independent support base.[12] National party leaders, who headed the major factions within the traditional parties, bargained with disparate, regional caudillos and used patronage as a tool for winning party primaries.[13]

Finally, electoral rules provided an institutional foundation for clientelism. Specifically, Colombia had electoral rules—the largest remainder system and the absence of vote pooling among candidates from the same party—which led parties to present multiple party lists in order to increase their representation in Congress. Electoral incentives resulted in a strategy called *Operación Avispa,* whereby parties would present multiple lists to "swarm" legislative seats like wasps, thereby winning each seat relatively cheaply.[14] The presentation of multiple party lists, in which typically only one candidate won from each list, created incentives for politicians to build personalistic and clientelistic loyalties.

Several points are worth drawing out from this brief discussion of clientelism prior to major institutional reform. Clientelism was organized through regional elites, who were linked to traditional parties. The dominance of the traditional parties and the reliance of party elites on regional brokers slowed the formation of a modern state. Institutions—electoral rules and patronage-ridden bureaucracies —reinforced these practices. Although clientelism was dynamic, and clientelistic networks changed over time as Colombia's economy industrialized and the state developed islands of bureaucratic capacity, clientelism was stabilized by the continuity of elections and organized around regional elites. While following *La Violencia* clientelism facilitated power sharing and peaceful coexistence between the traditional parties, it excluded multiple actors and prevented major state reform. It generated both social protest and guerrilla insurgency. It also generated a cadre of reformers who wanted to end these traditional practices and modernize the state.

Institutional Reforms to Reduce Clientelism

Since the 1960s, Colombia has witnessed several major efforts to check or eliminate clientelism, which was associated with inefficiency and wastefulness, exclusion of citizens outside of clientelistic networks, and a weak central state that lacked a monopoly on violence and hindered economic development. These reform efforts can be grouped into four major episodes: (1) the 1968 Constitutional Reform, (2) decentralizing changes beginning in the mid-1980s, (3) the 1990 Constitutional Convention, and (4) the 2003 electoral reform. Over time, these reforms demonstrated increasing boldness and cut increasingly close to the underlying institutional incentives that encouraged legislators to depend so heavily on clientelism. Taken together, however, these reforms not only have failed to curb clientelism, but they have in fact produced the new patron-client dynamics that we discuss in the next two sections.

Unlike later more radical attempts, the 1968 constitutional reform did not seek to make legislators less clientelistic. Instead, it simply sought to limit the damage caused by concentrating fiscal and monetary policymaking powers in the executive branch.[15] According to Eaton, "legislators gave up substantive input in the policy design process but preserved the right to demand the patronage they continued to need to satisfy their clientelist networks"—most importantly in the form of *auxilios* (congressional funds for constituency service) placed under the exclusive control of individual members of Congress.[16] Though legislators could have used their *auxilios* to finance local public goods, in practice they used them to finance the individual exchanges of private goods for votes that are the hallmark of clientelism. The 1968 changes did nothing to alter legislators' incentives, but the pragmatic logic of the reform does help explain the puzzle of how deeply entrenched clientelism in Colombia has gone hand in hand with a record of centrist macroeconomic policy making by relatively insulated technocrats.[17]

In contrast to the accommodating nature of the 1968 reform, in the mid-1980s Colombian politicians adopted a series of decentralizing changes that represented a more direct threat to established patterns of clientelism. At the top of the political system, decentralization appealed to reformers who sought, not to make legislators less clientelistic, but rather to re-assign resources and responsibilities in order to empower local officials whose proximity to local communities would presumably lead to better social policy outcomes. But decentralization and local control over service provision also emerged as a rallying cry "from below" in the 1970s and 1980s, both on the part of "outsiders" excluded from the benefits of clientelism and from "insiders" who complained about the quality of the services received from legislators to whom they had pledged their support. Rather than a one-shot deal, decentralization took place via numerous measures adopted over a seven-year period, starting with the adoption of mayoral elections in 1986, continuing with the introduction of gubernatorial elections in 1991, and culminating with 1993 legislation that transferred major social policy responsibilities to municipalities and departments (Colombia's intermediate level of government). If the recent literature on clientelism emphasized the importance of monopoly control by patrons who deliver goods and services necessary for the survival of potential clients,[18] then decentralization should constitute a threat to national patrons because it enables subnational governments to meet these needs instead.

Relative to the 1968 reform and to decentralization, the numerous changes introduced in the 1991 constitution can be understood as an attempt to wage a frontal assault on clientelism. Rather than trying to keep legislators out of the national policymaking process or to transfer their social policy responsibilities to subnational officials, the 1991 constitution represented a more direct attempt to make legislators less clientelistic. Most importantly, the new constitution replaced regional districts for the election of the Senate with a single nationwide district, a reform that sought to encourage senators to shift their energies from the maintenance of regional clientele networks toward the development of national policy interests and expertise. Although senators could and did continue to use clientelism to build regional voting blocs, the single national district appealed to reformers, who expected it to empower programmatic but territorially diffuse interests (which it has done, at the margin). Second, turning from the upper to the lower chamber, reformers used the 1991 constitution to undermine clientelism by eliminating the *auxilios* that had financed vote buying for over two decades. Third, the 1991 constitution mandated a new ballot system that bars parties from printing and distributing ballots—a practice widely believed to facilitate the monitoring capacity on which clientelism depends.[19] Together, these bold changes can be understood as the result of a decision to use non-traditional electoral rules to select the members of the constitutional convention, who were therefore less interested in perpetuating clientelism than representatives from the traditional parties would have been.[20]

Finally, reformers in 2003 secured a new electoral law in an attempt to lessen the incentives for clientelism. As it became increasingly clear that the 1991 constitution failed to dislodge clientelism from the legislature, the Pastrana and Uribe administrations set their sights on electoral reform. After years of debate, and under threat of a referendum on even more sweeping political reforms and the closing of the legislature, Congress agreed to a new electoral law in 2003 that went substantially beyond the 1991 constitution by barring parties from running multiple lists in elections.[21] Whereas list proliferation in the past gave legislators strong incentives to establish personalistic networks in order to distinguish themselves from co-partisans, the single list requirement substantially reduces these incentives. In contrast to Uribe's argument that the single list should also be a closed list, the 2003 law in fact enables parties to choose whether to run a closed or an open list. Open lists were used in almost all electoral districts in the 2006 and 2010 elections, which still preserves incentives for candidates to use clientelism to distinguish themselves from others of the same party. One could argue as a result that institutional reforms have simply not gone far enough in Colombia—after all, open lists still reward clientelistic behavior. But the significance of the reforms described in this section casts doubt on this view, particularly when combined with evidence below that institutional reforms themselves have generated qualitatively new and vibrant forms of clientelism.

Education: Sectoral Reforms and the Transformation of Clientelism

Since the beginning of the twentieth century, the education sector in Colombia was ridden with clientelism because it lacked prestige and because it was being rapidly expanded.[22] Various attempts to reform education and reduce clientelism—through both top-down institutional reform and bottom-up mobilization—met with some success; since the late-1970s, clientelism in the education sector has been confined to ever more restricted spaces. Still, clientelism has persisted and has morphed into new forms in response to institutional changes. Even more troubling, the teachers' union, an actor that led the fight against clientelism, now organizes new clientelistic networks. The decentralization of education, thought to bring government closer to citizens and break clientelistic linkages, has also engendered new clientelistic networks.[23]

During traditional party rule, the education sector was regulated almost entirely by particularistic exchange. Bogota, the capital and state center, could not set a coherent, national education policy at the departmental level. A patchwork of subnational, informal, and ad hoc administrative rules governed the education sector. The lack of formal administrative rules enabled regional party bosses to develop powerful political machines that exploited the education sector as a source of patronage.[24] Traditional party bosses wielded discretionary control over teacher hiring and firing and used teaching positions as sinecures for party activists who mobilized votes.[25] Teachers served as brokers who turned out the vote, since in lower-class communities teachers had considerable social status. Teachers were also the clients of party bosses; they needed a *palanca* (literally translated as a "lever," meaning a political connection) to get a teaching position. Because party bosses politicized the teaching profession, teachers faced arbitrary treatment, unequal salaries, meager or nonexistent fringe benefits, the uncertainty of the political business cycle, and high rates of turnover. Irregularities in salary payments meant that teachers could be paid in nonmonetary forms. Teachers could be compensated with bottles of *aguardiente* or tobacco products that they had to sell on their own time. Teachers, because of their low salaries and declared loyalty to party bosses, were called "political apostles."[26]

As working conditions deteriorated, teachers organized unions and demanded labor rights to protect themselves from clientelism. In 1959, teachers formed the Federation of Colombian Educators (FECODE). This organization emerged from regional teachers' unions organized by the traditional parties, particularly the Liberal party. Teachers' unions became increasingly autonomous from the traditional parties as leftist union leaders won power in FECODE's executive committee. After the union moved to the left, it mobilized major strikes in 1966, 1973–1974, and 1977—the "Civic Strike"—to demand a national labor code and to protest the clientelistic practices of party bosses. Through mobilization, FECODE merged multiple departmental unions. It became the overarching organizational structure that mobilized primary, secondary, technical, and university educators throughout Colombia. FECODE's centralized structure made it a potent interest organization that challenged the clientelistic practices of the traditional parties.

Ultimately, FECODE successfully negotiated policies that protected teachers from patronage. The *Teachers' Statute* of 1979—a civil service law—leveled teachers' salaries and made the national government (rather than departmental or municipal governments) responsible for hiring and paying teachers.[27] The *Teachers' Statute* also professionalized teachers and provided them with a "special" labor code that afforded them benefits—a salary scale, a disciplinary code, labor stability, and a pension—that were more generous than those received by other public servants.[28] This statute marked a major step forward in terms of setting national administrative rules in the education sector and ending the most egregious forms of clientelism.

Yet the *Teachers' Statute* had limitations; regional bosses were loath to abandon clientelism. While this law provided protection to already-hired teachers, some new teachers continued to be subject to political discretion. For example, loopholes in the law allowed subnational politicians to hire temporary teachers to fill under-staffed schools. Temporary teachers could be hired according to political criterion, and because they were paid by local or departmental governments, it was difficult for central authorities to monitor how they were hired.[29] In addition, teacher trans-fers and promotions could also follow a clientelistic logic. Teachers had to petition to be transferred from remote rural schools to more desirable urban schools, or to rise up the pay scale; authorities responded to these petitions based on clientelistic exchange. Clientelism, then, remained pervasive. In 1985, six years after the adoption of the *Teachers' Statute*, a minister of education raised controversy by noting: "One hundred percent of educators in Colombia have been named through political recommendations, and it is rare that a bureaucrat doesn't pick a teacher who doesn't have a letter of recommendation from an influential political leader."[30]

It was not until 2001–2002 that there was another major effort to curb clientelism in the education sector, beginning with the Law 715. Then President Alvaro Uribe was elected and appointed a technocrat to the Ministry of Education, María Cecilia Vélez White (2002–2010). The *New Teachers' Statute* was adopted for teachers hired after 2002. The primary aim of this new set of policies was to control costs and rationalize administration in the education sector. However, a secondary conse-quence was to introduce stronger rules governing teacher hiring and teacher trans-fers. A pre-service evaluation—a merit-based exam—became the basis for the hiring of all new teachers. Moreover, measures were adopted to only allow teacher transfers to schools where extra teachers were needed. The ministry claimed that before this reform was adopted clientelism enabled teachers to move to urban, and hence more desirable, schools, leading to a severe imbalance in the distribution of teachers be-tween rural and urban schools. In general, these reforms strengthened administra-tive rules and closed off some of the spaces previously used for clientelism.

Several points from this section are worth reinforcing. First, during traditional party rule teachers were located near the bottom of regional clientelistic networks. However, teachers formed labor unions and began to protest poor working condi-tions and mismanagement. This mobilization paid off, and teachers benefited from policies that, at least on paper, protected them from clientelistic abuses. Still, politi-

cians found ways to evade these laws and continued to use patronage in the education sector. The most recent efforts to reduce clientelism occurred in 2002, when
rules were adopted that regulated teacher hiring and transfers and further restricted
the space for clientelism.

The Limits of Reform: New Practices of Clientelism in the Education Sector

The persistence of clientelism in the education sector is remarkable. In the contemporary period, new forms of patronage plague the teaching profession and the
education sector. The growing electoral representation of the teaching profession
and efforts to decentralize education have created new spaces into which clientelism
has reappeared.

The increasing electoral representation of the teaching profession has contributed to the growth of clientelism. The Constitution of 1991—which brought political reform and a change in electoral law—promised to advance the representation
of the teaching profession and to weaken regional political machines. The constitution changed the arena of electoral competition for the Senate from departmental
districts to a single national district. Indeed, after this shift, the traditional parties
experienced a sharp decline, and the influence of traditional party bosses in the education sector receded. Meanwhile, territorially dispersed groups, such as teachers,
had space to win representation.[31] This electoral reform allowed voters to organize
across regions, and thus it positioned the teachers' union to expand its influence by
winning representation in the Senate.

Yet the increasing electoral participation of the teachers' union created new clientelistic networks. Leaders of FECODE pursued—and in many cases won—seats
in the Senate, the Chamber of Representatives, governorships, and municipal office.
Union leaders, who once used clientelism as the basis for teacher protests, began
to use clientelism as a strategy for winning votes. For example, after Jaime Dussan,
a former FECODE president, was elected to the Senate (1994–2010), allegations
surfaced that he used the union organization as a network for distributing benefits
and mobilizing votes and that he negotiated with regional elites to use their existing
networks to mobilize votes on his behalf.[32]

As the electoral participation of union leaders expanded, so did the usage of clientelism in political campaigns. The sequential entry of new Senate candidates who
were former leaders of FECODE created competition within the union for scarce
votes and electoral resources. From 1994 to 2010, nine different union leaders affili-
ated with FECODE had run for Senate, and all had appealed to teachers as their

core constituency. Increasing electoral competition had two consequences. First, politicians representing the teaching profession made more aggressive clientelistic appeals to teachers.[33] That is, because there were few programmatic differences among candidates campaigning to represent the teaching profession, clientelism became the primary strategy for out-competing rivals. Candidates with a large campaign war chest increasingly crowded out candidates with fewer campaign resources. Second, electoral coalitions began to form *within* labor organizations. That is, union leaders created their own electoral vehicles that competed for representation in the Labor Central, in the Teachers Federation, and in union locals. Patron-broker-client networks formed, involving politicians, union leaders, and rank-and-file teachers. Union leaders came to serve as brokers for politicians, and in exchange would later be nominated as candidates for public office themselves.

Politicians who represent the teaching profession in public office maintain particularistic exchange relations with their constituents. Senators linked to FECODE, for example, often pass laws and negotiate deals that benefit narrow segments of the teaching profession. Senators representing the teachers' union also offer "constituency services" that enable individual teachers to expedite bureaucratic transactions such as advancing on the salary scale and securing pensions.[34] Other rent-seeking activities, such as agreeing to vote on controversial legislation in exchange for side payments, also enable politicians to secure resources that help them to maintain their clientelistic networks.[35]

While the teachers' union has become a site of increasing clientelism, it is by no means the only actor that uses the education sector for particularistic exchange. The decentralization of education through the Laws 115 and 60 of 1993–1994 increased the role of departmental and municipal governments in education administration. Subnational governments have become a site of clientelism for a variety of actors, including local politicians, private providers, and NGOs. As improving education has become an increasingly urgent policy priority, spending on public education has often increased at the local level, creating new opportunities for clientelism. One such opportunity is packing local education bureaucracies with loyalists. While there are official procedures for hiring government workers, in practice informal referrals are still important, especially since there has been a reduction of the civil service and a growth in the hiring of temporary workers. Moreover, as the education sector has become increasingly differentiated and complex, there are more dark spaces into which clientelism can emerge. Policy experiments, pilot programs, and local initiatives, as well as the outsourcing of governmental functions through the expansion of "public-private partnerships," have all created opportunities for clientelism.

The case of Bogota nicely illustrates these problems. Bogota was heralded as a reformist city, where clientelism was significantly reduced during the late 1990s.[36] And
yet, during the mayoral administrations of Lucho Garzon (2003–2007) and Samuel
Moreno (2007–2011), allegations of clientelism in the education sector have resurfaced. The shifts toward hiring workers in the Secretariat with short-term contracts
and outsourcing governmental functions to private providers and NGOs rather
than performing functions "in house" have led to various high-profile investiga-
tions, audits, and pledges to root out clientelism.[37] Contracts—to both temporary
consultants and private providers—can be awarded according to the same logic
that governed the offering of temporary positions to teachers in the past.[38] The case
of Bogotá illustrates how "the decentralization of the administration of national
teachers to the local level has often resulted in the municipalization of clientelism
in public education."[39]

In sum, the old practices of blatant clientelism by regional party bosses have all
but disappeared, and institutional reforms have played a significant role in disrupt-
ing them. And yet, in response to institutional change, a new set of actors have
invented new, more subtle practices of clientelism that continue to plague the education sector.

Decentralization: Territorial Reforms and the Transformation of Clientelism

In this section, we shift from sectoral to territorial reforms by exploring three related
questions: (1) Why was social policy decentralized in Colombia? (2) How has decentralization changed the practice of clientelism? and (3) How did national politicians react when it became clear that mayors had used decentralization to transform
themselves from clients into patrons? Most of the literature that seeks to explain
why decentralization occurred in Latin America has emphasized strategic calculations by national political elites, including the decision by Colombian President
Belisario Betancur to decentralize because he believed that it would disproportionately benefit his own Conservative Party[40] and that it would encourage insurgent
groups to demobilize.[41] But the decision to decentralize in Colombia also reveals a
strong bottom-up dynamic, because these policy changes were adopted in response
to widespread (approximately 200) civic strikes (*paros cívicos*) in the 1970s and early
1980s.[42] These protests—which took the form of road blockades, work stoppages,
hunger strikes, and building occupations—exposed deep frustration with social
services that were deficient in quality and quantity, unequally distributed across
regional lines, and accessible only through clientelistic networks.[43] Protestors de-

manded that local governments play a more prominent role in service provision, rejecting as insufficient the de-concentration of the Colombian bureaucracy that had occurred in the early 1970s when field offices were established by over 90 central governmental agencies—without surrendering national control over the bureaucrats who staffed them.[44]

According to Collins, the civic strikes took two forms: protests in which participation was restricted to popular sectors and lower income groups, and protests in which middle- and upper-class groups—and even municipal councilors—also participated. Both types of protests encouraged reform-minded politicians to contemplate decentralization as a response, but for different reasons. The lower class–based civic strikes of the 1970s and 1980s resonated nationally precisely because the vertical practice of clientelism had been so successful in preventing horizontal organizing. In contrast, multiclass strikes resonated because they usually articulated a sharper set of territorially based grievances against other better-serviced and more economically developed regions.[45] While the civic strikes against clientelism and in favor of local service provision played a key role in convincing national politicians to decentralize social policy, one of the great ironies of the Colombian case is that decentralization in turn generated new forms of clientelism, as described below.[46]

Relative to prior institutional reforms, decentralization represented a major assault on clientelism as it was then practiced. Before decentralization, the appointment of mayors and governors operated as a highly valuable unit of clientelistic exchange through which vertical networks were built and sustained. Although formally the Ministro de Gobierno (Interior Ministry) appointed governors, and governors in turn appointed mayors, in fact Congress played a leading role as presidents awarded individual legislators the right to name these officials in exchange for supporting presidential initiatives.[47] While appointed mayors and governors enjoyed patronage powers in their own right and could use their offices to reward their own clienteles, they were expected to respect the clientelistic networks of the legislators responsible for their appointment. As an example of what happened when they did not, Eloisa Vasco reports an episode in 1976 during which seven of the department of Boyacá's ten national legislators wrote to the Ministro de Gobierno to complain that the governor's cabinet did not reflect the balance of factions in the department, after which the governor was sacked.[48] That mayoral and gubernatorial appointments were subject to contestation among rival brokers can be seen in the high turnover rate of these offices, with mayors often serving for no more than three months.[49] Appointed mayors could be fired whenever they sought to transcend their identities as clients and to act instead more like patrons. According to Jairo Blanco, who served as mayor of Mogotes in the department of Santander both before and after the introduction of elections, "When I was an appointed mayor I only lasted six months because I refused to give positions to individuals recommended by local *gamonales*."[50]

In three key dimensions, decentralization rescued appointed mayors from their traditional and subordinated roles as clients. First, reformers opted to introduce direct elections for mayors and to hold these elections non-concurrently with national elections. This decision made it possible for mayors not just to win elections by establishing their own clienteles, but to ensure that these clients respond to them rather than to the higher-level politicians that are elected at a different point in the electoral calendar. Second, fiscal decentralization included a programmed schedule of generous and increasing monetary transfers to both municipal and departmental governments without specifying how exactly the governments should spend these transfers.[51] Patrons need their own resources to be effective, and unearmarked transfers are more useful in this respect than transfers that are conditioned on the choices of higher-up officials. Third, administrative decentralization transferred responsibilities for health and education to subnational governments that formerly played little role in social policy (other than the local *Juntas de Acción Comunal* that operated with central funds beginning in 1958). Although departments were initially favored relative to municipalities—in part due to the anti-decentralization stance of FECODE—by 2001 municipalities were completely free to petition for the transfer of services.[52] The key point here is that decentralization transferred to local officials authority over the very policies that lend themselves to clientelistic abuses.

In other words, as a result of Colombia's comprehensive approach to political, fiscal, and administrative decentralization, mayors now have significant revenues under their control, real responsibilities for social services that used to lie with the national government, and far less interest in delivering vote blocs to national legislators in exchange for resources that the legislator might steer toward the municipality. The cumulative effect of these measures constitutes a major rupture in clientelism.

The Subnational Consequences of Decentralization

In the more than two decades since its adoption, decentralization has altered the practice of clientelism in Colombia. The decentralization of social policy has resulted in new forms of "subnational clientelism," according to which mayors and governors—no longer only senators—now serve as heads of clientele networks with greatly expanded patronage capabilities. Even more negatively, decentralization has also made possible the strengthening of "armed clientelism," a term that describes the exchange of votes for material benefits distributed through local governments that are under the control of armed actors on the left and right.[53]

If mayors and governors previously needed to balance their dual roles as clients and patrons, decentralization has made it possible to shed their former status as clients and to more fully develop their stature as patrons. While mayors with aspirations to higher office may still see themselves as clients of regional brokers, the proliferation of party lists until 2003 meant that they could just as easily leverage their patronage powers as mayors into successful campaigns for Congress on their own lists (most of which only elected one or two legislators). According to the evidence emerging over the last fifteen years, subnational officials have used decentralization to expand two classic forms of clientelism: vote buying and patronage. Consider examples from the health sector, where the policy shift from supply-side approaches (for example, state payment to hospitals) to demand-side approaches (such as state transfers to individuals) has produced new opportunities for clientelism. Specifically, Law 100, passed in 1993, created a system of subsidies for lower-income Colombians, whose eligibility is determined by a national index (*Sistema de Selección de Beneficiarios,* or SISBEN), and who use subsidies to purchase health insurance from private insurers called *Administradoras del Régimen Subsidiado* (ARS) that are under contract with the municipality. According to Oscar Fresneda, while the National Planning Department controls SISBEN, mayors have the authority to add additional beneficiaries into the system at their discretion, which they appear to do using political criteria. Fresneda's surveys among health officials at the departmental level suggest that inclusion in SISBEN at the discretion of mayors has been used to buy votes in nearly two-thirds of all municipalities.[54]

In addition to exchanging votes for health subsidies, mayors can also now use clientelistic criteria to give jobs to workers in municipal health departments. Just as the expansion of the national bureaucracy in the 1960s and 1970s triggered new attempts by national politicians to secure jobs for their clients,[55] the expansion of the *subnational* bureaucracy generated new opportunities for *subnational* politicians. Subnational patronage has depressed health outcomes in at least two ways. First, while health coverage has improved in Colombia, the quality of care now provided at the municipal level has suffered due to a lack of technical expertise. According to Molina and Spurgeon, the problem is not that mayors do not have sufficient funds for hiring, but rather that they hire too few doctors and nurses and too many staff for nontechnical administrative tasks like billing and auditing.[56] In some municipalities, the number of personnel who directly attend to patients has actually declined. Second, like their counterparts at the national level, mayors prefer the use of short-term contracts when they hire clients so that these contractors can be removed from their positions as mayoral patronage needs evolve. High turnover has wreaked havoc on planning efforts in municipal health departments across Colombia. As a reflection of the political dividends they have derived from the decentralization of health, at the end of the 1990s subnational officials joined with unions and legislators in vetoing reform efforts that sought, unsuccessfully, to reduce the number of patronage employees in the health sector.[57]

In what can be thought of as a virulent subvariety of subnational clientelism, Colombia has also witnessed the expansion of "armed clientelism" in local governments controlled by guerrillas and paramilitaries.[58] On the Left, decentralization encouraged Colombia's two most powerful and tenacious guerrilla groups—the FARC (Fuerzas Armadas Revolucionarias de Colombia, or Revolutionary Armed Forces of Colombia) and ELN (Ejército de Liberación Nacional, or National Liberation Army)—to literally come down from the mountains in the 1990s and to focus on controlling municipalities—not just militarily but politically as well. After decentralization, the size of fiscal transfers is a better indicator in predicting the FARC's territorial presence than the objective conditions (i.e., poverty, unequal access to land) that gave rise to the insurgency in the first place.[59] When citizens exchange their votes for social services in municipalities whose mayors are allied with the guerrillas, subnational clientelism gives these groups the opportunity to play what look like traditional governing roles in Colombia. Fiscal and administrative decentralization was particularly important in the resurrection of the ELN in the 1980s and 1990s, after its practice of forced peasant contributions proved unpopular in the 1970s. In municipalities under its control, many of which also receive oil royalties in addition to revenue transfers, the ELN no longer needs to extract local war taxes and can instead direct social services toward supporters.[60]

Decentralization has similarly enabled paramilitary groups on the right, like their adversaries on the left, to combine the use of force with the exercise of what look like very familiar (though now subnational) practices of clientelism. On the country's Caribbean coast, the region in Colombia where paramilitaries are strongest, only a single candidate ran for mayor in more than two hundred municipal elections in 2002.[61] According to Mauricio Romero, of the five candidates who ran for governor of Meta in 2002, the paramilitaries forced three to withdraw and then assassinated a fourth candidate after his defeat by the paramilitary-endorsed candidate.[62] Using coercive methods to prevent the election of mayors and governors whom they do not control, the paramilitaries can then selectively administer social services to supporters. In addition to their use of decentralization to build local clienteles, paramilitaries also undermine social policy outcomes through other negative practices. For example, in regions where paramilitaries dominate, investigators have uncovered evidence of contracts between municipal governments and bogus ARS health insurance companies. In what amounts to a serious misappropriation of decentralized health funds, these companies submit bills for services they have not provided, and the municipalities then reimburse the companies in exchange for a cut of the proceeds.[63]

The Center Reacts to the Consequences of Decentralization

Subnational clientelism in the wake of decentralization has created political problems for legislators and presidents alike. Mayors and governors use control over social provision to build their own clientele networks, profoundly threatening legislators who fear that their service as brokers is thereby rendered obsolete. Furthermore, every peso decentralized is one peso less in the annual appropriations process that legislators attempt to influence in Bogotá. The decentralization of social policy would have been less threatening if it were not for the more or less simultaneous failure of reform efforts that sought to make legislators less dependent on clientelism. For example, despite the shift to a single nationwide district meant to encourage more programmatic politics in the Senate, most senators still cultivate regionally concentrated vote bases that are held together through clientelism.[64] In the lower chamber, clientelism remained an essential practice for legislators, who continued to face intra-party competition until the 2003 electoral reform and who continue to favor clientelistic strategies due to the use of open-lists by most parties since 2003. Moreno and Escobar-Lemmon find worrisome evidence (from the standpoint of legislators) that former mayors in congressional elections fared especially well in the competitive dynamics created by list proliferation in pre-2003 Colombia.[65] In addition to reducing available financing for clientelistic networks headed by national legislators, decentralization was particularly challenging for Conservative and Liberal legislators because it facilitated the decline of Colombia's traditional two-party system.

If the (electoral) need for clientelism did not diminish, neither did legislators withdraw from the social policy-making process in Colombia. Despite the adoption of automatic revenue sharing to finance social services, legislators continued to appropriate additional monies that they could claim credit over as brokers—a phenomenon referred to as "double spending." When the 1991 constitution eliminated the *auxilios* that they previously used for clientelistic purposes, legislators responded by introducing "co-financing" schemes (*fondos de co-financiación*). According to Cristina Escobar, "the process is certainly much more complex than the previous system of *auxilios* and requires a great deal of maneuvering by Congressmen, [who] have to secure the faithful support of the mayors to ensure that the latter will publicly acknowledge the Congressmen as the ones responsible for interceding on behalf of the communities."[66] Legislators who refused to reduce their involvement in social provisioning in response to decentralization help account for the doubling of social spending that occurred in the 1990s. Combined with the Russian and Asian financial crises, unsustainable social expenditure widened budget deficits and contributed to Colombia's worst economic crisis since the 1930s.[67] In the late 1990s, Fresneda reports a crisis-induced decline in access to health care by lower income groups for whom subsidies were no longer sufficient to purchase health insurance.[68]

In addition to threatening legislators, decentralization has also created challenges for presidents, who can no longer use the appointment of mayors and governors as a tool to build congressional support for their bills. During the term of President Samper in the mid-1990s, finance ministers consistently complained about the threat to Colombia's famed macroeconomic stability posed by fiscal transfers that amounted to 46.5% of annual revenue by 2001. Rather than rein in "double spending" by legislators, President Andres Pastrana proposed, and legislators endorsed, major cuts in the size of fiscal transfers in 2001, buoyed by the growing consensus that decentralization may have improved coverage of social services but not their quality or efficiency. Thanks to recentralization, which eliminated transfers as a percentage of current revenue and legislated instead an inflation-adjusted fixed sum to be transferred, by 2005 departments and municipalities were receiving 37.2% rather than 46.5% of current revenue—a savings for the national government that amounted to 3.7% of GDP.[69] Recentralization further gained steam under President Alvaro Uribe, who extended the 2001 cuts until 2016, proposed a reduction in the number of municipalities, and imposed stricter administrative controls on subnational governments through the creation of a Special Administrative Unit in 2008 to monitor the use of transfers.[70]

When mayors used the assets provided by decentralizing reforms to assert themselves as patrons and not just clients, they also triggered a counter-reaction by national politicians who responded by seeking to reverse the reforms that had originally made possible this decentralization of power. Two caveats are in order, however. First, though aggressive, recentralization has only been partial, and Colombia has not returned to its pre-decentralization days. Mayors are still elected rather than appointed, still have responsibility for important social services, and still receive automatic transfers (even if these are now smaller than before). Subnational clientelism is alive and well, just less generously funded.

Second, thanks to the centralization of social policy within the office of the president—which Uribe implemented—not only has the center reasserted itself relative to subnational tiers, but within the national government the president has become increasingly dominant compared to the national legislature. In other words, if senators and representatives were displaced as power-brokers by mayors and governors when decentralization occurred, under Uribe they were crowded out by the president himself. Though the Colombian president has always effectively been the patron-in-chief, historically he served this function by focusing on appointments, for example, by appointing a senator's preferred candidate to political office in order to secure that senator's legislative support in Congress. In contrast, through the Presidential Agency for Social Action, which he created and expanded, Uribe transformed the role of the president by engaging more directly in the provision of social services.

Consider, for example, Colombia's conditional cash transfer program *Familias en Acción*. Initiated in 2000 with multilateral funding and located under the auspices of the Office of the President, enrollment in *Familias en Acción* grew rapidly to 2.5 million families by 2010.[71] To date, policy evaluations report that this program has contributed to positive outcomes in terms of human capital formation, including increases in school enrollment, vaccination rates, height and weight figures, and food consumption.[72] Yet despite positive evaluations, the political logic behind this program has been seriously questioned, emerging as a major point of controversy in the 2010 elections.[73] According to ex-minister of Hacienda, Juan Camilo Restrepo, the fact that the president has exclusive control of this program makes governors and mayors dependent on the president's largesse and thereby creates opportunities for clientelistic exchange.[74] In one city, Bucaramanga, officials allegedly pressed program beneficiaries to attend a campaign rally for presidential candidate Juan Manuel Santos.[75] The program's uneven expansion is also suspect: departments with the most poverty, such as Choco, have fewer participants than relatively well-off departments, such as Caldas, allegedly because the director of *Acción Social* has ties to a senator from Caldas.[76] Though *Familias en Acción* requires further study, the program appears to represent yet another example of the persistence of clientelism in Colombia.

Institutional Reform and Clientelism: Lessons from the Colombian Case

Our analysis of Colombia offers insights into theoretical debates about the relationship between institutional reform and clientelism. We agree with Kitschelt and Wilkinson's assertion that "as long as socioeconomic, competitive, and political economic configurations are conducive to clientelism, politicians may come up with tactics to implement such linkages under all sorts of formal institutional arrangements."[77] Formal institutional rules have repeatedly changed in Colombia over the last half century, but clientelism has remained a mainstay of the country's politics. Whether politicians make programmatic or clientelistic appeals to voters appears to be determined independently of institutions. Clientelism, then, should be understood primarily in terms of its embeddedness in social relations, party organizations, and politician-voter linkages; the right institutional reforms cannot eliminate clientelism.

While institutions do not determine *whether* clientelism is used, they do shape *how* it is practiced and how this practice changes through time. Institutional changes can disrupt established clientelistic networks, even if new ones may form in their stead. Better diagnoses of how clientelism is practiced may in turn generate better strategies for how it can be overcome—even if the Colombian case strongly suggests that these strategies will not be exclusively institutional in form. With respect to both teachers and mayors, our analysis shows that institutional changes in Colombia contributed to the weakening of regional political bosses. We do not suggest that institutional reform either (1) rendered regional political bosses completely irrelevant, or (2) was the only factor that contributed to the decline of these bosses. Still, we do see that the transformation of mayors from clients into patrons, as well as the growth of political bosses within the teachers' union, came at the expense of established party bosses and as the direct result of institutional reform.

Finally, our institutional analysis shows that, while sectoral and territorial reforms unwittingly facilitated new practices of clientelism, these reforms had different effects on teachers and mayors, and understanding these consequences requires a rather fine-grained focus on the particularities of institutional design. With respect to teachers, even as FECODE developed into a clientelistic organization, clientelism has become less prevalent in the education sector. While clientelism persists, it is now more restricted than during the period of traditional party rule, since goods—such as teaching positions and teacher transfers—can no longer be allocated on a purely discretionary basis. In contrast, if sectoral reforms partially constrained the scope for clientelism in education, the story is much less positive in the case of territorial reforms. Decentralization worsened clientelism in at least three significant ways: (1) by enabling mayors to emerge as patrons in their own right, (2) by encouraging national legislators to respond to this threat by "doubling down" on their own clientelistic appeals to voters, and (3) by prompting fundamentally new forms of presidential clientelism through which the patron-in-chief himself now seeks to negotiate direct deals with local officials in ways that appear to circumvent national legislators. Clientelism continues to evolve in Colombia, and institutional perspectives help to illuminate its meaning and significance for political life.

NOTES

1. Ronald Archer, "The Transition from Traditional to Broker Clientelism in Colombia: Political Stability and Social Unrest" (Working Paper no. 140, Kellogg Institute for International Studies, University of Notre Dame, Notre Dame, IN, July 1990), 12–24.

2. Miguel Urrutia, "On the Absence of Economic Populism in Colombia," in *Macroeconomic Populism in Latin America,* ed. Rudiger Dornbusch and Sebastian Edwards (Chicago: University of Chicago Press, 1991), 370–80.

3. David Collier and Ruth Collier, *Shaping the Political Arena* (Princeton, NJ: Princeton University Press, 1991), 459–61.

4. On the persistence of clientelism over time, and its changing forms, in Brazil as well as in Kenya, Zambia, and other African cases, see Frances Hagopian, *Traditional Politics and Regime Change in Brazil* (Cambridge: Cambridge University Press, 1996); and Nicolas Van de Walle, "Meet the New Boss, Same as the Old Boss? The Evolution of Political Clientelism in Africa," in *Patrons, Clients, and Policies: Patterns of Democratic Accountability and Political Competition,* ed. Herbert Kitschelt and Steven Wilkinson (Cambridge: Cambridge University Press, 2007), 50–67.

5. Archer, "Transition from Traditional to Broker Clientelism"; Fernán E. González, Ingrid J. Bolívar, and Teófilo Vázquez, *Violencia Política en Colombia: De la Nación Fragmentada a la Construcción del Estado* (Bogotá: CINEP, 2002); Jonathan Hartlyn, *The Politics of Coalition Rule in Colombia* (Cambridge: Cambridge University Press, 1988); Francisco Leal Buitrago and Andres Davila, *Clientelismo: El sistema política y su expresión regional* (Bogotá: Tercer Mundo, 1990); John Martz, *The Politics of Clientelism: Democracy and the State in Colombia* (New Brunswick, NJ: Transaction Publishers, 1999); and Steffen W. Schmidt, "Bureaucrats as Modernizing Brokers? Clientelism in Colombia," *Comparative Politics* 6 (1974): 425–50.

6. González, Bolívar, and Vázquez, *Violencia Política en Colombia,* 270–72.

7. Martz, *Politics of Clientelism,* 243–47.

8. Archer, "Transition from Traditional to Broker Clientelism," 9.

9. Urrutia, "Absence of Economic Populism," 378.

10. Fernán Gonzalez and Silvia Otero, "¿Hasta que punto el clientelismo hace ilegitimo el sistema politico colombiano?" in *Governanza y conflicto en Colombia: Interaccion entre gobernantes y gobernados en un contexto violento,* ed. Claire Launay-Garna and Fernan Gonzalez (Bogotá: Universidad Javeriana, 2010), 41.

11. Schmidt, "Clientelism in Colombia," 433–35.

12. Urrutia, "Absence of Economic Populism in Colombia," 383.

13. Martz, *Politics of Clientelism,* 654. After the National Front, national leaders, who were often ex-presidents, gained salience. In the Conservative Party, Laureano Gómez and Mariano Ospina represented the two primary factions. In the Liberal Party, Alfonso López Pumarejo, Carlos Lleras Restrepo, and Julio Cesar Turbay Ayala led the primary factions.

14. Erika Moreno and Maria Escobar-Lemmon, "Mejor Solo Que Mal Acompanado: Political Entrepreneurs and List Proliferation in Colombia," in *Pathways to Power: Political Recruitment and Candidate Selection in Latin America,* ed. Peter Siavelis and Scott Morgenstern (University Park: Pennsylvania State University Press, 2008), 121.

15. Ronald Archer and Matthew Shugart, "The Unrealized Potential of Presidential Dominance in Colombia," in *Presidentialism and Democracy in Latin America,* ed. Scott Mainwaring and Matthew Shugart (New York: Cambridge University Press, 1997).

16. Kent Eaton, *Politicians and Economic Reforms in New Democracies* (University Park: Penn State University Press, 2002), 275.

17. Urrutia, "Absence of Economic Populism in Colombia," 384.

18. Beatriz Magaloni, Alberto Díaz-Cayeros, and Federico Estévez, "Clientelism and Portfolio Diversification: A Model of Electoral Investment with Applications to Mexico," in *Patrons, Clients, and Policies,* ed. Kitschelt and Wilkinson, 182–205; and Luis Fernando Medina and Susan Stokes, "Monopoly and Monitoring: An Approach to Political Clientelism," in *Patrons, Clients, and Policies,* 68–83.

19. Steven Taylor, "The Evolution of the Ballot in Colombia" (paper presented at the Southern Political Science Association Conference, New Orleans, 2008).

20. Daniel Nielson and Matthew Shugart, "Constitutional Change in Colombia: Policy Adjustment through Institutional Reform," *Comparative Political Studies* 32 (1999): 313–41.

21. Matthew Shugart, Erika Moreno, and Luis Fajardo, "Deepening Democracy by Renovating Political Practices: The Struggle for Electoral Reform in Colombia," in *Peace, Democracy and Human Rights in Colombia,* ed. Christopher Welna and Gustavo Gallon (Notre Dame, IN: Notre Dame University Press, 2006), 26–33.

22. Jesús Duarte, "State Weakness and Clientelism in Colombian Education," in *Colombia: The Politics of Reforming the State,* ed. Eduardo Posada-Carbó (New York: St. Martin's Press, 1998); and Jesús Duarte, *Educacion publica y clientelismo en Colombia* (Medellin: Editorial Universidad de Antioquia, 2005).

23. Educational outcomes in Colombia remain bleak as measured by national standardized tests such as SABER and international standardized tests such as TIMSS and LLECE (see J. Guillermo Ferrer and Patricia Arregui, "Las pruebas internacionales de aprendizaje en América Latina y su impacto en la calidad de la educación: Criterios para guiar futures aplicaciones" [PREAL Document No. 26, Partnership for Educational Revitalization in the Americas, 2003]: 14–17). To be sure, clientelism is one of *multiple* factors that explain the low quality of public education. Still, the politicization of teachers does not bode well for improved pedagogy.

24. Duarte, *Educacion publica y clientelismo en Colombia,* 90.

25. According to Pamela Lowden, "teachers were hired *en masse* at election time, with little or no regard to the availability of funding (far less actual need)." See Pamela S. Lowden, "Education Reform in Colombia: The Elusive Quest for Effectiveness," in *Crucial Needs, Weak Incentives: Social Sector Reform, Democratization, and Globalization in Latin America,* ed. Robert R. Kaufman and Joan M. Nelson (Washington, DC: Woodrow Wilson Center Press, 2004), 353.

26. Carlos Pardo, *Adalberto Carvajal: una vida, muchas luchas* (Bogotá: Editorial Pijao, 1985).

27. Law 43 and the *Teachers' Statute* Decree 2277 of 1979 cemented these changes. See

Abel Céspedes Rodríguez, *La Educación Despues de la Constitución del 91. De la Reforma a la Contrarreforma* (Bogotá: Editorial Magisterio, 2002), 25.

28. The Estatuto Docente states: "*El presente Decreto establece el régimen especial para regular las condiciones de ingreso, ejercicio, estabilidad, ascenso y retiro de las personas que desempeñan la profesión docente en los distintos niveles y modalidades que integran el sistema Educativo nacional, excepto el nivel superior que se regirá por normas especiales.*" Decreto 2277 de 1979, Estatuto Docente, Ministerio de Educacion (Ministry of Education), Colombia, September 14, 1979, www.mineducacion.gov.co/1621/articles-103879_archivo_pdf.pdf.

29. Duarte, "State Weakness and Clientelism in Colombian Education," 151.

30. *La Opinion*, May 17, 1985, quoted in and translated by Duarte, "State Weakness and Clientelism in Colombian Education."

31. Brian Crisp and Rachael E. Ingall, "Institutional Engineering and the Nature of Representation: Mapping the Effects of Electoral Reform in Colombia," *American Journal of Political Science* 46 (2002): 736.

32. Christopher Chambers-Ju, "The Electoral Dilemma Revisited: The Colombian Constitution of 1991 and the Policy Influence of Colombia's Teachers' Union" (working paper, University of California, Berkeley, 2011), 32–33.

33. Chambers-Ju, "Electoral Dilemma Revisited," 32–33.

34. Duarte, "State Weakness and Clientelism in Colombian Education," 141.

35. Chambers-Ju, "Electoral Dilemma Revisited," 30.

36. Lowden, "Education Reform in Colombia."

37. Carlos Malaver, "'Mientras esté, ni puestos ni contratos': Secretario de Educación," *El Tiempo* (Bogotá), June 12, 2012.

38. Juan Camilo Maldonado and Laura Ardila Arrieta, "¿Qué hay detrás del intento de moción de censura al secretario de Educación?" *El Espectador* (Bogotá), June 7, 2012.

39. Duarte, "State Weakness and Clientelism in Colombian Education," 148.

40. Kathleen O'Neill, *Decentralizing the State* (New York: Cambridge University Press, 2005).

41. Kent Eaton, "The Downside of Decentralization: Armed Clientelism in Colombia," *Security Studies* 15 (2006): 533–62.

42. John Dugas, Angelica Ocampo, Luis Javier Orjuela, and Germán Ruiz, *Los Caminos de la Descentralización* (Bogotá: Universidad de los Andes, 1992); and Tulia G. Falleti, *Decentralization and Subnational Politics in Latin America* (New York: Cambridge University Press, 2010).

43. Charles Collins, "Local Government and Urban Protest in Colombia," *Public Administration and Development* 8 (1988): 424.

44. Timothy Campbell, *The Quiet Revolution: Decentralization and the Rise of Political Participation in Latin American Cities* (Pittsburgh, PA: University of Pittsburgh Press, 2003), 45.

45. Collins, "Local Government and Urban Protest in Colombia," 425.

46. Despite the hope that decentralization would reduce clientelism, there are good reasons to expect that it would worsen the practice by making it easier for incumbents to monitor votes in (municipal) districts that are smaller and more homogeneous than in the departmental districts where national legislators have traditionally been elected in Colombia. See Medina and Stokes, "Monopoly and Monitoring," 82.

47. Buitrago and Davila, *Clientelismo.*

48. Eloisa Vasco Montoya, *Clientelism y Minifundio: Bases Socio-Economicas del Poder Politico en un Municipio Minifundista* (Bogotá: Editorial CINEP, 1978), 69.

49. Pilar Gaitán and Carlos Moreno, *Poder Local: Realidad y Utopia de la Descentralización en Colombia* (Bogotá: Tercer Mundo, 1991).

50. "Tendencia centralista del Gobierno amenaza avances de eleccion popular de alcaldes, dicen expertos," *El Tiempo* (Bogotá), June 1, 2008.

51. Departamento Nacional de Planeación (National Planning Department, Colombia), *Evaluación de la Descentralización Municipal en Colombia: Balance de una Década* (4 vols., 2002).

52. Iván Jaramillo, "La salud en el gobierno de Uribe," *Revista Foro* 52 (February 2005): 86.

53. Although we argue that mayors across Colombia have been able to transition from clients to patrons as a result of decentralization, it is important to note that this policy apparently had the opposite effect in Bogota. According to Eleonora Pasotti, the introduction of direct elections and fiscal transfers facilitated the emergence of leaders who attacked clientelism aggressively, including Mayors Antanas Mockus and Enrique Peñalosa. More recently, however, the resurgence of clientelism under Mayor Samuel Moreno (2007–2010) has exposed the limitations of reform projects that depend so heavily on mayoral leadership. See Eleonora Pasotti, *The Decline of Machine Politics in Bogota, Naples, and Chicago* (Cambridge: Cambridge University Press, 2010).

54. According to Córdoba's (2003, 40) discussion of the politicization of SISBEN, people with the ability to pay for insurance often appear on the subsidized list, and some people appear more than once. See Oscar Fresneda, "El sistema de selección de beneficiaries y el regimen subsidiado de salud en Colombia," *Comercio Exterior* 53 (2003): 577, 581.

55. Steffen W. Schmidt, "Bureaucrats as Modernizing Brokers? Clientelism in Colombia" *Comparative Politics* 6 (1974): 438.

56. Gloria Molina and Peter Spurgeon, "La Descentralizacion del Sector Salud en Colombia," *Gestión y Política Pública* 16 (2007): 181.

57. Eric Hershberg, "Technocrats, Citizens and Second-Generation Reforms: Colombia's Andean Malaise," in *State and Society in Conflict: Comparative Perspectives on the Andean Crises,* ed. Paul Drake and Eric Hershberg (Pittsburgh, PA: University of Pittsburgh Press, 2006).

58. Alfredo Rangel, "El Poder Local: Objetivo de la Guerrilla," in *Descentralizacion y Orden Publico,* ed. Fundacion Friedrich Ebert (Bogotá: Mileno, 1997); and Eduardo Pizarro, *Una Democracia Asediada: Balance y Perspectivas del Conflicto Armado en Colombia* (Bogotá: Norma, 2004).

59. Fabio Sánchez and María del Mar Palau, "Conflict, Decentralisation and Local Governance in Colombia: 1974–2004" (*Documento CEDE* 2006–2020, May 2006).

60. Andres Peñate, "El sendero estrategico del ELN: del idealismo guevarista al clientelismo armado," in *Reconocer la Guerra para Construer la Paz,* ed. Malcolm Deas and Maria Victoria Llorente (Bogotá: Norma, 1999).

61. Eaton, "Downside of Decentralization," 533–62.

62. Mauricio Romero, ed., *Para Política: La Ruta de la Expansion Paramilitar y los Acuerdos Políticos* (Bogotá: Corporacion Nuevo Arco Iris, 2007), 20.

63. "Raponazo de los 'paras' al erario público," *El Espectador* (Bogotá), Sept. 26–Oct. 2, 2004.

64. Romero, ed., *Para Política*.

65. Moreno and Escobar-Lemmon, "Mejor Solo Que Mal Acompanado," 142.

66. Cristina Escobar, "Clientelism and Citizenship: The Limits of Democratic Reform in Sucre, Colombia," *Latin American Perspectives* 29 (2002): 36.

67. Hershberg, "Technocrats, Citizens and Second-Generation Reforms."

68. Oscar Fresneda, "El sistema de selección de beneficiaries y el regimen subsidiado de salud en Colombia," *Comercio Exterior* 53 (2003): 584.

69. Fabio Velásquez, "La Descentralización en Colombia: Trayectoria, Realidades y Retos" (unpublished manuscript, Universidad Nacional, 2010).

70. Another example of recentralization in the health sector is the new (2004) FOSYGA mechanism, which retains transfers from certain municipalities and directs them toward the Finance Ministry (Jaramillo 2005).

71. Agencia Presidencial para la Acción Social y la Cooperación Internacional—Acción Social (Presidential Agency for Social Action and International Cooperation—Social Action, Colombia), "Familias en Acción: Informe de Estado y Avance Segundo Semestre de 2010" (report presented in Bogotá, February 2011).

72. Orazio Attanasio and Alice Mesnard, "The Impact of a Conditional Cash Transfer Programme on Consumption in Colombia," *Fiscal Studies* 27 (2006): 421–42; and Fábio Veras Soares, Rafael Perez Ribas, and Rafael Guerreiro Osório, "Research Notes: Evaluating the Impact of Brazil's Bolsa Familia Cash Transfer Programs in Comparative Perspective," *Latin American Research Review* 45 (2010).

73. In the election, rumors swirled that Santos's campaign threatened participants that voting for opposition candidate Antanas Mockus would result in the loss of their benefits. See "Cómo cambió la política," *Semana* (Bogotá), July 31, 2010, www.semana.com/nacion/como-cambio-politica/142438-3.aspx; "Familias en Acción ¿plataforma para la reelección?" *Cambio* (Bogotá), July 9, 2008, www.cambio.com.co/panoramacambio/784/4369276–pag-2_2.html; and "Dudas en Acción," *Semana* (Bogota), June 12, 2010, www.semana.com/nacion/dudas-accion/140234-3.aspx.

74. In 2008, the Constitutional Court also investigated the legality of giving the presidency exclusive managerial control over such large pots of money. NGOs, including Global Exchange, issued a report correlating the expansion of *Familias en Acción* and an increase in the electoral support for Alvaro Uribe and Juan Manuel Santos in 2006 and 2010. See "Análisis del Programa Familias En Acción en el Marco de los Procesos Electorales en Colombia" (Final Report, Global Exchange), www.globalexchange.org/countries/americas/colombia/ColomInformeFinalESP.pdf; and "Familias en Acción."

75. "Dudas en Acción."

76. "Dudas en Acción."

77. Kitschelt and Wilkinson, eds., *Patrons, Clients, and Policies*, 43.

CHAPTER FIVE

Lessons Learned
While Studying Clientelistic Politics
in the Gray Zone

JAVIER AUYERO

It has been 10 years since the publication of *Poor People's Politics* and 15 since I began the first ethnographic study of "political clientelism" in Argentina. During this decade, scholarship on the subject has expanded substantially. We now know much more about the factors associated with patronage spending and about the relationship between unemployment programs, cash transfer programs, and clientelism. We also have models that seek to account for the logic of political machines and qualitative studies on the intricate relationships between clients, brokers, and patrons that examine the "system of incentives" at work within patronage networks.[1] In this chapter I seek to (1) describe what I call the double life of clientelism; (2) highlight what I believe are the most important substantive and analytic shortcomings in recent studies; and (3) analyze the relationship between clientelism and collective action, paying particular attention to what I call "the gray zone" of politics.

The chapter makes one analytical, one substantive, and one methodological contribution. In analytical terms, I argue that we should pay empirical and theoretical attention to "the gray zone," the area of clandestine relations where everyday life, routine politics, and collective violence meet and mesh. In substantive terms, I argue that clientelism owes its durability to the consolidation and legitimation of two types of practices in two different but interrelated arenas—the political field, and the daily life of the dispossessed. These practices are, respectively: (1) the personalized distribution of resources to obtain votes and participants for the political machine (including its shock troops); and (2) the nature of poor people's problem-solving strategies that revolve around the offering of votes and support. In methodological terms, I suggest that the social-scientific study of clientelism needs more political ethnography, which is understood as research based on close observation, in real time and space, of political actors and institutions, in which the investigator embeds him/herself near—or within—the phenomenon to detect how and why agents in the setting act, think, and feel the way they do. Political ethnography allows us to transcend the intrinsic limitations of opinion surveys and to grasp the objective support and the subjective experience of patronage politics—both as a mechanism of political domination and as a problem-solving strategy. However, my methodological choice does not deny the potential advantages of using both sociological/anthropological and political science research methods.

The Double Life of Political Clientelism

Political clientelism has been one of the strongest and most recurrent images in the study of political practices of the urban and rural poor in Latin America, almost to the point of becoming a sort of "metonymic prison"[2] for the region. Used (and abused) to explain the reasons why poor and destitute people sometimes follow populist leaders and at other times authoritarian or conservative ones, the notion of political clientelism has been understood as one of the central elements of the populist appeal but has also been defined as a mode of vertical political inclusion distinct from populism. Political clientelism is also recurrently associated with the limitations of Latin America's unceasingly fragile democracies. It is seen as one of the pillars of oligarchic domination that reinforce and perpetuate the rule of traditional political elites and as a practice that remains at the core of party behavior. With neoliberal emphasis on "targeted" social programs, political clientelism has been defined as one of the main obstacles that the modern lean state must overcome to reach the poorest of the poor.

Understood as the distribution (or promise) of resources by political office holders or political candidates in exchange for political support, clientelism has exhibited, to cite Robert Merton's still insightful analysis of political machines in the United States, "a notable vitality" in many parts of the modern world.[3] In the words of the authors of the most recent survey on this resilient sociopolitical phenomenon, clientelism is a particular form of party-voter linkage: "a transaction, the direct exchange of a citizen's vote in return for direct payments or continuing access to employment, goods, and services."[4] According to these authors, patronage-based voter-party linkages are still operating—and sometimes expanding—not only in the new democracies of Latin America, post-communist Europe, South and Southeast Asia, and parts of Africa but also, contrary to the predictions of those who saw clientelism as a "holdover from pre-industrial patterns that would gradually disappear in the modernizing West,"[5] in many industrial democracies such as Italy, Austria, and Japan.[6]

It is common knowledge that clientelistic exchanges concatenate into pyramidal networks comprising asymmetrical, reciprocal, and face-to-face relationships. The structure of what David Knoke calls "domination networks"[7] and the key actors within them (patrons, brokers, and clients) are well-studied phenomena of popular political life both in urban and rural settings.[8] One general agreement in the extensive literature on the subject is that patron-broker-client relationships are as far from any kind of Simmelian sociability ("the purest, most transparent, most engaging kind of interaction—that among equals"[9]) as a Roman *societas leonina* (a partnership in which all the benefits go to one side). The vast range of literature concurs that clientelistic relations are a complex cocktail of the four different forms of social interaction identified by George Simmel in his classic *On Individuality and Social Forms:* exchange, conflict, domination, and prostitution. Clientelistic relations are seen as hierarchical arrangements, as bonds of dependence and control based on power differences and inequality. Being highly selective, particularistic, and diffuse, they are "characterized by the simultaneous exchange of two different types of resources and services: instrumental (economic and political) and associational or expressive (promises of loyalty and solidarity)."[10]

With its particularized favors, the patron-broker network offers alternative channels for "getting things done," while avoiding bureaucratic indifference. As Robert Gay and Gerrit Burgwald convincingly show in their studies of two *favelas* (shantytowns) in Rio de Janeiro and a squatter settlement in Quito, clientelistic mediation is an effective way of obtaining many urban services that are otherwise unavailable for those without contacts.[11] With its informal rules of promotion and reward (similar to an informal party structure), and its low-cost access to state jobs, the clientelistic network also offers one of the few remaining channels of upward social mobility. In contexts of dwindling economic opportunities, sustained and loyal engagement in the party machinery can assure participants access to jobs and influence in the distribution of public resources.[12]

Most studies still focus on clientelism as a form of getting the vote and as a form of political domination. Without denying the fact that this particular political practice is useful (with limitations) as an electoral strategy, as a means of solving organizational problems for a party, and as a form of political power over dispossessed populations, I believe we miss a lot of "where the action is" (to borrow from E. Goffman) and remain blind to the reasons clientelism persists and thrives, if we fail to examine patronage as a strategy for solving the problems of the poor. We need to shift the central focus of studies of political clientelism and concentrate on the place this political arrangement occupies in the lives of the most destitute citizens. How important is patronage as a problem-solving strategy among the urban poor? How does it compete (or fail to compete) with other problem-solving strategies (markets, state welfare, etc.)? We know that patronage is, for party leaders and brokers, a way of buying the vote and buying turnout.[13] What does clientelism represent for clients? Testimonies about the workings of clientelism are usually gathered from opposition politicians, journalists, or community leaders who are against this "way of doing politics." We also commonly "learn" about the pervasiveness of patronage through opinion polls that rarely go beyond the surface of the actual exchange of votes for favors (asking basic questions such as: What is your opinion about clientelism? Did you or your neighbor ever receive a favor from a local politician during an election season?). Only sporadically do we listen to the so-called clients, to the reasons they give for their behavior (supporting a particular patron or broker, attending rallies, etc.), and to their own judgments concerning what others label "anti-democratic" procedures. The viewpoints of clients, which can be reconstructed through ethnographic fieldwork, are crucial to understanding and explaining the objective and subjective underpinnings of political clientelism as both a mechanism of political domination and as a problem-solving strategy among the urban poor. One analytical lesson (and avenue for further research) that I learned over years of close examination of grassroots politics is that we need to do more and better work to describe and explain the points of view of clients.

Patronage politics is not solely about the distribution of material resources in exchange for political support. A line of research inspired by the sociology of Pierre Bourdieu has noted that clientelism not only lives an objective life of network exchange, but it also it lives a second, subjective life in the dispositions it inculcates in some of its actors—dispositions that ensure the reproduction of this arrangement.[14] This research argues that the automatic appearance of the exchange of "support for favors" that is often noted in the literature should be interpreted not in mechanistic terms but as the result of the habituation it generates in beneficiaries or clients. This body of research shows that the everyday workings of clientelistic problem-solving networks produce a set of dispositions among those who receive daily favors from patrons and brokers. I emphasize the regular, routine operation of this network to highlight that this relationship transcends singular acts of exchange. In her analysis of the emergence of activism among Filipino workers, Rosanne Rutten labels this dispositional toolkit "clientelist habitus."[15] These schemes of perception, evaluation, and action are in turn reconfirmed by the symbolic actions that patrons and brokers routinely perform in their public speeches (emphasizing, for example, the "love" they feel for their followers and their "service to the people") and in their personalized ways of giving (stressing their efforts to obtain goods and thus creating the appearance that in their absence such benefits would not be delivered).[16] In other words, clientelistic politics are not limited to material problem solving. The "way of giving" that brokers and patrons enact—in which the patron or the brokers (be they Chicago precinct captains, Mexican *caciques,* Argentine *punteros,* or Brazilian *cabo eleitorals*) portray themselves as "just one of us, who understands what it's all about"[17]—is a central dimension in the workings and persistence of patronage. The "humanizing and personalizing manner of assistance to those in need," as Robert Merton famously put it, is therefore a constitutive element in the functioning and durability of clientelism.[18] Much more detailed, close-up, and systematic work needs to be done on the formation, reproduction of, and possible challenges to the clients and politicos' clientelistic habitus.

Patronage politics might thus be based on material resources, but it has a crucial symbolic dimension that is entirely missed by most analysts, who repeatedly predict a looming crisis of machine politics (a crisis that has now presumably been in the making for decades). The daily social order of the machine has durable effects via the dispositions it instills in client beliefs. The authority of specific patrons and brokers might well come from the resources they wield, but the authority of machine politics and the authority of brokers and patrons in general comes from habituation to the everyday workings of the network. In the daily workings of patronage, what matters most is not short-term, quid-pro-quo exchanges but diffuse, long-term reciprocity based on the embedding of the machine operators (brokers, and through them, patrons) in poor people's everyday lives.

If I have learned one thing after years of fieldwork and writing, it is that patronage owes its durability to the consolidation and normalization of two types of practices in two different but (sometimes) intertwined spheres, namely, the political field and the daily life of the urban poor. Much more needs to be examined about the emergence, consolidation, and legitimation of this way of politics and problem solving.

Some of the possible consequences of political clientelism have been well researched: politicized bureaucracies, corruption, electoral manipulation, political inequality, and weak institutions, for example.[19] Clientelism erodes democracy, but it can also, paradoxically, complement it by closing the distances between elites and those excluded from the polity.[20] The causes,[21] logic,[22] and impact on public policy[23] of clientelism are still the object of intense academic debate. This is not the place to review more than a decade's worth of scholarship on the subject. I do, however, want to highlight that much of the research on patronage politics still reproduces a dichotomy that, in my view, acts as a pernicious premise and obscures much of the dynamic of popular politics.[24]

Patronage and Collective Action

Among the most established findings in social movement and collective action research are the notions that "prior social ties operate as a basis for movement recruitment and that established social settings are the locus of movement emergence."[25] Existing scholarship agrees on the key role played by indigenous organizations or associational networks in the emergence of a movement.[26]

Far from being a realm of possible cooperation, patronage networks are, on the contrary, considered a demobilizing structure.[27] Conceptualized as what Julian Pitt-Rivers famously called "a lopsided friendship,"[28] patron-client bonds are seen as the exact opposite of the horizontal networks of civic engagement believed to foster a truly civic community that "make democracy work"[29] and make social movement possible. Embeddedness in clientelistic relationships is understood as a suppressor of participation in the more horizontal relational contexts that have been found to be "conducive to various forms of collective engagement."[30]

Research conducted in urban poverty enclaves (shantytowns, *favelas,* squatter settlements, *colonias,* etc.) and on poor people's movements in Latin America show that patronage and collective mobilization can indeed coexist in the same geographical place, albeit usually in a conflictive way.[31] In their chronicle of the emergence and development of the *piquetero* movement in Argentina (the social movement that grouped the unemployed and that used road-blockades, called *piquetes,* as their main tactic) Maristell Svampa and Sebastian Pereyra, assert that picketer organizations represent the "first concrete challenge against *punteros* (political brokers)" of the Peronist party clientelistic machine.[32] Another recent example is found in the work of Claudio Holzner. Writing about the "stubborn resilience of clientelistic organizations and practices in Mexico despite a strengthening civil society and growing electoral competition at all levels," he notes the emergence of "rival" forms of political organization—one that is hierarchical and clientelistic, and another that emphasizes democratic participation, political autonomy, and "actively resists political clientelism."[33]

Although pointing to the complexity of poor people's politics and the diversity of problem-solving strategies used by the destitute, all of these studies depict clientelistic and mobilizing networks as two different and opposing fields of political action—two spheres of social interaction and exchange that seldom overlap and that usually "rival," "resist," or "challenge" each other.[34] The dominance of patronage politics among the poor, the extant research agrees, frustrates collective claims-making and isolates and atomizes citizens, thereby preventing the organizational and the relational work at the basis of collective action.

But the literature also agrees that in one particular case (that of the breakdown of clientelistic arrangements) protest can, in fact, emerge from patronage—and it usually does so in explosive ways. When a well-oiled system of patron-client relationships, crucial for the survival of the local population, fails to deliver or suddenly collapses, "reciprocity [can] change to rivalry."[35] Scholars are familiar with these situations of mass mobilization originating in the abrupt malfunctioning of routine social and political relations. Political scientist James Scott examined one of its iterations when writing about the collective revolts caused by the swift changes in the "balance of reciprocity" between landlords and tenants (a balance that, as Scott examined in detail, was the normative foundation of clientelistic networks in agrarian societies).[36] Historian E. P. Thompson uncovered an analogous case when dissecting the eighteenth-century English food riots as manifestations of the rupture in the "moral economy of the poor" and the "consistent traditional view of social norms and obligations, of the proper economic functions of several parties within the community."[37] An affront to these moral assumptions—caused by an unexpected alteration in the "particular equilibrium between paternalist authority and the crowd"[38]—was, in Thompson's view, "the usual occasion for direct action."[39]

Most of the scholarship on patronage networks points to their potential malfunction as a generator of sudden grievances, which creates the opportunity for collective action. Only recently, well-functioning clientelistic networks have been analyzed as a key relational support for collective action. In these studies, vertical networks do not need to break down in order for collective action to emerge; some of their key actors (patrons, brokers, or clients) may for a variety of reasons (ranging from threats to existing arrangements to attempts at improving their position in the political field) become organizers of collective (and in some cases violent) action.

Students of civil wars show, for example, that disputes between operating clientelistic networks can be at the basis of violent contention. Writing about the mass killings that took place in Indonesia between 1965 and 1966, Stathis Kalyvas asserts that although they were "ostensibly articulated around the communism/anticommunism cleavage . . . a sustained examination of regional massacres unearthed all kinds of local conflicts. . . . [I]n Bali they were associated with long-standing rivalries between patronage groups."[40] Patronage networks have also been identified as the crucial relational support of collective violence in Colombia. As Steffen Schmidt argues, "Colombia's political violence...is in great part due to the existence of widespread, competitive, aggressive, patron-client based politics."[41]

But the relationship between patronage and contention need not take a violent form. In his study of environmental protest in eight communities in southern Japan, Jeffrey Broadbent notes the presence of what he calls "breakaway bosses" (local leaders who join protesters).[42] These bosses are indicative, in Broadbent's analysis, of the existing vertical ties between citizens and elites that shape local political opportunities. Local political bosses, he writes, "formed a vertical structure of social control [which] penetrated into the community through the political party, government, and big business."[43] Much like a precinct captain in the Chicago political machines analyzed by Guterbock,[44] or a *cabo eleitoral* in a Brazilian *favela*,[45] these local bosses build their local power through patronage, by "presenting generous contributions at funeral and weddings, holding sake parties to build camaraderie, distributing small bribes at election time, finding jobs and even marriage partners for [constituents'] children."[46] Patronage networks pose "a formidable barrier to mobilization in village context" unless a boss breaks free: "[O]nce a traditional boss broke from his bosses in favour of resistance, he was able to carry much of his subordinate networks 'automatically' (structurally) into the protest movement."[47]

Thus more than two opposed spheres of action or two different forms of sociability, patronage and contentious politics can be mutually imbricated. When it malfunctions or when it thrives, clientelism may lie at the root of collective action—an embeddedness that studies of repertoires of contention have indeed anticipated but have failed to explore in detail.[48]

The available evidence focusing on what I call the "support scenario" is limited and scattered for a reason. This form of recursive relationship between patronage and collective action has not been examined in depth, either theoretically or empirically. There is no need of a collapse or interruption in the flow of clientelistic exchanges for contention to occur. Well-functioning patronage networks can be purposively activated to conduct politics by other collective—and sometimes violent—means. We need much more empirical and theoretical work on the various ways in which patronage and contention are mutually imbricated. Inattention to the recursive relationship between both phenomena risks missing many of the dynamics of both routine and extraordinary forms of popular politics. An empirical focus on the area in which they meet and mesh should afford a better view of two processes that have been identified as crucial to many forms of contentious politics. These two processes are brokerage—here understood simply as "the forging of social connections between previously unlinked persons or sites"[49]—and certification—understood as "the validation of actors, their performances, and their claims by external authorities."[50] One particularly challenging area of research on this topic is the one that focuses on the "gray zone" of popular politics.

The Gray Zone

The empirical evidence on "gray areas" in the making of collective violence is mounting and is increasingly unequivocal. What Charles Tilly calls "violent specialists"— that is, actors who specialize in inflicting physical damage—play a key, though sometimes not quite discernible, role in the origins and the course of the collective violence.[51] Some of these specialists (police and soldiers, for example) are part of the state apparatus; others (such as thugs, gangs, and vigilante groups), however, enjoy important but often clandestine connections with established power-holders. These "shadowy ties" between state actors and perpetrators of violence define what in previous work I call "the gray zone of politics" and challenge the easy and simplistic state-society distinctions (among government agents, repressive forces, challengers, polity members, etc.) that most of the literature on collective action still takes for granted.[52]

Although far from being a clearly delimited area of inquiry, the relationship between clandestine political connections and collective violence has been the subject of increasing scholarly attention. For example, research on the origins and forms of communal violence in Southeast Asia highlighted the hidden links between partisan politics and collective violence.[53] Paul Brass's notion of "institutionalized riot systems" appositely describes these obscure connections. In these riot systems, Brass points out, "known actors specialize in the conversion of incidents between members of different communities into ethnic riots. The activities of these specialists, who operate under the loose control of party leaders, are usually required for a riot to spread from the initial incident of provocation."[54] Sudhir Kakar's analysis of a *pehlwan,* a wrestler/enforcer who works for a political boss, further illustrates this point: the genesis of many episodes of collective violence is located in the area where the actions of political actors and specialists in violence are secretly intertwined.[55]

Steven Wilkinson's *Votes and Violence* is perhaps the most systematic study to date of the connections between party politics (electoral competition) and collective violence (ethnic riots). Wilkinson convincingly shows that "ethnic riots, far from being relatively spontaneous eruptions of anger, are often *planned* by politicians for a clear electoral purpose. They are best thought of as a solution to the problem of how to change the salience of ethnic issues and identities among the electorate in order to build a winning political coalition."[56] Throughout his detailed and insightful study, Wilkinson calls attention to the instances in which political elites "cause," "foment," or "instigate" riots "in order to win elections" and brings to the fore what is often the state's complicity in failing to prevent violence.[57] The state's response, he argues, is very much conditioned by the "instructions" that politicians give to other

state officials on "whether to protect or not protect minorities."[58] Political elites
and organizers often "incite" violence and prevent repressive forces from responding once riots break out. Why? Wilkinson's conclusions are straightforward. Political leaders in some Indian states "impress upon their local officials that communal
riots and anti-Muslim pogroms must be prevented at all costs"[59] because of electoral
incentives.

Historical accounts of "race riots" in the United States point to a similar dynamic
between members of established political parties and the instigation (or absence) of
collective violence. Janet Abu-Lughod, for example, documents the attacks committed by the Ragen's Colts—young party hacks who were financially supported
by Frank Ragen, a well-known Democratic Cook County commissioner—on African Americans during the 1919 riots in Chicago. Years later, during the 1943 riots
in Detroit, whites who attacked blacks could count "on police protection and even
assistance."[60]

That party leaders and state officials might be "behind"—rather than against—
such episodes of collective violence should hardly surprise students of Latin American politics. In a detailed study of "la violencia"—the wave of political violence
that killed 200,000 people in Colombia in the 1940s and 1950s—historian Mary
Roldán shows that in the state of Antioquía "partisan conflict provided the initial
catalyst to violence."[61] She argues that not only did state bureaucrats "promote" the
violence that shocked the region, but police and even mayors actively participated in
the partisan attacks. Political elites, she points out, did not simply tolerate or instigate the violence; they were its perpetrators. While party members organized attacks
on places and peoples, the police acted as partisan shock troops. In words that should
ring true to those studying political violence in other parts of the world, Roldán
states: "While many citizens attributed the escalation of violence to the absence of
official forces, these forces were so often the perpetrators of violence between 1946
and 1949 that one wonders why anyone bothered to suggest that the presence of the
authorities could have been of much help."[62] Clandestine ties, Roldán demonstrates,
outlast specific episodes of violence and show durable, structure-like properties.

Historian Laurie Gunst and sociologist Orlando Patterson uncover the relationships between local patronage networks in Jamaica, or what the latter calls "garrison
constituency" and gang violence. Patterson points out how these gangs, which were
"initially formed for political purposes, now also serve the drug trade . . . [and have]
increasingly worked to generate unrest as a political tactic." Gunst, meanwhile, argues that the origins of Jamaican drug gangs in New York can be traced to these
same *posses,* native to Jamaica, which were armed by party members linked to prime
ministers Seaga or Manley.[63] Recent ethnographies authored by Donna Goldstein

and E. D. Arias about Rio de Janeiro's *favelas* provide further evidence of collusion between state actors, members of political parties, and violent entrepreneurs such as gang members who are associated with the drug trade.[64] Finally, Luis Astorga's historical reconstruction of the intertwining of the political field with the field of illicit drug production and trafficking in twentieth-century Mexico offers another excellent example of the (concealed and often illegal) connections between actors inside and outside the official political system—relations that must be rigorously examined if we are to explain seemingly random upsurges of violence.[65]

What do all these cases have in common? They all portray the activation of clandestine connections among political actors well entrenched within the polity and others located outside of it. When faced with such gray areas, most of the categories that scholars of collective action routinely operate within (categories that are very much informed by empirical analyses carried out in the United States and Europe) proved useless, if not misleading. As much as the literature agrees that the interactions between political elites, agents of social control, and protagonists of civil disorder matter, these remain discrete entities. The imaginary political anthropology of social movement and collective action scholarship lives in a world in which there are clear boundaries between insurgents and authorities, and dissidents or challengers and state actors, which are located in different regions of the social and political space (such as the "protest side" and the "repression side"). There is an almost complete silence about the possible participation of authorities, either elected officials or police agents, in the direct promotion of mobilization and/or the straightforward perpetration of collective violence. In part, the notion of the gray zone of clandestinity seeks to address this problem by calling attention to the existing continuities between state actions, routine politics, and extraordinary massive violence.

Political analysts should do a better job of integrating "gray zone" relations into the study of "normal" politics. Inattention to these clandestine connections has effects that are analogous to the inattentiveness to "informal institutions" noted by political scientists Gretchen Helmke and Steven Levitsky. In both cases, political analysis "risks missing much of what drives political behavior and can hinder efforts to explain important political phenomena."[66] Rather than dismissing them as aberrant or denouncing them on moralistic grounds, the challenge for a proper social scientific analysis is to feature such robust relations in our standard models of political action—an analytic integration that should in turn allow us to better incorporate violence into the study of popular politics, something that, as the late Charles Tilly argued, most political analysis still neglects. Much theoretical and empirical work lies ahead.

Conclusions

Political clientelism has been thoroughly scrutinized for more than three decades from both a macro and a micro perspective. This essay has reviewed some of the main agreements in the existing scholarship and pointed to some areas in need of further study. Given the resiliency of this particular political arrangement, I believe we should pay closer attention to the cultural dimension of patronage politics as well as to the intricate and little-understood connections that patronage establishes with collective action. Further research should also be conducted on the clandestine relationships between clientelistic networks, established political actors, and organizers and perpetrators of violent action.

NOTES

1. See Ernesto Calvo and María Victoria Murillo, "Who Delivers? Partisan Clients in the Argentine Electoral Market," *American Journal of Political Science* 48 (2004): 742–57; Karen Remmer, "The Political Economy of Patronage: Expenditure Patters in the Argentine Provinces, 1983–2003," *Journal of Politics* 69 (2007): 363–77; R. Weitz-Shapiro, "Partisan and Protest: The Politics of Workfare Distribution in Argentina," *Latin American Research Review* 41 (2006): 122–47; Agustina Giraudy, "The Distributive Politics of Emergency Employment Programs in Argentina," *Latin American Research Review* 42 (2007): 33–35; Susan Stokes, "Perverse Accountability: A Formal Model of Machine Politics with Evidence from Argentina," *American Political Science Review* 99 (2005): 315–25; Simeon Nichter, "Vote Buying or Turnout Buying? Machine Politics and the Secret Ballot," *American Political Science Review* 102 (2008): 19–31; and Mariela Szwarcberg, "Clientelismo en democracia: Lecciones del caso argentino," *Nueva Sociedad* 225 (2010): 139–55.

2. Arjun Appadurai, "Putting Hierarchy in its Place," *Cultural Anthropology* 3 (1988): 36–49.

3. Robert Merton, *Social Theory and Social Structure* (Glencoe, IL: Free Press, 1949), 71.

4. Herbert Kitschelt and Steven Wilkinson, eds., *Patrons, Clients, and Policies: Patterns of Democratic Accountability and Political Competition* (New York: Cambridge University Press, 2007), 2.

5. Kitschelt and Wilkinson, eds., *Patrons, Clients, and Policies,* 3.

6. For evidence of its endurance in Mexico, see also Claudio Holzner, "The End of Clientelism? Strong and Weak Networks in a Mexican Squatter Movement," *Mobilization, An International Quarterly* 9 (2004): 223–40; Magdalena Tosoni, "Notas sobre el clientelismo politico en la ciudad de México," *Latinoamericanos* 29 (2007): 47–49; E. D. Arias, "Trouble en Route: Drug Trafficking and Clientelism in Rio de Janiero Shantytowns," *Qualitative Sociology* 29 (2006): 427–45; V. Bursco, M. Nazareno, and S. Stokes, "Vote Buying in Argentina," *Latin American Research Review* 39 (2004): 66–88; Steven Levitsky and Lucan Way, "Linkage, Leverage and the Post-Communist Divide," *East European Politics and Societies*

27 (2007): 48–66; Sian Lazar, *El Alto, Rebel City: Self and Citizenship in Andean Bolivia* (Durham, NC: Duke University Press, 2008); David Smilde, "The Social Structure of Hugo Chavez," *Contexts* 7 (2008): 38–43; A. Schneider and R. Zuniga-Hamlin, "A Strategic Approach to Rights: Lessons from Clientelism in Rural Peru," *Development Policy Review* 23 (2005): 567–84; and Steven Wilkinson, "Explaining Changing Patterns of Party-Voter Linkages in India," in Kitschelt and Wilkinson, *Patrons, Clients, and Policies,* 110–40.

7. David Knoke, *Political Networks: The Structural Perspective* (Cambridge: Cambridge University Press, 1990).

8. For examples, see James Scott, "Political Clientelism: A Bibliographical Essay," in *Friends, Followers, and Factions: A Reader in Political Clientelism,* ed. Steffen Schmidt et al. (Los Angeles: University of California Press, 1977), 483–505; James Scott and Ben Kerkvliet, "How Traditional Rural Patrons Lose Legitimacy (in Southeast Asia)," in *Friends, Followers, and Factions,* ed. Schmidt et al., 483–507; Lazar, *El Alto, Rebel City;* Javier Auyero, *Poor People's Politics: Peronist Survival Networks and the Legacy of Evita* (Durham, NC: Duke University Press, 2000); and Holzner, "The End of Clientelism?" 223–40.

9. George Simmel, *On Individuality and Social Forms* (Chicago: University of Chicago Press, 1971).

10. Luis Roniger and Ayşe Güneş-Ayata, eds., *Democracy, Clientelism, and Civil Society* (Boulder, CO: Lynne Rienner, 1994); see also Sydel Silverman, "Patronage and Community-Nation Relationship in Central Italy," *Ethnology* 4 (1965): 172–89; Thomas Guterbock, *Machine Politics in Transition: Party and Community in Chicago* (Chicago: University of Chicago Press, 1980); M. Bodeman, "Relations of Production and Class Rule: The Hidden Basis of Patron-Clientage," in *Social Structures: A Network Approach,* ed. Barry Wellman et al. (Cambridge: Cambridge University Press, 1988); Robert Gay, "Rethinking Clientelism: Demands, Discourses, and Practices in Contemporary Brazil," *European Review of Latin American and Caribbean Studies* 65 (1998): 7–24.

11. Robert Gay, "Community Organization and Clientelist Politics in Contemporary Brazil: A Case Study from Suburban Rio de Janeiro," *International Journal of Urban and Regional Research* 14 (1990): 648–66; Robert Gay, *Popular Organization and Democracy in Rio de Janiero: A Tale of Two Favelas* (Philadelphia: Temple University Press, 1994); Gerrit Burgwald, *Struggle of the Poor: Neighborhood Organization and Clientelist Practice in a Quito Squatter Settlement* (Amsterdam: CEDLA, 1995).

12. See Kitschelt and Wilkinson, *Patrons, Clients, and Policies,* 19. As Kitschelt and Wilkinson write, clientelism is usually carried out through multifaceted and enduring webs of reciprocal exchange: "In many systems characterized by relatively high levels of poverty—such as Thailand, India, Pakistan, or Zambia—patrons directly purchase clients' votes in exchange for money, liquor, clothes, food, or other immediately consumable goods. . . . Much more frequently than single-shot transactions of this nature, however, are webs of exchange, obligation, and reciprocity sustained over a longer period, in which patrons provide private goods or club goods to their clients."

13. Stokes, "Perverse Accountability," 315–25; Nichter, "Vote Buying or Turnout Buying?" 19–31.

14. Rosanne Rutten, "Losing Face in Philippine Labor Confrontations: How Shame May Inhibit Worker Activism," in *New Perspectives in Political Ethnography,* ed. Lauren Joseph et

al. (New York: Springer, 2007); Auyero, *Poor People's Politics;* Javier Auyero, *Routine Politics and Violence in Argentina: That Gray Zone of State Power* (Cambridge: Cambridge University Press, 2007).

15. Rutten, "Losing Face in Philippine Labor Confrontations."

16. For an analysis of this symbolic dimension of patronage networks, see Auyero, *Poor People's Politics.*

17. Merton, *Social Theory and Social Structure,* 75.

18. Ibid.

19. Remmer, "Political Economy of Patronage," 363–77.

20. Tina Hilgers, "Who Is Using Whom? Clientelism from the Client's Perspective," *Journal of Iberian and Latin American Research* 15 (2009): 51–76.

21. Remmer, "The Political Economy of Patronage," 363–77.

22. Nichter, "Vote Buying or Turnout Buying?" 19–31; Stokes, "Perverse Accountability," 315–25.

23. Weitz-Shapiro, "Partisan and Protest," 122–47; Giraudy, "Distributive Politics of Emergency Employment Programs in Argentina," 33–35.

24. Javier Auyero, Fernanda Page, and Pablo Lapegna, "Patronage Politics and Contentious Action: A Recursive Relationship," *Latin American Politics and Society* 51 (2009): 1–31.

25. Mario Diani and Doug McAdam, eds., *Social Movements and Networks: Relational Approaches to Collective Action* (New York: Oxford University Press, 2003), 7.

26. Doug McAdam, *Political Process and the Development of Black Insurgency, 1930–1970* (Chicago: University of Chicago Press, 1985); Aldon Morris, *The Origins of the Civil Rights Movement: Black Communities Organizing for Change* (New York: Free Press, 1984); M. Osa, "Creating Solidarity: The Religious Foundations of the Polish Social Movement," *East European Politics and Societies* 11 (1997): 339–56; Doug McAdam, Sidney Tarrow, and Charles Tilly, *Dynamics of Contention* (Cambridge: Cambridge University Press, 2001).

27. David Rock, "Machine Politics in Buenos Aires and the Argentine Radical Party, 1912–1930," *Journal of Latin American Studies* 4 (1972): 233–56; David Rock, *Politics in Argentina, 1890–1930: The Rise and Fall of Radicalism* (Cambridge: Cambridge University Press, 1975); Claudio Holzner, "The End of Clientelism?" 223–40.

28. Julian Pitt-Rivers, *The People of the Sierra* (New York: Criterion Books, 1954), 110.

29. Robert Putnam, *Making Democracy Work* (Princeton, NJ: Princeton University Press, 1993).

30. Diani and McAdam, eds., *Social Movements and Networks,* 2; see also Mustafa Emirbayer and Jeff Goodwin, "Network Analysis, Culture, and the Problem of Agency," *American Journal of Sociology* 99 (1994): 1411–54; Pamela Oliver, "'If You Don't Do It, Nobody Else Will': Active and Token Contributors to Local Collective Action," *American Sociological Review* 49 (1984): 601–10; Doug McAdam and Roberto Fernandez, "Microstructural Bases of Recruitment to Social Movements," *Research in Social Movements, Conflict and Change* 12 (1990): 1–33; Florence Passy, "Social Networks Matter. But How?" in *Social Movements and Networks,* ed. Diani and McAdam; Ann Mische, "Cross Talk in Movements: Reconceiving the Culture-Network Link," in *Social Movements and Networks,* ed. Diani and McAdam.

31. Robert Gay, "Community Organization and Clientelist Politics in Contemporary Brazil," 648–66; Lazar, *El Alto, Rebel City.*

32. Maristell Svampa and Sebastian Pereyra, *Entre la ruta y el barrio: la experiencia de las organizaciones piqueteras* (Buenos Aires: Editorial Biblos, 2003), 93.

33. Holzner, "The End of Clientelism?" 77.

34. For a recent and illuminating exception on the ways in which citizens, in their attempt to solve pressing survival problems, may shuttle back and forth between "opposing" networks, see Julieta Quiros, *Cruzando la Sarmiento: Los piqueteros en la trama social del sur del Gran Buenos Aires* (Buenos Aires: IDES, 2006).

35. Rene Lemarchande, "Comparative Political Clientelism: Structure, Process, and Optic," in *Political Clientelism, Patronage and Development,* ed. S. N. Eisenstadt and Rene Lemarchand (London: Sage, 1981), 10.

36. Scott, "Political Clientelism: A Bibliographical Essay," 483–505.

37. E. P. Thompson, *Customs in Common* (New York: New Press, 1993), 188.

38. Ibid., 249.

39. More recently, sociologist Magdalena Tosoni (2007) dissects another occurrence, focusing her attention on contemporary urban Mexico. She describes the process by which residents of colonia San Lázaro (a working class neighborhood in Mexico City) campaigned, supported, and voted for a candidate who had promised to help solve a land ownership problem in the district. On taking office, the broker "forgot" about his clients and failed to deliver what had been agreed upon. As a result, the multitude mobilized and staged a massive road blockade and protest. See Tosoni, "Notas sobre el clientelismo politico en la ciudad de México."

40. Stathis Kalyvas, "The Ontology of 'Political Violence': Action and Identity in Civil Wars," *Perspectives on Politics* 1 (2003): 478.

41. Steffan Schmidt, "The Transformation of Clientelism in Rural Colombia," in *Friends, Followers and Factions,* ed. S. Schmidt et al., 109.

42. Jeffrey Broadbent, *Environmental Politics in Japan: Networks of Power and Protest* (Cambridge: Cambridge University Press, 1998); and "Movement in Context: Thick Social Networks and Environmental Mobilization in Japan," in Mario Diani and Doug McAdam, eds., *Social Movements and Networks.*

43. Broadbent, "Movement in Context," 219–20.

44. Guterbock, *Machine Politics in Transition.*

45. Gay, "Community Organization and Clientelist Politics in Contemporary Brazil."

46. Broadbent, "Movement in Context," 222.

47. Ibid., 223, 221.

48. Charles Tilly, *The Contentious French* (Cambridge, MA: Harvard University Press, 1986); Charles Tilly, *Popular Contention in Great Britain, 1758–1834* (Cambridge, MA: Harvard University Press, 1995); Charles Tilly and Sidney Tarrow, *Contentious Politics* (Boulder, CO: Paradigm Publishers, 2006).

49. Ronald Burt, *Brokerage and Closure: An Introduction to Social Capital* (New York: Oxford University Press, 2005).

50. McAdam, Tarrow, and Tilly, *Dynamics of Contention;* see also Tilly and Tarrow, *Contentious Politics.*

51. Charles Tilly, *The Politics of Collective Violence* (New York: Cambridge University Press, 2003).

52. See Javier Auyero, *Routine Politics and Violence in Argentina.*

53. Veena Das, ed., *Mirrors of Violence* (New York: Oxford University Press, 1990).

54. Paul Brass, *Theft of an Idol* (Princeton, NJ: Princeton University Press, 1997), 12.

55. Sudhir Kakar, *The Colors of Violence: Cultural Identities, Religion, and Conflict* (Chicago: University of Chicago Press, 1996).

56. Steven Wilkinson, *Votes and Violence: Electoral Competition and Ethnic Riots in India* (New York: Cambridge University Press, 2004).

57. Ibid., 236.

58. Ibid., 65, 85.

59. Ibid., 137.

60. Janet L. Abu-Lughod, *Race, Space, and Riots in Chicago, New York, and Los Angeles* (New York: Oxford University Press, 2007), quotation on 148.

61. Mary Roldán, *Blood and Fire: La Violencia in Antioquia, Colombia, 1946–1953* (Durham, NC: Duke University Press, 2002): 22.

62. Ibid., 82.

63. Orlando Patterson, "The Roots of Conflict in Jamaica," The New York Times Online Edition, January 23, 2001; Laurie Gunst, *Born Fi' Dead: A Journey Through the Jamaican Posse Underworld* (New York: Henry Holt & Co., 1995).

64. Donna Goldstein, *Laughter Out of Place: Race, Class, Violence, and Sexuality in a Rio Shantytown* (Berkeley, CA: University of California Press, 2003); E. D. Arias, "Trouble en Route: Drug Trafficking and Clientelism in Rio de Janeiro Shantytowns," *Qualitative Sociology* 29 (2006): 427–45.

65. Luis Astorga, *El Siglo de las Drogas* (Mexico City: Plaza y Janés, 2005).

66. Gretchen Helmke and Stephen Levitsky, eds., "Informal Institutions and Comparative Politics," *Perspectives in Politics* 2 (2004): 725.

CHAPTER SIX

Political Clientelism and Social Policy in Brazil

SIMEON NICHTER

Clientelism undermines social policy in contemporary Brazil and is a serious problem that the innovative Bolsa Familia program only partially addresses. Most researchers agree that Bolsa Familia, the world's largest conditional cash transfer program, is relatively well insulated from clientelistic pressures and has contributed to Brazil's recent decline in poverty and income inequality. Despite the program's substantial successes, I argue that Bolsa Familia is by no means a panacea, since many Brazilians continue to depend on exchange relationships with politicians for basic needs. Based on extensive fieldwork in Northeast Brazil, this chapter suggests that insufficient health care and employment opportunities often lead to a citizen strategy of clientelism that I term "declared support." This strategy reveals an important way in which contingent benefits can distort the political voice of poor citizens.

Whereas most literature on clientelism focuses exclusively on the strategies of politicians, this chapter also considers strategic behavior by citizens. Even in contexts with strong ballot secrecy, such as Brazil, voters may choose to declare their support publicly before an election. For example, voters may campaign on behalf of a candidate, attend rallies, put banners on their houses, wear party t-shirts, and so forth. However, in the context of clientelism, declaring support for a candidate is risky. If a voter's declared candidate wins, the voter may expect favored treatment with respect to social policies once that candidate takes office. But declaring support for a candidate can also leave a voter worse off. Fieldwork discussed below suggests that elected politicians in small communities often disfavor voters who declared for the opposition. For this reason, a voter may expect disfavored treatment if his or her declared candidate loses the election and thus choose to remain undeclared, a less-risky strategy. The overall point is that when social policy programs are not entirely insulated from clientelism, citizens often carefully consider the consequences when choosing whether to declare support and for whom.

The Context of Clientelism in Brazil

Before investigating the citizen strategy of declared support more extensively, we first examine the overall context of clientelism and the impact of Bolsa Familia. Over the years, many scholars have examined the prevalence and persistence of clientelism in Brazil. Until the latter part of the twentieth century, most Brazilians lived in rural areas where exchange relations tend to be particularly rife; for instance, 69% of the population lived in rural areas in 1940, compared to only 14% today.[1] During the oligarchic Old Republic (1889–1930), many citizens in rural municipalities voted as instructed by powerful *coroneis,* local political bosses (with titles from the National Guard) who provided sustenance but often demanded clients' political voice in return.[2] The political agency of such blocs of citizens was so restricted that observers typically called them *votos de cabresto* (halter votes) or *currais eleitorais* (electoral corrals), in obvious reference to equipment used to lead and contain livestock. Such exchange relations continue to evolve and play a significant role in Brazilian politics. For example, even though the military regime that oversaw Brazil's most recent authoritarian period (1964–1985) viewed clientelism as one of the "systemic obstacles to economic growth and ultimately political stability," this regime increasingly relied on existing patterns of exchange relations to garner political support at the local level.[3] In contemporary Brazil, various researchers provide evidence that politicians frequently forgo ideological appeals and instead provide contingent benefits to gain political support.[4]

As in many other regions of the world, clientelism has long undermined social policies in Brazil. In many cases, politicians manipulate programs for clientelistic purposes, delivering benefits in contingent exchange for electoral support. To provide just one example, rural poverty alleviation programs have been particularly afflicted by patterns of exchange relations. For instance, consider recent prosecutions of clientelism in Canudos, a small municipality in Northeast Brazil. After winning reelection in 2004, the mayor and vice-mayor of Canudos were impeached for electoral clientelism.[5] The electoral commission of the state of Bahia found these two politicians guilty of manipulating the distribution of a rural poverty alleviation program, delivering 65 solar kits and constructing 78 residential bathrooms in exchange for votes during the election. More specifically, the politicians manipulated a community-driven development (CDD) program in which individuals form community associations to propose projects that are then vetted by municipal councils. Such CDD programs, which are funded in part by the World Bank throughout much of Latin America, are designed to improve development outcomes by fostering citizen involvement and devolving decision-making power over the selection of project proposals to communities. Yet in Canudos, politicians sabotaged this bottom-up process in order to politicize the distribution of CDD benefits. To obtain benefits that could then be distributed using political criteria, the head of the mayor's party formed a community association that even shared the same name as the governing political coalition, "Unidos por Canudos." According to court documents, the total value of the solar kits and residential bathrooms distributed in exchange for votes totaled R$199,000 ($115,000). The state electoral commission removed both officials from office and fined them R$10,641 ($6,200) each.[6] Given the *Ficha Limpa* (clean slate) law implemented in 2010, such politicians will now be ineligible to run for political office for eight years from the date of conviction. While few rigorous studies examine the extent to which clientelism affects specific social policy programs in Brazil, findings from many other researchers suggest that this example from Canudos is far from an isolated account.[7]

Bolsa Familia

When compared to many other social programs in Brazil, Bolsa Familia is relatively well insulated from clientelistic pressures and has contributed substantially to Brazil's recent decline in poverty and income inequality. Bolsa Familia provides benefits to poor households across Brazil and is the largest conditional cash transfer (CCT) program in the world. CCT programs provide money to poor families contingent on specified behaviors, such as sending children to school and getting medical checkups, and are thus seen as a way of reducing poverty while at the same time investing in human capital development. In the mid-1990s, Brazil and Mexico pioneered the use of CCTs.[8] Currently, these programs operate in 30 countries, including Indonesia, Nigeria, Turkey, and almost every country in Latin America.[9]

Bolsa Familia was launched in October 2003 during Lula's first presidency by integrating four existing cash transfer programs: Bolsa Escola (a CCT for education), Bolsa Alimentação (a CCT for health and nutrition), Cartão Alimentação (a CCT for food consumption), and Auxilio Gas (compensation for phasing out cooking gas subsidies). After its introduction, Bolsa Familia expanded quickly, with expenditures reaching R$8.2 billion ($4.8 billion) in 2006, compared to only R$2.4 billion ($1.4 billion) spent on all CCTs in 2002.[10] The number of families receiving Bolsa Familia transfers more than doubled between 2004 and 2006, from 5.0 million to 11.1 million families.[11] Bolsa Familia currently serves over 12 million families, which corresponds to approximately 50 million Brazilians, more than a quarter of Brazil's entire population. Overall, between 2003 and 2010, the program has distributed R$60.2 billion ($35.5 billion).

Bolsa Familia currently provides families with a monthly stipend of up to R$200 ($116). Extremely poor families, measured as those with per capita monthly incomes up to R$70, receive a base stipend of R$68 per month even if they have no children. In addition, the program offers variable benefits to both extremely poor individuals and families (those with per capita monthly incomes up to R$140). Families receive R$22 per month for each child 15 years or younger. This benefit is only offered for up to three children, partly to avoid potential incentives for increased fertility. In 2008, Bolsa Familia was expanded to create incentives for increasing the educational attainment of older children.[12] Overall, the average monthly value of benefits paid to Bolsa Familia recipients is currently R$96 per month, which represents an average of 47% of the family income of recipients.

As a CCT program, Bolsa Familia requires beneficiaries to meet specific education and health conditionalities in order to maintain benefits. Parents must enroll their children aged 6 to 15 in school and attendance cannot fall below 85%. To receive benefits, school attendance of children aged 16 and 17 must be at least 75%. Families must take children up to the age of 6 to local medical clinics for vaccinations and periodic checkups. In addition, pregnant women must visit health clinics for pre and post-natal visits.[13] A study found that Bolsa Familia has relatively frequent monitoring, but compared to CCTs in other countries, penalties for non-compliance are "light."[14]

Bolsa Familia is relatively well insulated from clientelistic pressures. Across Latin America and beyond, such CCT programs "limit opportunities for political abuse of antipoverty money."[15] Rather than provide local politicians a high level of discretion, recipients of Bolsa Familia are selected by a federal agency (the Ministry of Social Development). This agency established quotas for how many families in each municipality would receive benefits, based on estimates of poverty from household survey data. To allocate benefits across families *within* a given municipality, self-declared income is employed.[16] Each municipality conducts interviews of potential participants and enters the data into a national household registry (*Cadastro Unico*). Beneficiaries are then selected by the federal agency—rather than by local officials—by comparing data entered in the registry with eligibility criteria.

Some opportunities for clientelistic manipulation remain. For example, some politicians and citizens interviewed in Bahia suggested that officials could purposely fail to enter opposition voters' data into the registry or could pressure local school or health officials to refrain from reporting when supporters fail to meet conditionalities. Furthermore, the national registry used for Bolsa Familia asks for citizens' voter ID numbers and what precinct they vote in, data that provide some (aggregated) information about whether an applicant is a supporter. Electoral results are released for each precinct, which typically have about 400 voters but occasionally have fewer than 50 voters. If a citizen votes in a precinct that almost entirely votes for the mayor, he or she can be fairly confident the citizen is a supporter (or vice versa).

Such considerations notwithstanding, when compared to other social policy programs in which local politicians hold wide discretion regarding who receives benefits, the design of Bolsa Familia is relatively robust against clientelistic interference. Overall, most researchers concur with Borges's assertion that Bolsa Familia "cannot be considered an instance of clientelism, for the selection of beneficiaries is based on universalistic criteria."[17]

Bolsa Familia is typically viewed not only as relatively insulated from clientelism but also as fairly well targeted. Using household survey data, Lindert et al. (2007) found that the poorest quartile of Brazilians received 80% of Bolsa Familia outlays; of the remaining 20% of funds, 85% went to the next poorest quartile.[18] This level of leakage is low in comparison to transfer programs in many countries, and suggests better targeting than many other CCTs. In a 2010 report, Soares finds that 45% of Bolsa Familia recipients are ineligible because their current income is actually greater than the allowed maximum.[19] However, Soares argues that this finding reflects income volatility rather than poor targeting: the poor often experience fluctuating income and thus may not always fall below a specified level.[20]

While studies tend to agree that Bolsa Familia is relatively well targeted, the exclusion of eligible families continues to be a concern. For example, Soares et al. estimates that the program fails to reach 59% of households meeting the eligibility criteria.[21] The recent expansion of Bolsa Familia has improved its coverage, though Soares suggests that the program would need to reach 15 million recipients to serve all of its target population.[22]

With respect to the program's impact, Bolsa Familia is widely regarded to have made considerable advances in reducing poverty and inequality in Brazil.[23] As figure 6.1 demonstrates, the decline of poverty and inequality in Brazil in recent years has been substantial. Poverty rates fell 56% between 1995 and 2009, and the Gini index of income inequality declined an average of 0.70 points (on a 100-point scale) annually between 2001 and 2008.[24] Bolsa Familia clearly contributed to these declines, though estimates of precisely how much vary. Some evidence also suggests that Bolsa Familia has improved food consumption, education, and health; but such findings are relatively less well identified than with some other CCTs, including Mexico's *Oportunidades* program.[25]

Although Bolsa Familia is relatively well insulated from clientelism and has helped to reduce poverty and inequality, the program is by no means a panacea. As Diaz-Cayeros and Magaloni explain when discussing social policy in Latin America,

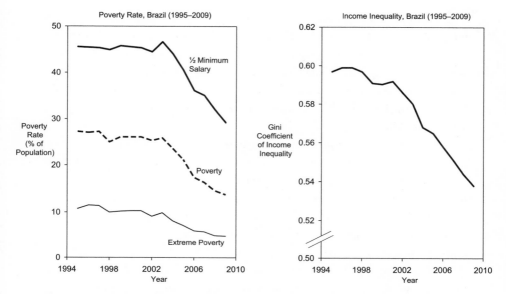

Figure 6.1. Poverty Rate and Income Inequality in Brazil, 1995–2009. *Note:* Poverty lines based on levels commonly used in Brazil: "½ minimum salary" is R$232 ($137) per month, "poverty" is R$131 ($78) per month, and "extreme poverty" is R$66 ($39) per month. *Source:* Instituto de Pesquisa Econômica Aplicada (IPEA), "Primeiras Análises: Distribuição de Renda entre 1995 e 2009," *Comunicados de IPEA* 63 (2010).

"Although the introduction of CCTs is a step in the right direction, it is hard to imagine successful poverty relief based solely on these policies."[26] Even though Bolsa Familia reaches over one quarter of the population of Brazil, many citizens continue to depend on exchange relationships with politicians for basic needs. While it is true that the program contributed to the decline of dominant state political machines in Brazil's North and Northeast regions,[27] clientelism continues to play a central role in local politics and in the lives of many poor Brazilians. The remainder of this chapter explores this key point through a discussion of fieldwork in Bahia. More specifically, I examine how insufficient health care and employment opportunities lead to a citizen strategy of clientelism, which I call "declared support."

Description of Fieldwork

Prior to and after the October 2008 municipal elections, during 18 months of fieldwork in Brazil, I conducted a total of 110 formal interviews on clientelism in the state of Bahia. These formal interviews included 55 interviews of community members and 55 interviews of elites. All interviews were conducted in Portuguese, lasted an average of 70 minutes, and were taped and transcribed. In addition, I conducted informal interviews of another 350 citizens and elites. Bahia, where the interviews were conducted, is the most populous state in the Northeast region of Brazil with nearly 15 million citizens.[28] The Northeast is also the poorest region of Brazil, with approximately one-third of the income level of Southeast region of Brazil.[29] Bahia has one of the lowest social indicators with respect to both health and education across all Brazilian states.[30]

Whereas most studies on clientelism in Brazil focus on the federal or state level, the research discussed below focuses on clientelism at the municipal level. For example, an extensive body of literature on the Brazilian context focuses on contingent rewards distributed by deputies who are elected to represent particular states. Such deputies submit thousands of budgetary amendments each year, and most researchers agree that in doing so they target specific municipalities to gain voters' electoral support.[31] In contrast with these studies, my fieldwork focuses on exchange relations between municipal politicians (mayors and city councilmen) and citizens. Given that the poor in Brazil directly interact with municipal administrations more than with any other level of government, this focus provides important insights into understanding clientelism in Brazil.

Also in contrast to most existing research on clientelism in Brazil, my research focused on small municipalities, defined as those with 100,000 citizens or fewer. Almost all qualitative research on clientelism in Brazil focuses on large metropolitan areas. Although this focus continues to offer substantial contributions, the limited extent of research on smaller communities is unfortunate, given that so much of Brazil's population lives in such environments. As shown in figure 6.2, 46% of Brazilians live in municipalities with 100,000 citizens or fewer, and 95% of Brazilian municipalities are of this size.[32]

In order to identify potential themes, develop interview questions, and field test citizen and elite interview protocols, I began qualitative research in a municipality of 10,000 citizens in central Bahia, where I lived for approximately five months. An additional six municipalities were selected for further interviews, employing a stratified random sample. Overall, the municipalities spanned each of Bahia's seven "mesoregions," which are defined by Brazil's national census bureau (IBGE) as areas that share common geographic characteristics. The population sizes of the seven municipalities selected were approximately 10,000, 15,000, 30,000, 45,000, 60,000, 80,000, and nearly 100,000.

Within each selected municipality, individuals for community member interviews were selected randomly using stratified sampling. Inclusion/exclusion criteria for individuals included the following: (1) at least sixteen years of age (the voting

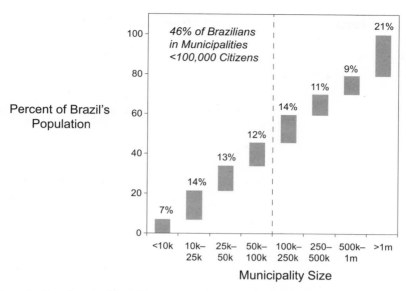

Figure 6.2. Population of Brazil by Municipality Size, 2009. *Source:* Based on population statistics available on the Brazilian census webpage (Instituto Brasileiro de Geografica e Estatistica or IBGE), www.ibge.gov.br.

age in Brazil); (2) had lived in the municipality since the previous mayoral election in 2004; and (3) not a member of the same household as any other interviewee. The sample was stratified to ensure balanced representation across gender, age, and urban/rural mix.

With respect to elites, a range of perspectives were obtained by interviewing 10 mayors and former mayors, 28 city councilmen (*vereadores*), 3 vice-mayors, 6 party heads, 5 heads of social services, and several other elites. These interviews were balanced to include a combination of elites both allied and opposed to the current administration. Given that mayors likely face different incentives if ineligible for reelection, the random sample of municipalities was stratified to include several municipalities with second-term mayors.

Declared Support in Brazil

Fieldwork suggests that social policy is often undermined by the uneven treatment of citizens by local politicians. Politicians at the municipal level have substantial discretion over expenditures in Brazil, given the country's high level of political and fiscal decentralization.[33] Many citizens and elites explained that benefits often differ according to whether or not one declared his or her support publicly before the previous election. As this section explores, this pattern of clientelism has important effects on citizen strategies during political campaigns. Expressing one's political voice entails strategic decisions about potential benefits and risks and thus does not simply convey underlying preferences about programmatic platforms and candidates. For example, citizens assess (1) the relative benefits that candidates promise to give declared supporters and declared opponents once elected, (2) the credibility of these promises, and (3) each candidate's relative probability of winning the election.

Before exploring evidence about the contingency of benefits and effects on citizen strategies, we need to investigate the logic behind the strategy of declared support more closely. Figure 6.3 presents a simplified game tree of declared support. Unlike most other studies of clientelism, which tend to focus on elite strategies, we examine the strategies of citizens. Consider a citizen, whom we call Maria. Assume there are two candidates, A and B, in an upcoming election. In the first node of the tree, Maria has three potential actions before the election: (1) declare for A, (2) remain undeclared, or (3) declare for B. In the next node, the election occurs and either candidate A or B wins. In the final node, the winning candidate distributes goods, services, and employment during her mandate and has three options with respect to Maria: (1) favor her, (2) disfavor her, or (3) neither favor nor disfavor her (be neutral).[34] Observe that the phenomenon of declared support requires some level of discretion over benefit targeting by politicians, which as discussed below is the case in Brazilian municipalities.

This simplified game tree suggests many possible outcomes (represented by the terminal nodes), but interview respondents indicate that three sets of outcomes (shaded) are most common: (1) politicians favor voters who declared their support for them before the election ("declared supporters"); (2) politicians disfavor voters who declared their support for opposing candidates before the election ("declared opponents"); and (3) politicians neither favor nor disfavor voters who remain undeclared ("undeclared voters").

During interviews with both citizens and elites, respondents frequently discussed how declaring one's support could influence the benefits one received after the election. Many explained, sometimes giving specific examples from their own personal experiences, that politicians favor voters who publicly declared support for them before the election. Respondents identified various ways in which declared supporters would be favored. Many examples related to health and employment.

With respect to health, respondents frequently reported that declared supporters have easier access to health care. For example, although Brazil's 1988 Constitution established a public health system intended to be universal and comprehensive, in practice medicines are often out of stock or otherwise unavailable at the pub-

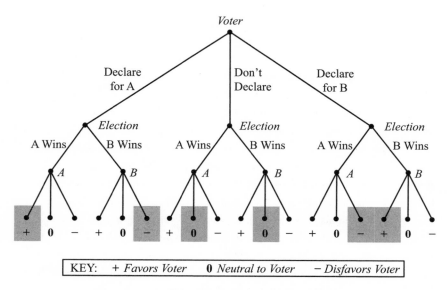

Figure 6.3. Simplified Game Tree of Declared Support

lic pharmacy. According to interviewees, politicians often buy such medicines for their declared supporters at private pharmacies, either using public funds (especially mayors) or out of their own salaries (especially city councilmen). As is discussed below, the logic of declared support requires political operatives to be embedded in social networks so that they can collect information about the actions of citizens. The dependence of the poor on direct medical assistance from politicians becomes clearer when considering how few Brazilians have insurance to cover purchases at private pharmacies. According to a federal registry, as of June 2010 only 9.0 million Brazilians, or 4.7% of the population, have private insurance (i.e., insurance paid by a family or private employer) that covers medical assistance. Within small communities in Bahia, the rate of coverage is even lower: 3.4% in municipalities under 100,000 citizens, and 2.5% in municipalities with under 20,000 citizens.[35]

Interviewees suggest that citizens who declared support for a winning candidate not only receive help purchasing medicines at private pharmacies, but also enjoy preferred access to health-related transportation. More specifically, declared supporters reportedly have an easier time obtaining access to ambulances during emergencies, and rides or bus fare for consultations and surgeries in distant cities. Such uneven access is particularly worrisome because health-related transportation is a crucial yet underserved need for the poor in small municipalities. Recognizing the lack of reliable ambulance coverage in many regions of Brazil, the federal Ministry of Health launched a national fleet of ambulances (Serviço Móvel de Urgência, or SAMU/192) in 2003. This program has expanded rapidly but still fails to reach all citizens in small municipalities; it currently reaches 108 million Brazilians (56% of the population) in 1,365 of country's 5,564 municipalities.[36] Beyond ambulances, the poor in small municipalities are also dependent on transportation to other municipalities for much of their health care. For example, consider the case of municipalities with fewer than 20,000 citizens, which comprise 59% of municipalities in Bahia and 20% of the state's population. Only 44% of such municipalities have even a single medical x-ray machine.[37] In addition, only 40% of municipalities of this size have an ultrasound machine, and only 52% of such municipalities have a dental x-ray machine. Moreover, treatment for serious illnesses, such as cancer, is often outsourced to distant cities such as Salvador. Even when treatment and patient transportation is covered by the public system, politicians often help by paying for the bus fare and lodging for families to visit patients in other cities. During interviews, numerous politicians discussed how they help supporters with health care. For example, a city councilman emphasized his provision of medical benefits to supporters by explaining: "If you spend four years in office giving this help to a voter, then you can be more or less certain that he's not going to deny you in the hour that you also need him."

Given that social policy in the health care sector is often inadequate, exchange relations with politicians often play an important role and influence the strategy of declared support. This importance is emphasized by citizens such as Carlos, a 50-year-old married man who has several children and works as a mason.[38] When asked to whom he would turn if he needed a costly medical procedure, he explains:

A quem pediria?
Aos político que eu votei.

Whom would you ask?
The politicians I voted for.

E por que pra eles e não pra outros?
Porque eu acho que aquele que eu votei, eu votei com confiança, e ele sabe que eu votei pra ele. Aí eu vou pedir pra eles.

Why ask them and not others?
Because I think that who I voted for, I voted with trust, and he knows that I voted for him. So I will ask them.

Como eles sabem que você votou neles?
Ah, sabem. Porque eu declaro meu voto antes de eu votar.

How do they know that you voted for them?
Oh, they know. Because I declare my vote before voting. [Points to a candidate's banner displayed on his house]

Então por isso eles vão ajudar?	*And because of that they will help?*
Confio que sim, né. Eu já voto	I trust that they will. I even also vote
prevendo uma precisão também, né.	foreseeing a need. I don't vote just
Eu não voto só porque chegou a hora	because the time comes to vote. I
de votar não. Eu acho assim que o	think that the poor need to vote well
pobre tem que fazer uma boa votação	because, if we're poor, at any time we
porque, se a gente é pobre, qualquer	need them too.
hora tem precisão deles também.	

With respect to employment, interviewees often explained that politicians favor declared supporters for short-term employment contracts. Although many public sector jobs require public competitions, in practice, politicians still have discretion over a considerable number of temporary positions. Numerous respondents explicitly reported declaring their support in the hopes that they would be rewarded with a temporary position if their candidate won. Respondents also gave various examples of other selective benefits, such as financial assistance for utility bills, building materials, and subsidized housing.

On the other hand, citizens and elites also often mentioned the negative consequences of declaring one's vote for a candidate who ends up losing the election. Respondents frequently used the term *marcação,* which directly translates to "marking" or "branding," to describe the ways in which politicians label and disfavor their declared opponents. According to many interviewees, *marcação* occurs in various spheres of life, including health and employment.

With respect to health, interviewees reported numerous ways in which declared opponents are disfavored. Some respondents explained that those who declared against the winning candidate would have more difficulty obtaining transportation to treatments in Salvador, the distant state capital. As Jose, the vice-mayor in a municipality with 60,000 citizens, explains:[39]

Muitos indecisos têm medo de dizer	Many undecided people are afraid of
quem vai acompanhar ou quem vai	saying who they're going to accompany
votar, porque se disser que vai votar	or vote for, because if you say you're
com aquele e aquele perder, o de cá	going to vote for someone who loses, the
marca. Você fica marcado. Você é	other labels. You become labeled. You're
de lá, então aqui você não tem vez.	on that side, so here you don't have a
Porque o que assume, na verdade, ele	chance. Because the person who takes
devia governar pra todos, mas ele não	office should really govern for everyone,
governa pra todos. Ele governa pra	but doesn't govern for everyone. He
todos naquilo que é possível. Mas nas	governs for everyone in what's possible.

vantagens, ele só governa pra aqueles que o acompanharam.

Por exemplo?

Por exemplo, se tiver um emprego, eu vou ver quem votou comigo. Vou dar um outro exemplo que é vexatório, que é até grosseiro, é desumano, mas é verdade. Você votou comigo, ele votou contra. Acontece que o carro virou e tinha um parente seu e um parente dele. E os dois precisam urgente ir pra Salvador, e a ambulância só conduz um. O dele não vai, vai o seu primeiro, entendeu?

But with advantages, he only governs for those who accompanied him.

For example?

For example, if there's a job, I'll look at who voted for me. I'm going to give another example that is disgraceful, that's even vulgar, that's inhumane, but is true. You voted for me, he voted against me. A car happens to flip and there's one of your relatives and one of his relatives. And the two need to go urgently to Salvador [distant state capital], and the ambulance only transports one. His doesn't go, yours goes first, you understand?

In addition to transportation, declared opponents sometimes have more difficulty getting help to buy medicine that is unavailable in the public pharmacy. Other respondents reported that they had to wait longer at or were turned away from the health clinic because they declared against the mayor in the last election. As one interviewee explained, "For example, here there is a dentist. . . . I only obtained a ticket once, only because I was never on their side. Every time I arrived: 'Oh, it's already full, there are already many people!' And other people who arrived after I did obtained them."[40] Another interviewee also suggested inequalities in dental treatment, explaining that while a declared supporter might get a root canal from the public dentist, a declared opponent in the same condition would have his tooth pulled. As a party head explained the difficulties faced by citizens who declared against winning candidates: "If you need a benefit from any public health office . . . they already know—'Ah, you're from the other party!'—and then it's more difficult for you."[41]

Citizens who declare support for a losing candidate are often also disfavored with respect to employment. By law, mayors cannot hire or fire permanent public employees (*concursados*), who are chosen by competitive exams.[42] However, most respondents reported that people who declared their vote against a winning mayoral candidate are excluded from temporary employment. In the words of Yasmin, a 23-year-old hairdresser:[43]

O que pode acontecer com quem declara seu voto?

Quem declara? O que pode acontecer? O que pode acontecer é que se o

What can happen with someone who declares his vote?

Someone who declares? What can happen? What can happen is that

outro partido ganhar, aquela pessoa que declarou o seu voto não vai ter as oportunidades assim que precisa, né.	if the other party wins, that person who declared his vote won't have the opportunities as soon as he needs them.
Pode dar um exemplo? Um exemplo? Assim se você . . . se alguém conseguir algum trabalho pra você, aí a pessoa vai dizer—"ah, você não votou em mim, eu já sei em quem você votou, então a vaga é do que votou em mim."	*Can you give an example?* An example? Like if you … if someone gets a job for you, then the person will say, "oh, you didn't vote for me, I already know who you voted for, so the opening is for someone who voted for me."

In addition, some interviewees explained that mayors also punish *concursados* who declared against them during a previous election. For example, teachers are sometimes transferred from the center of a municipality to schools only reachable by an hour bus ride. Even within the center, *concursados* who declared against winning candidate are also sometimes transferred to less desirable positions. As one respondent explained, they "take them from a higher position and put them in a lower one . . . take the person from that city and put him in the countryside, far from family. This happens a lot."[44]

In daily conversations after the municipal election, citizens would commonly refer to others as *marcado* ("marked," "branded," or "labeled") if they declared support for a candidate that lost. In most municipalities visited, there were also words in the local vernacular that people frequently used to refer to those who declared for a losing candidate, such as *jacu* (the name of a bird) and *baleado* (a person who has been shot). Most respondents report that politicians and others remember if one is *marcado* for a long time, often until the next election. As one respondent explained: "They will be labeled, you know for how many years? Four years. There are four years of government!"[45]

Many respondents reported that partly because of the risk of being *marcado*, it was better to remain undeclared. These respondents focused on the possible consequences of declaring instead of the potential benefits. Some interviewees discussed not wanting to risk future employment opportunities. For example, Rafael explained: "If you vote for your party and go after a job, there are people who say, 'No, this one here voted against us, so don't give the job to him.' There's that. So it is better to keep quiet. This is persecution, it's called."[46]

Interviewees discussed the desire to remain undeclared because politicians might not help them in a time of need if they declared against them during the campaign. Elected officials reportedly refer people who declare against them to go to "their candidates" for help, even though "their candidates" have lost the election and thus do not have access to municipal resources. Such political discrimination is not exercised without exception, so citizens declaring for a candidate who fails to win the election do not necessarily lose complete access to resources. And in some cases, losing politicians still provide benefits to their declared supporters, using their own private funds. However, the availability of such benefits is far smaller than that of the public funds controlled by the victorious politicians. Numerous interviewees emphasized that their poverty made them rely on politicians during emergencies, making it too risky to declare support for a particular candidate. In the words of Felipe, a 37-year-old man who works in a small fast food restaurant:[47]

Você declara o seu voto?	*Do you declare your vote?*
Não. Eu não gosto não. Eu não digo pra quem vou votar não. No dia, eu sei pra quem vou votar e voto. Mas não gosto de sair falando com A e B não, que aí fica manjado, né?	No. I don't like to. I don't tell for whom I am going to vote. On the day, I know who I am going to vote for, and I vote. But I don't like to go out saying with A or B, because then you end up well-known, right?
Pode explicar mais? Porque você não gosta de declarar?	*Can you explain more? Why don't you like to declare?*
Porque fica manjado. Depois a pessoa precisa e não sabe quem que vai ganhar. A pessoa fraca precisa deles tudo, de quem ganhar.	Because you end up well-known. Later, the person needs, and he doesn't know who is going to win. The weak person needs everything from them, from those that will win.
Se você declara e seu candidato não ganha, o que acontece então?	*If you declare and your candidate doesn't win, what happens then?*
Se não ganha? É isso que eu quero dizer. O negócio é que a pessoa fica manjada, né?	If he doesn't win? It's what I want to say. The deal is that the person ends up well-known, right?
Manjada?	*Well-known?*
Manjada é a pessoa, às vezes, precisar, se cair doente, vai procurar ele e ele vai dizer "Você não votou pra mim."	Well-known is the person, at times, he needs, if he falls sick, he goes to look for him and he will say, "you didn't vote for me."

Those who prefer to remain undeclared are often highly secretive about whom they support. Many avoid such questions even in casual conversation with acquaintances by responding that they are "still in doubt" (*ainda tô em dúvida*) or "on the fence" (*tô em cima do muro*). Others may tell friends who they support but avoid using candidate banners, wearing stickers, and attending rallies. Others are wary about making their support known to anyone aligned with a candidate they declared against. Ana Paula, a single 23-year-old vendor, explains why she didn't tell campaign workers who she supported:[48]

Perguntaram em quem você ia votar? Perguntavam.	Did they ask for whom you were going to vote? They asked.
Contou? Não, com certeza!	Did you tell? Absolutely not!
Por que não contou? Porque aqui, se eu não votar nele, amanhã eu precisar de algum serviço, ele não vai me ajudar porque vai dizer—"você votou em outro candidato." Aí a gente prefere ficar calado pra poder não se prejudicar no futuro.	Why didn't you tell? Because here, if I don't vote for him, and tomorrow I need some service, he won't help me because he'll say, "you voted for another candidate." So we prefer to remain quiet to be able to not harm ourselves in the future.

It should be noted that the informational assumptions underlying the logic of declared support differ from those in the existing literature on clientelism. The strategy relaxes some assumptions about parties, such as their ability to violate the secret ballot and observe political preferences. But on the other hand, because it views citizens as strategic actors, declared support makes new assumptions about citizens, such as their ability to observe elite promises and threats.

Most studies of clientelism assume that parties have the ability to observe, albeit imperfectly, vote choices. However, the assumption that parties can monitor actions within the voting booth is often too stringent. Declared support relaxes the assumption that elites can violate the secret ballot. Within the context of Brazil, politicians might be expected to have a more difficult time violating the secret ballot, given that in 2000 it became the first country to have fully electronic voting. During interviews of citizens in Bahia, 42 of 52 individuals (81%) responding to the question believed that voting is secret.

Declared support also relaxes the assumption that parties can observe political preferences. This often unrealistic assumption—that parties know citizens' ideal points—is frequently made in the formal literature on clientelism,[49] as well as in formal studies of distributive politics.[50] But parties don't actually observe underlying preferences; they observe declared preferences. And in the context of clientelism, declared preferences are strategically determined. How does a party really know that a citizen attends a rally because her ideal position is aligned with the party? Might she not attend the rally because she believes that future selective benefits depend on attendance? This issue remains, even if the party observes declared preferences over an extended period of time. Unlike the assumption made in the broader literature, the strategy of declared support assumes that parties observe only declared preferences.

On the other hand, declared support involves several assumptions that are distinct from those employed in many other studies of clientelism. For example, the logic of declared support assumes that clientelistic parties are able to observe, to a reasonable extent, who publicly declares support for them. In practice, this means that parties must be able to observe who campaigns on behalf of the party, attends rallies, puts banners on their homes, wears party t-shirts or stickers, and so forth. Otherwise, voters would not be expected to engage in declared support as a strategy to obtain selective benefits (though they might declare for other reasons). After all, voters might face the risk of punishment if their declared choice loses, without the possibility of benefits if their declared choice wins. In most cases, this assumption requires elites to be "socially proximate" to their supporters,[51] in that their embeddedness in social networks enables them to collect information about the actions of citizens. This discussion has also assumed that elites too have the ability to monitor, albeit imperfectly, who declares against them. This assumption reflects evidence from Northeast Brazil, but note that a different form of declared support may be possible even if parties cannot monitor who declares against them.

Declared support also involves informational assumptions about citizens, who, as strategic actors, keep in mind how elites will react when they make decisions. The strategy requires citizens to observe the promises that candidates make about the selective benefits they will distribute to declared supporters once elected. In addition, it is assumed that they observe threats that candidates make about how, once elected, they will punish citizens who declared against them. Moreover, citizens are assumed to have beliefs about the credibility of each candidate's promises and threats. Finally, with the strategy of declared support, citizens are assumed to have beliefs about candidates' relative probability of winning the election. As citizens gain new information about how well candidates' campaigns are performing, they are expected to update these beliefs.

In sum, there is sound evidence about the strategy of declared support. Although most scholars focus exclusively on the strategies of elites, citizens also often engage in strategic behavior. In contexts where social policies are applied unevenly, citizens consider carefully the likely reactions by candidates when they choose whether—

and for whom—to declare. Interviewees report that: (1) politicians often favor declared supporters; (2) politicians often disfavor voters who declared against them; and (3) politicians neither favor nor disfavor voters who remain undeclared.

Conclusions

This chapter has argued that, despite the substantial successes of Bolsa Familia, clientelism continues to undermine social policy in Brazil. Although it has significantly reduced poverty through conditional cash transfers, Bolsa Familia often does not eliminate the dependency of the poor on politicians. Evidence suggests that many Brazilians continue to rely heavily on exchange relationships with politicians for basic needs.

When the state fails to ensure equality in public services, the political voice of poor citizens is often distorted. Based on extensive fieldwork in Bahia, this chapter argues that insufficient health care and employment opportunities often lead to "declared support," a *citizen* strategy of clientelism. Contingent benefits can lead the poor to make strategic decisions about political participation, in that they weigh potential benefits and risks of declaring support for a particular candidate. This phenomenon has pernicious effects on the quality of democracy, since it suggests that patterns of political participation may reflect strategic behavior rather than underlying preferences about programmatic platforms and candidates. Declared support may be a particular concern in highly decentralized contexts, where subnational politicians yield considerable influence over social programs.

Overall, this chapter suggests that while conditional cash transfer programs can contribute to development outcomes, they are far from a silver bullet. CCTs strive to circumvent clientelism through a market-based approach, providing cash directly to the poor rather than using public agencies in the direct provision of goods and services. But given that the market can never entirely supplant the state in social policy, further innovations are required to curb the role of clientelism in public agencies.

One area for further exploration would be the increased role of audits. For instance, municipalities could be subjected to additional scrutiny if rigorous econometric evidence suggested that a mayor's bailiwicks received significantly more medical care than other areas.[52] Also beneficial would be educational campaigns to inform citizens about their rights as well as about the responsibilities of the state. Such campaigns could reduce the extent to which poor citizens interpret public services as favors from politicians. As one city councilman explained, "Health and education are a duty of the state, a right of the citizen. But not everybody knows that."[53]

Further electoral regulations could also play an important role. For example, officials who play a direct role in choosing who receives benefits arguably should not be permitted to play an active role in campaign activities. At one political rally I attended, the Secretary of Social Services helped to organize supporters for the mayor's reelection campaign and greeted people as they disembarked from the bus provided to attend the rally. Overall, these and many other strategies could help to reduce the influence of clientelism in social policy.

NOTES

1. Instituto de Pesquisa Econômica Aplicada (IPEA), "Primeiras Análises: Distribuição de Renda entre 1995 e 2009," *Comunicados de IPEA* 63 (2010).

2. Victor Nunes Leal, *Coronelismo, Enxada e Voto* (Sao Paulo: Alfa e Omega, 1975); and Eul-Soo Pang, *Coronelismo e Oligarquias, 1889–1934: a Bahia na Primeira República Brasileira* (Rio de Janeiro: Civilização Brasileira, 1979).

3. Frances Hagopian, *Traditional Politics and Regime Change in Brazil* (New York: Cambridge University Press, 1996), 2, 14–15.

4. Barry Ames, "Electoral Strategy under Open-List Proportional Representation," *American Journal of Political Science* 39 (May 1995): 406–33; Kurt Weyland, *Democracy Without Equity: Failures of Reform in Brazil* (Pittsburgh: University of Pittsburgh Press, 1996); Scott P. Mainwaring, *Rethinking Party Systems in the Third Wave of Democratization: The Case of Brazil* (Stanford, CA: Stanford University Press, 1999); David J. Samuels, "Pork Barreling Is Not Credit Claiming or Advertising: Campaign Finance and the Sources of the Personal Vote in Brazil," *Journal of Politics* 64 (August 2002): 845–63; Robert Gay, *Popular Organization and Democracy in Rio de Janeiro: A Tale of Two Favelas* (Philadelphia: Temple University Press, 1994); and Robert Gay, "The Even More Difficult Transition from Clientelism to Citizenship: Lessons from Brazil," in *Out of the Shadows: Political Action and the Informal Economy in Latin America,* ed. Patricia Fernández-Kelly and Jon Shefner (Princeton, NJ: Princeton University Press, 2006).

5. Evidence was collected by the author in the archives of Bahia's state electoral commission (Tribunal Regional Eleitoral da Bahia, Acórdão No. 1335/2006, December 4, 2006).

6. To expedite the removal of such politicians, Law 9840 of 1999 created civil penalties for clientelism that are imposed by courts within the electoral commissions. Criminal proceedings, which may involve jail sentences, take numerous years to process.

7. Octavio Damiani, *Report for the Government of Brazil–World Bank Commission: Rural Poverty* (Cambridge: MIT Press, 1996); Judith Tendler, "The Rise of Social Funds: What Are They a Model Of?" (monograph, MIT/UNDP Decentralization Project, January 1999); and Robert Gay, "Lessons from Brazil."

8. A predecessor of Bolsa Familia, the Bolsa Escola program, initially emerged from two pilot programs launched in cities of Brasilia and Campinas in 1995. These successful experiences were the first CCTs in the world, since they offered cash benefits with educational conditionalities. Other municipalities and states soon developed similar CCTs, and by 1997 the federal government provided transfers for these local programs.

9. Ariel Fiszbein and Norbert Schady, "Conditional Cash Transfers: Reducing Present and Future Poverty" (World Bank Policy Research Report, Washington, DC, 2009); and World Development Indicators, The World Bank, www.worldbank.org/.

10. Anthony Hall, "Brazil's Bolsa Familia: A Double-Edged Sword?" *Development and Change* 39 (September 2008): 799–822.

11. Unless otherwise noted, all Bolsa Familia information is taken directly from the website of *Ministério do Desenvolvimento Social e Combate à Fome*, www.mds.gov.br.

12. More specifically, families can now receive R$33 for each of up to two children aged 16 and 17 who attend school.

13. Other conditionalities also exist—for example, pregnant recipients must attend health seminars where available.

14. Fiszbein and Schady, "Conditional Cash Transfers."

15. Alberto Díaz-Cayeros and Beatriz Magaloni, "Aiding Latin America's Poor," *Journal of Democracy* 20 (October 2009): 36–49.

16. Unlike CCTs in many other Latin American countries, Bolsa Familia employs unverified means testing, which has often been criticized. However, it should be noted that data in the registry are cross-checked with other federal databases to identify discrepancies. See Fábio Veras Soares, Rafael Perez Ribas, and Rafael Guerreiro Osório, "Evaluating the Impact of Brazil's *Bolsa Família*: Cash Transfer Programmes in Comparative Perspective," *Latin American Research Review* 45 (2010): 173–90.

17. André Borges, "Rethinking State Politics: The Withering of State Dominant Machines in Brazil," *Brazilian Political Science Review* 1 (2007): 133.

18. Kathy Lindert, Anja Linder, Jason Hobbs, and Bénédicte de la Brière, "The Nuts and Bolts of Brazil's Bolsa Familia Program: Implementing Conditional Cash Transfers in a Decentralized Context" (Social Protection Discussion Paper 0709, World Bank, May 2007).

19. Sergei Soares, "Targeting and Coverage of the Bolsa Família Programme: What Is the Meaning of Eleven Million Families?" (One pager No.117, International Policy Centre for Inclusive Growth, October 2010).

20. This fluctuation is a particular issue when using household survey (PNAD) data, because income earned in the previous month often involves substantial variation.

21. Soares, Ribas, and Osório, "Evaluating the Impact of Brazil's Bolsa Familia."

22. Soares, "Targeting and Coverage of the Bolsa Família Programme."

23. Ricardo Barros, Mirela de Carvalho, and Samuel Franco, "Determinantes da Queda Recente no Grau de Desigualdade de Renda no Brasil" (PowerPoint, Instituto de Pesquisa Economica Aplicada, Brasilia, April 2006); Fábio Veras Soares, Sergei Suarez Dillon Soares, Marcelo Medeiros, and Rafael Guerreiro Osorio, "Cash Transfer Programmes in Brazil: Impacts on Inequality and Poverty" (Working Paper #21, International Poverty Centre, June 2006); Anthony Hall, "Brazil's Bolsa Familia," 799–822; Marcelo Medeiros, Tatiana Britto, and Fábio Veras Soares, "Targeted Cash Transfer Programmes in Brazil: BPC and the Bolsa Familia" (Working Paper #46, International Poverty Centre, June 2008); and Soares, "Targeting and Coverage of the Bolsa Família Programme."

24. Instituto de Pesquisa Econômica Aplicada (IPEA), "Primeiras Análises."

25. Fiszbein and Schady, "Conditional Cash Transfers."

26. Díaz-Cayeros and Magaloni, "Aiding Latin America's Poor," 36–49.

27. André Borges, "The Decline of Political Bosses: Unstable Clientelism, Vertical Competition and Electoral Change in the Brazilian states" (paper presented at the Latin American Studies Association Congress, Rio de Janeiro, Brazil, 2009).

28. Instituto Brasileiro de Geografica e Estatistica (IGBE), 2009, www.ibge.gov.br.

29. Instituto de Pesquisa Econômica Aplicada (IPEA), "Primeiras Análises."

30. Based on data from the Índice Firjan de Desenvolvimento Municipal (IFDM), 2007.

31. Barry Ames, review of *Elections and Democratization in Latin America, 1980–85*, edited by Paul W. Drake and Eduardo Silva, *Journal of Interamerican Studies and World Affairs* 29 (Autumn 1987): 125–27; Ames, "Electoral Strategy Under Open-List Proportional Representation," 406–33; Barbara Geddes, *Politician's Dilemma: Building State Capacity in Latin America* (Berkeley: University of California Press, 1994); and Mainwaring, *The Case of Brazil*.

32. Note the distinction in Brazil between rural areas and small communities: many municipalities are located hours from large cities and have fewer than 10,000 citizens but are considered only one-quarter rural if 7,500 citizens live in the "centro" (center of the municipality).

33. Celina Souza, *Constitutional Engineering in Brazil: The Politics of Federalism and Decentralization* (New York: St. Martin's Press, 1997); and Tulia G. Falleti, *Decentralization and Subnational Politics in Latin America* (New York: Cambridge University Press, 2010).

34. Of course, favoring one individual implies that another individual is disfavored if resources are fixed. I distinguish here between individuals who only suffer from this implicit loss ("neutral to voter") and those who are explicitly disfavored ("disfavored voters").

35. Data from the Sistema de Informação da Atenção Básica Cadastramento Familia, Datasus, 2010. Also note that out-of-pocket health care expenditures represent 59% of total expenditures on health in Brazil (see the World Bank's World Development Indicators, 2007, http://data.worldbank.org/products/data-books/WDI-2007).

36. Data from the Ministry of Health, 2010.

37. Data analyzed by author from the Cadastro Nacional de Estabelecimentos de Saúde, 2010.

38. Interview conducted in a municipality with 80,000 citizens on November 21, 2008 (Code #1121-3). All names are changed to protect the anonymity of respondents.

39. Interview conducted in a municipality with 60,000 citizens on November 5, 2008 (Code #1105-VP-2).

40. Interview conducted in a municipality with 10,000 citizens on October 22, 2008 (Code #1022-1). *"Por exemplo, aqui tem uma dentista . . . Eu consegui ficha uma vez, só porque eu nunca fui do lado deles. Sempre que eu chegava . . . 'Ah, já tá cheio, já tem muita gente!' E outra pessoas que chegava após eu chegar, conseguiam."*

41. Interview conducted in a municipality with 15,000 citizens on January 15, 2009 (Code #0115-H-2).

42. City councilmen have relatively less control over employment, but can still appoint various individuals to become employees within the city council for the duration of their four-year mandate. These positions are only given to declared supporters (usually to those who campaigned on their behalf as well).

43. Interview conducted in a municipality with 15,000 citizens on January 12, 2009 (Code #0112-2).

44. Interview conducted in a municipality with 10,000 citizens on October 1, 2008 (Code #1001-1). "*Tira de um cargo mais alto e põe num mais inferior . . . tira a pessoa daquela cidade e bota pra zona rural, distante da família. Isso acontece muito.*"

45. Interview conducted in a municipality with 60,000 citizens on November 3, 2008 (Code #1103-1). "*Vão ficar marcados, sabe quantos anos? Quatro anos. São quatro anos de governo!*"

46. Interview conducted in a municipality with 10,000 citizens on October 1, 2008 (Code #1001-3). "*Se você vota no seu partido e vai atrás de um emprego, tem gente que fala 'não, esse aí votou contra a gente, então não dou o emprego a ele.' Tem isso. Então é melhor você ficar quieto. Isso é a perseguição, que chama.*"

47. Interview conducted in a municipality with 10,000 citizens on October 16, 2008 (Code #1016-2).

48. Interview conducted in a municipality with 80,000 citizens on November 21, 2008 (Code #1121-2).

49. See Susan C. Stokes, "Perverse Accountability: A Formal Model of Machine Politics with Evidence from Argentina," *American Political Science Review* 99 (August 2005): 315–25; Thad Dunning and Susan C. Stokes, "Clientelism as Mobilization and as Persuasion" (unpublished typescript, Yale University, 2008); Simeon Nichter, "Vote Buying or Turnout Buying? Machine Politics and the Secret Ballot," *American Political Science Review* 102 (February 2008): 19–31; Jordan Gans-Morse, Sebastian Mazzuca, and Simeon Nichter, "Varieties of Clientelism: Machine Politics During Elections" (CDDRL Working Paper #119, Stanford University, October 2010).

50. See Gary W. Cox and Mathew D. McCubbins, "Electoral Politics as a Redistributive Game," *Journal of Politics* 48 (May 1986): 370–89; Avinash Dixit and John Londregan, "The Determinants of Success of Special Interests in Redistributive Politics," *Journal of Politics* 58 (November 1996): 1132–55; and Assar Lindbeck and Jörgen W. Weibull, "Balanced-budget Redistribution as the Outcome of Political Competition," *Public Choice* 52 (1987): 273–97.

51. Susan C. Stokes, "Pork, by Any Other Name . . . Building a Conceptual Scheme of Distributive Politics" (paper presented at the Annual Meeting of the American Political Science Association, Toronto, Canada, 2009).

52. Of course, identification strategies would need to address obvious concerns about endogeneity.

53. Interview conducted in a municipality with 60,000 citizens on November 4, 2008 (Code #1104-V-01).

PART TWO

LESSONS IN CLIENTELISM
FROM OTHER REGIONS

CHAPTER SEVEN

Patronage, Democracy, and Ethnic Politics in India

KANCHAN CHANDRA

India's democracy has developed over time into a "patronage-democracy"—a democracy in which elections function as auctions for the sale of government services. The most basic goods that a government should provide—security of life and property, access to education, provision of public health facilities, a minimum standard of living—have become, for large numbers of citizens, market goods rather than entitlements. Such marketization has become routinized in everyday imagination and is no longer perceived as illegitimate.

At the same time, India's democracy has also been both covertly and overtly dominated by the politics of ethnicity. Voters formulate preferences across parties by ignoring the issues that parties represent and looking instead at the distribution of co-ethnics who occupy positions of power within those parties. Parties, in turn, have over time invested less in differentiating their policy positions and more in sending signals about which ethnic categories they are likely to favor when in power. When overt coalitions have indeed been mobilized, they have been organized around ethnic categories: Hindus, Other Backward Castes, and the "Bahujan" at the national level, and other coalitions based on region, religion, tribe, language, and caste at the state level.

Both of these phenomena have been interpreted as anomalies for empirical democratic theory, which predicts that economic underdevelopment—of which patronage politics is often seen as an indicator—and ethnic diversity independently threaten democratic stability. Yet democracy is deeply consolidated in India, which has held fifteen parliamentary elections over five decades, hundreds of elections at the state level, and, since 1993, thousands of elections for village-level governments. These elections have been accompanied by increasing participation by members of subordinate social groups; incumbents have frequently lost; the losses in seats have often been large; and all sides have peacefully accepted the verdict. Along with the

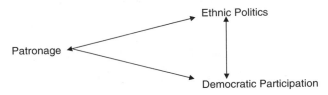

Figure 7.1. The Reinforcing Relationship between Patronage, Democratic Participation, and Ethnic Politics

politics of patronage and the politics of ethnicity, democracy in India has come to be understood as business as usual.

Synthesizing arguments that I have made in my previous work, I argue here that patronage, ethnic politics, and democratic consolidation are mutually reinforcing.[1] The politics of patronage creates and sustains the roots of both ethnic politics and democratic politics in India. Furthermore, it sustains an especially fluid form of ethnic politics in which ethnic categories are continually redefined by politicians seeking to win the democratic game. Once created, both ethnic politics and democratic politics in turn strengthen the politics of patronage. The links can be seen in figure 7.1.

I use this argument to speculate about the political implications of one aspect of the economic reforms introduced since 1991: the expansion of the private sector. This has the potential, I argue, both to transform the nature of ethnic politics in India by making it more rigid and to weaken the foundations of democratic legitimacy by reducing the proportion of the population that has a stake in the democratic system.

The Concept of "Patronage-Democracy"

I use the term "democracy" here in a minimal sense to mean simply a system in which the political leadership is chosen through competitive elections.[2] By the term "patronage-democracy," I mean a democracy in which the state has a relative monopoly on jobs and services and in which elected officials enjoy significant discretion in the implementation of laws allocating the jobs and services at the disposal of the state. The term "patronage-democracy" may apply to a political system as a whole or to a subsystem within it.

The key aspect of a patronage-democracy is not simply the size of the state but the power of elected officials to distribute the vast resources controlled by the state to voters on an *individualized* basis through their discretion in the implementation of state policy. This individualized distribution of resources, in conjunction with a dominant state, I argue, makes patronage democracies a distinct family of democracies with distinct types of voter and elite behavior. A democracy is not patronage-based if the private sector is larger than the public sector as a source of jobs and provider of services or if those who control the distribution of state resources and services cannot exercise discretion in the implementation of policy concerning their distribution.

In a patronage-democracy, obtaining control of the state is the principal means of obtaining both a better livelihood and higher social status. Elected office or government jobs, rather than the private sector, become the principal source of employment. Because elected office or government jobs place individuals in a position of power over the lives of others, control of the state also brings with it higher status. Those who have the capital to launch a political career in patronage-democracies, therefore, seek political office. For those who do not, obtaining access to those who control the state becomes the principal source of both material and psychic benefits. Proximity to a state official increases a voter's chances of obtaining valued state resources and services. At the same time, it affords the voter the chance to bask in the reflected glory of his patron's power. Patronage-democracies, therefore, produce an overwhelming preoccupation with politics on the part of both elites and voters seeking both material and psychic goods.[3]

India as a Patronage-Democracy

For most of the years since its independence, the Indian state has controlled approximately two-thirds of the jobs in the organized economy. Table 7.1 summarizes the percentage of the labor force in the organized economy that worked in the public sector from 1961 to 2008. As the table indicates, the public sector provided the lion's share of employment opportunities in the organized economy. This share was on an increasing trajectory between 1961 and 1991: the public sector provided little more than half of the jobs in 1961, but it had acquired control over two-thirds of the available jobs by 1991. The public sector has contracted following the economic reforms of 1991, albeit slowly. Although it still controls almost two-thirds of the jobs in the organized economy, it has shrunk by more than a tenth since 1991.

Public sector jobs are classified into four categories based on an income criterion: Class I (or Group A), Class II (or Group B), Class III (or Group C), and Class IV (or Group D). Class I is the highest-paid category and includes employees of the prestigious Indian Administrative Service (IAS), the India Foreign Service (IFS), the Indian Police Service (IPS), and related central government services. Class II employees, who fall into the next income bracket, include, among others, officers of

TABLE 7.1.
Size of the Indian public sector

Year	Public sector	Private sector
1961	58.3%	41.7%
1971	61.4	38.6
1981	67.7	32.3
1991	71.3	28.7
2001	68.9	31.1
2008	63.3	36.4

Source: Statistical Outline of India 1997–98 for the years
1961–1991; Economic Survey of India 2010–11, table A52
for 2001 and 2008.

the state civil service cadre. The Class III and Class IV categories include relatively low-income posts.

Selecting authorities have relatively little discretion in the recruitment of Class I and Class II positions, which are typically filled by competitive exams and an interview conducted by a collective body. The exams produce a first cut of applicants based on educational and technical qualifications. Although another elimination round occurs at the interview stage, the influence of any individual member of the interview board over the selection of candidates is limited, since each needs the consent of others to approve any candidate. Class III and Class IV jobs, however, are filled according to less rigorous procedures.[4] It is in the allocation of these Class III and Class IV jobs, therefore, that the selecting authorities and those who influence them can exercise the greatest discretion.

The significance of this discretion in the allocation of Class III and Class IV jobs becomes clear when we look at the sheer volume of these positions. Table 7.2 provides a snapshot of the distribution of jobs across the four categories of central government employment for the Union Government.

Although the figures in table 7.2 refer to 1994, the profile in the present is much the same, as is the distribution of state-level government jobs across the different categories. Economic reforms introduced in 1991 changed the nature of India's state-based economy. However, such change is limited. Successive governments have been reluctant to privatize. As a result, the public sector continues to dominate the organized economy, controlling over two-thirds of jobs post-reform. Figure 7.2 charts the continuing dominance of the public sector since 1991, using annual data from the Economic Survey of India. Successive governments have placed limits on investments and hiring in the public sector, and after expanding rapidly since

TABLE 7.2.
Profile of central government employment in India
(1994 figures)

Class	Percentage employed
Class I or Group A	2.2
Class II or Group B	3.3
Class III or Group C	66.8
Class IV or Group D	27.2
Total	99.5*

Source: Report of the Fifth Central Pay Commission,
January 1997, p. 223
  *The figures do not add to a hundred because of
rounding error.

independence, it has now begun to contract from controlling 71% of public sector jobs in 1991 to 63% in 2008. And while the absolute share of public and private sector employment has remained relatively stable, the relative rates of growth of the two have changed. The greater opportunities and incentives now provided by the government to the private sector, combined with restrictions on the expansion of the public sector, cause the private sector to grow at a faster rate.

The size and expansion of the private sector varies across states in India as shown in figure 7.3. The private sector dominates employment in the organized economy of four states—Kerala, Gujarat, Maharashtra, and Assam. All four states have recorded increases in the size of the private sector since 1999. In several other states, concentrated in the south and west—Karnataka, Andhra Pradesh, Goa, Haryana, Tamil Nadu, and West Bengal—the private sector is almost as large as the public sector. But the public sector still dominates the economy of states in northern and eastern India—over 70% of jobs in the organized economies in Jammu and Kashmir, Uttar Pradesh, Madhya Pradesh, Bihar, Orissa, and the northeast are in the public sector, and in several of these states, employment in the private sector has actually decreased since 1998.

The full magnitude of the expansion of the private sector in India—both nationally and regionally—is difficult to establish in the absence of data on employment in the unorganized economy, which employs the vast majority of the Indian population. But by all accounts it is considerable. We might take the figures on the organized economy, therefore, as the lower boundary of private sector activity.

In the unorganized economy, especially agriculture, the state does not directly control access to jobs. However, public officials exercise discretionary control over the livelihoods of cultivators through the power they wield in the supply of inputs—land

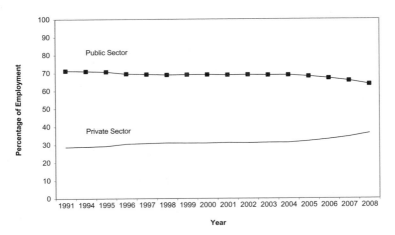

Figure 7.2. Public and Private Sector in India, 1991–2008. *Source:* Economic Survey of India.

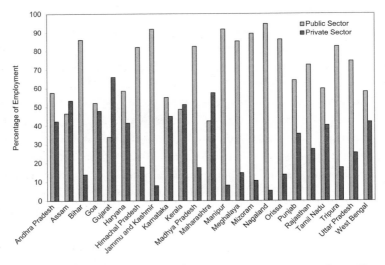

Figure 7.3. Employment in Public and Private Sectors Statewise, 2004. *Source:* Statistical Abstract of India.

security, roads, electricity, water, and credit. Quite apart from jobs and inputs, the state also dominates the everyday business of existence, especially in rural India, and especially for the poor. Citizens require a minimum set of goods to attest to their existence and then to survive—birth certificates, death certificates, caste certificates, land titles, appointment letters, ration cards, hospital beds, loans, drinking water, electricity, sanitation, and so on—and procuring each of these requires contact with the state, which in turn can be influenced by politicians. The standard promise of the candidate at the constituency level, therefore, is "Vote for me, and I will get your work done."

Take the example of the marketization of security of life and property. It is now routine for candidates from across the political spectrum to campaign in Muslim areas on a single-point promise: "Vote for me, and I will make sure that no one harms a hair on your head." The import of such a promise is extraordinary. Security is a minimum good that all governments, democratic or not, should provide to all citizens as a basic guarantee. Yet it is selectively provided (and withdrawn) in India by political parties in return for political support. The Bharatiya Janata Party (BJP) seeks votes by covertly encouraging violence or, at a minimum, by withdrawing the protection of BJP-led governments from the potential targets of that violence. Just as importantly, "secular" parties also gain from the conversion of security from an entitlement to a market good. As long as citizens are forced to obtain this good through bargaining on the electoral market, politicians can obtain support at relatively low cost simply by promising to do what a government should do in any case—that is, not look the other way during communal riots.

The freedom to vote has become another good that many citizens must often purchase, ironically, by giving up their freedom of choice. For many Scheduled Caste voters in Uttar Pradesh, for instance, the security of their voting rights depends on striking a bargain with politicians from dominant castes either through an umbrella party or an umbrella alliance. Without such a bargain, they cannot vote. As one such voter put it: *"Dabane vala aur dabne vala ek hi party main hain to theek hai. Agar alag party main ho gaye to mushkil hoti hai."* [If those who oppress and those who are oppressed are in the same party, it is all right. If they end up in different parties, then there is a problem.]

Statements such as these, while not made with equal frequency across different states in India, are commonplace in Uttar Pradesh. Despite the reforms introduced by the Election Commission in recent years, those whom I interviewed had no expectation that the state could intervene effectively. Why, I asked, did voters not complain to the District Magistrate (DM)? *"DM kya kar sakta hai? Har aadmi ko suraksha chahiye—aur iske liye majboot hona chaihiye."* [What can the DM do? Each man needs security—and for this it is important to be strong.]

A third example is the marketization of the basic implementation of government policy. Again, this marketization of basic services is an accepted political fact. Voters believe they can count on state services only when the politicians they have paid with votes are in power and not otherwise. One Scheduled Caste youth, facing resistance from a local bureaucrat in obtaining an appointment letter for a government job, put it philosophically: "It's because *our* government has fallen. If our government was in power, he would have given me that letter in two minutes." By *our* government, he meant a Bahujan Samaj Party BSP government. The idea that an administration led by a different party might also have provided the same service was not taken seriously either by him or any others present.

Such marketization does not affect all citizens equally. Those it affects most are those who are most vulnerable. The higher that individuals rank on the ladder of income and education, the easier it is to opt out of the electoral market through exit options in the private sector or international migration. When they cannot escape dependence on the state, they possess several tools other than the vote—status, bribes, personal connections—to get state officials to use discretion in their favor. But the lower an individual's standing in terms of income and education, the more his fate depends upon access to state-provided goods and the more likely it is that the vote is his primary channel of influence. Because class and ethnicity intersect, those affected come disproportionately from subordinate ethnic groups (defined by caste, religion, tribe, and language), and especially from the poorer subgroups within these ethnic groups.

Patronage-Democracy and Democratic Participation

The dominance of the state means that for most citizens, especially those from subordinate groups, elections are a high-stakes affair. Those who can obtain office can significantly alter their life chances and those of their dependents. And those who cannot can at least use their vote as currency to obtain access to entitlements that they might otherwise not receive.

Not surprisingly, then, the rates of political participation in India, as measured both by voter turnout and office-seeking activity, are high. Figure 7.4 summarizes changes in voter turnout and the average number of candidates per constituency in national elections between 1951 and 2009. As we see, voter turnout has risen from 45% in 1951 to 58% in 2009. This does not indicate a steady increase: the aggregate turnout rate has hovered around 60% for the last thirty years. But even when the aggregate rate is the same, there has been a change in the composition of voters who turn out, with rising rates of participation among subordinate groups in India.[5] Additionally, there is

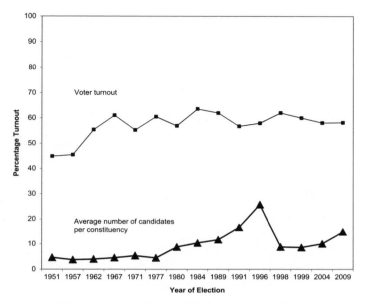

Figure 7.4. Political Participation in National Elections in India, 1951–2009. *Source:* Election Commission of India.

a dramatic increase in office-seeking activity, as measured by the total number of parties competing in an election and the average number of candidates per constituency.

Increasing participation has also been accompanied by increasing competitiveness. Incumbents frequently lose elections. At the national level, incumbents have lost elections in 1977, 1980, 1989, 1996, 1998, and 2004. The turnover at the state level has been more pronounced, and the number of parties entering the fray has increased dramatically. Figure 7.5 summarizes the number of parties registered to compete in national elections between 1951 and 2009. As we see, there is an increasing trend in the number of parties competing in the elections, which more than quadrupled from 53 in 1951 to 342 in 2009.

This high level of participation on the part of voters and elites has been idealistically interpreted as the "maturing" of Indian democracy, implying that some kind of normative commitment to the democratic idea has taken root among the Indian electorate.[6] It has also been indulgently interpreted as a ritual, a celebration, and even "in a beautiful way . . . the greatest sport in India."[7] The more cynical interpretation suggests that the "continuously expanding circle of participants"[8] in Indian politics represents less a normative commitment or a spirit of celebration, and more the intensification of struggle over the scarce resources provided by the state, where the stakes are high and the outcome makes an immediate difference to the lives of elites and voters and the like.

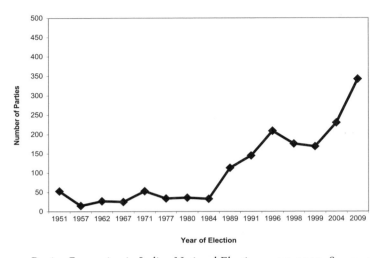

Figure 7.5. Parties Competing in Indian National Elections, 1951–2009. *Source:* Election Commission of India.

Still, the existence of large sections of the population with a vested interest in participation in democracy is as good a basis for democratic legitimacy as any other. Democracies become consolidated when all sides respect the rules of the game.[9] Democratic politics in India is indeed characterized by respect for these rules, if not for their own sake, then because expanding sections of the population have come to believe that they benefit by following them.

The argument that the legitimacy, and therefore the consolidation, of India's democracy rests on the vested interests of social groups that benefit from it is not new. Pranab Bardhan first made it in 1984, arguing that the maintenance of a democratic structure in India stemmed from a bargain struck between India's "democratic proprietary classes"—industrial capitalists, rich farmers, and white collar workers and professionals—who "remain seriously interested in the maintenance of democratic processes, if only for the sake of their own bargaining procedures."[10] Where I differ with Bardhan is in my characterization of the actors who have developed a vested interest in democracy and in my characterization of the dynamic nature of this process. Bardhan sees class-based groups as being the beneficiaries and therefore advocates of patronage-democracy in India, whereas I argue that the relevant actors are defined principally on the basis of ethnicity rather than class. Although a middle class within each ethnic category is typically the principal beneficiary of patronage, class identities are typically enfolded within ethnic identities and often rendered invisible by them. Furthermore, while Bardhan describes a relatively static picture of the class actors in question, I argue that the ethnic actors that have a stake in the perpetuation of democracy in India have so far been continually redefined by democratic politics. I elaborate on this point in the next section.

Patronage-Democracy and the Incentives for Ethnic Mobilization

In a patronage-democracy, political parties win elections by making open promises about whom they want to favor in the distribution of state jobs where they can, and when they cannot, by sending covert signals about whom they will favor in the distribution of patronage. Competing parties and politicians in a patronage-democracy have incentives to make both types of promises by mobilizing ethnic identities—and because ethnic identities are most effectively mobilized by identifying ethnic "outsiders," ethnic mobilization translates into ethnic polarization. By the term "ethnic identities," I mean, in the Indian context, identities based on caste, religion, tribe, language, and region.

Politicians can signal whom they expect to favor in the allocation of state jobs by using three policies outlined in the Indian constitution: affirmative action, language, and statehood. Each of these policies privileges ethnic mobilization and hinders non-ethnic mobilization.

The Indian constitution promises affirmative action in jobs, education, and to a lesser extent, representative institutions, to three categories: the Scheduled Castes, the Scheduled Tribes, and the "Other Backward Classes." Each of these categories is defined as a collection of ascriptive groups, that is, castes or tribes. Even the term "Other Backward Classes" is intended as, and has been accepted as, a euphemism for the "Backward Castes." However, the constitution does not specify which castes and tribes are to be included in each category and which are to be excluded. This is for the central or state governments to decide through simple majority legislation, and is open for periodic review. The ambiguity over inclusion, and the ease with which the lists are revised, creates an incentive to mobilize on the basis of caste or tribal identity and demand placement in one of the three lists. Politicians also have an incentive to mobilize individuals on the basis of caste or tribe. The politicization of identities based on non-ethnic categories is in no one's interest, and it has resulted in the massive mobilization of groups—often a majority of the population—which demand inclusion in these lists. There are states in India where more than 80% of the population is classified as eligible for affirmative action benefits on some basis or another.

The second policy that encourages the politicization of ethnic identity is language policy. There is a hierarchy of official languages in India. At the top are the official languages of the union, which offer the best career prospects in India's civil services. At the next level are the official languages of the federal units—the Indian states—which provide access to all Indian civil services, as well as the vast pool of jobs controlled by the states. At the third level are mother tongues, which do not offer any access to state jobs. State level governments may add, subtract, or replace one or more official languages at the state level through simple majority legislation. If the Indian government clearly specified this hierarchy, it would provide an incentive to individuals to learn the official languages of the state. But since official language policy is treated as an unsettled issue in India, marginalized individuals have incentives to mobilize as linguistic groups and demand that their own language be upgraded to the status of official language, and that another language be downgraded to the status of mother tongue. As a result, linguistic mobilization has been a recurrent issue at the state level in post-colonial Indian politics.

Finally, there is the policy on recognition of statehood. India is a federation of states, and the constitution empowers the Union government to carve out new states from existing ones simply by passing a law and without obtaining the assent of the affected state. The central government has established two precedents for granting statehood. First, statehood is only accorded on the basis of ethnic criteria, predominantly to three kinds of ethnic groups: linguistic groups, regional groups, and tribal groups. Second, statehood is granted only in response to the mobilization of substantial sections of the population. These constitutional precedents encourage politicians to mobilize individuals on an ethnic basis to demand a state of their own.

The result of these three institutional devices—affirmative action, official language policy, and recognition of new states—has been the activation of ethnic identities and the deactivation of other forms of self-definition. Mobilization on non-ethnic dimensions such as class, sector, or income has certainly occurred in India, but it is effective only in lobbying for policy concessions in certain issue areas. So, for example, farmers' movements have been successful in winning and maintaining subsidies, and trade unions have been successful in extracting wage increases. However, non-ethnic mobilizations are crippled in the struggle for control of the state, and the state in India is where the opportunities lie.

The key aspect of voting in a patronage-democracy is that it occurs in an environment shrouded by lack of information. The main consideration in the mind of a citizen when deciding how to vote is not what a politician says about policy legislation but who a politician is likely to favor in the distribution of patronage resources. Politicians typically cannot openly make promises about whom they will favor in patronage transactions. Trading policy implementation for votes in the open market would constitute a serious violation of the norms of modern government and violate the laws of most modern democracies.

As an illustration, let us take the example of public health facilities. A bed in a public hospital is a scarce commodity, and the waiting rooms of MPs and MLAs in India are routinely filled by favor seekers to secure beds for their friends and relatives. However, no politician could openly promise to favor some voters in the allocation of hospital beds over others. Selective allocation of basic services such as public health, to which all citizens should have equal access in principle, would be indefensible on both normative and legal grounds. The normative and legal constraints of modern democratic government ensure that politicians only send surreptitious signals about favoritism in the implementation of policy and signal their intent by unofficial action, not by open declaration in the official political sphere.

As a result of these policies, voters typically have extremely superficial information about the beneficiaries of patronage transactions. They learn about beneficiaries by observing hangers-on at party offices, hearing rumors about past favors, or reading the names of job appointees in the newspapers, but they seldom know them intimately. The limited information available to voters biases them toward an ethnic classification of beneficiaries. Consequently, watchful voters surveying patronage transactions see beneficiaries through an ethnic prism and conclude that politicians allot favors on the basis of ethnic identity, whether or not ethnic favoritism actually influenced the decision.

To illustrate, consider some examples. In Uttar Pradesh, there was a widespread perception that Chief Minister Mulayam Singh Yadav favored members of the Yadav ethnic group in his distribution of patronage. The belief was based on newspaper reports that mentioned such favoritism. As one such article noted, "720 out of 900 teachers appointed by Mulayam Singh Yadav reportedly belonged to the Yadav caste."[11] How did the author of this article make this assessment? A reporter or an ordinary observer might easily ascertain from a list of names of appointees the caste, religious, or linguistic memberships of Mulayam Singh's appointments. But it would be hard to ascertain their class memberships or ideological affinities from such information. Suppose, for instance, that the basis for these appointments was poverty—that Mulayam Singh favored low-income individuals in his appointment of teachers, and because of the imperfect correlation between income and class, many of these low-income individuals happened to be Yadav. Even if the "true" criterion had been income, we can see that it would have been difficult for the reporter (or others confronted with the list of job appointees) to "see" this criterion. Caste, on the other hand, is immediately visible.

In another example in the state of Bihar, observers have noted that when Jagannath Mishra, a Maithil Brahmin, was chief minister, "the Maithil Brahmins acquired important positions in the political system."[12] How might an observer come to such a judgment? Mishra might well have favored Maithil Brahmins in his administration. But suppose that this was not his intention—suppose that in allotting these posts, the true criterion he employed was personal loyalty. Without detailed information on the relationship between Mishra and his employees, an observer would not have been able to detect this "true" relationship. However, it would be easy to ascertain by looking at a list of cabinet names and favored ethnic groups. No wonder, then, that the calculus of voters in India is routinely described as "voting for the surname."[13]

Because individual voters perceive beneficiaries and politicians only on an ethnic basis, it follows that politicians will only distribute patronage benefits on an ethnic basis. From the point of view of politicians, there is no payoff to helping individuals based on a non-ethnic category since such an act would simply be discounted. The political entrepreneur knows that the only credible promises he can make are to help someone based on their ethnicity. Consequently, he has no option but to allot favors on an ethnic basis. As long as the politician is forced to favor a certain ethnic category, he will, at a minimum, help members of his own group, since it gives him a comparative advantage over his competitors. However, when his own ethnic category is not sufficiently large enough to produce a favorable outcome, he may also attempt to channel patronage benefits to some broader mosaic of ethnic groups. However, watchful voters will observe that politicians always favor voters from their own ethnic category. Accordingly, in a self-fulfilling cycle, they will conclude that their best hope of access to patronage benefits depends upon having their own man in power.

Both at the level of open promises and at the level of covert signals, then, politics in India is overwhelmingly ethnic. It is a common misconception that ethnic politics is one of fixed identities, in which a single ethnic majority dominates one or more ethnic minorities. In India, the politics of ethnicity is astonishingly fluid—constrained politicians who signal voters along ethnic lines have a multitude of possibilities at their disposal. Not surprisingly, then, we find that they are constantly attempting to manufacture new ethnic majorities based on tribe, caste, region, language, and religion—and the attempt to mobilize the population on one identity dimension promptly produces a reaction on a competing dimension. During the mid-1950s, for instance, language was especially salient in Indian national politics. Language gave way to caste in the 1970s, and caste remained relevant in the 1980s, but the categories of caste were transformed from local, *jati* configurations to nationwide aggregates such as OBCs (Other Backward Classes) and others. These caste-based majorities were activated in response to the attempt by the BJP to invoke the Hindu majority in the 1980s. In the 1990s, the interlocking attempts to bid for the support of ethnic majorities based on the cross-cutting dimensions of caste and religion were supplemented by the increasing salience of the dimension of region. As a result, although politics is overwhelmingly ethnic, it is also overwhelmingly fluid—and any single ethnic majority is unstable and vulnerable to the manufacture of a new one.

Implications for Democratic Participation and Ethnic Politics

Although the patronage-economy described above looms large over Indian society as a whole, some groups and some regions are less dependent on it than others. In particular, the development of the private sector has expanded the proportion of the population that can purchase an exit option from the patronage economy. This is the so-called new middle class, numbering hundreds of millions of people by most estimates.[14] The middle class is unlikely to be independent of the patronage economy altogether, but it does not depend upon that economy for survival goods or livelihoods.[15]

Although this class is not homogeneous by any means, it is disproportionately composed of privileged ethnic categories: Hindu upper castes, and to a lesser extent Hindu backward castes. A recent national-level survey of class and class mobility in India found that Hindu upper castes made up almost half of the salaried workers (47%) and business classes (42%) in the sample, with Hindu backward castes coming a distant second (25% and 29%, respectively). Scheduled Castes, Scheduled Tribes, and Muslims make up only a small proportion of this middle class.[16]

If, as I have argued, patronage sustains the roots of democracy by giving many citizens a stake in participation, then the weakening of patronage ties should also erode the ties to democracy by diminishing citizen participation. Writing in 1984, Bardhan noted that democracy survived in India because it delivered the spoils to these middle classes. But democracy no longer delivers the spoils—the economy does, and the economy is now more separate from democratic politics than it has ever been. To the extent that the private sector continues to grow, the argument I have made here implies that we should see declining rates of participation and perhaps declining support for democracy as we move up the class hierarchy. Furthermore, because class and ethnicity are imperfectly correlated, there should be some correlation between declining participation rates by class and by ethnicity.

The claim here, it is important to emphasize, is not that the new middle classes may not support democracy for normative reasons, but that they now have less of a vested interest in it. Over time, this weakened interest may fray a normative commitment. Indeed, if we look at survey data on *attitudes* toward democracy in India, the proportion of those who claim to prefer democracy over dictatorship is highest in the middle of the class ladder: only 37% of the lowest class, 46% of the lower class, 58% of the middle class, 58% of the upper class, and 50% of the highest class prefer democracy to dictatorship.[17] But if we look at *turnout* rates across class, the opposite is true. The poor are more likely to vote than the middle classes, and rural areas (where the poor are disproportionately located) report higher turnout than urban areas (where the middle classes are disproportionately located).[18] This decline in turnout rates among the middle classes followed privatization. In 1971, the last date for which figures are given prior to the economic reforms, the middle classes were more likely to vote than the poor. But since 1996, they have become less likely to vote.[19] Regardless of their normative commitment, in other words, middle classes are less likely to participate in democratic structures in the aftermath of economic reforms than they were previously.

The implications of the argument for ethnic politics also give some reason for pessimism. If the politics of ethnicity is produced by the politics of patronage, then the shrinking of the scope of patronage politics should also shrink the scope of ethnic politics. However, the fluid form of ethnic politics that accompanies shrinkage is also likely to become more rigid.

The fluid form of ethnic politics that has accompanied patronage politics in India so far is derived from the stakes involved. In a political environment in which voters and politicians play for high stakes and the main signals they send are ethnic ones, each has an incentive to manipulate their ethnic categories to maximize their chances of winning. Losing politicians have incentives to continually propose new forms of ethnic self-definition to the electorate in order to attract new votes to their side—and given a choice between multiple ethnic identities, voters have incentives to choose those categories which put them in a winning position—and to change their forms of self-definition when the winning configuration changes. But to the extent that large sections of the electorate, and therefore the parties that they support, are no longer competing for patronage, they do not have the incentive to compete by redefining ethnic identities. This may introduce a reification of ethnic categories that, although a standard feature of politics in colonial India, has so far been absent from post-independence Indian politics.

Consider the examples of Gujarat and Uttar Pradesh. In 1991, the electorate in both states was polarized on a Hindu-Muslim basis, with the Hindu "majority" mobilized by the BJP ranged against a Muslim minority. In the intervening years, however, the pattern of ethnic politics in both states changed. In Uttar Pradesh, the formulation of a majority based on religion was quickly followed by the manufacture of a new majority based on caste. The caste-based majority of "Other Backward Castes" was first undermined by the fabrication of still more caste categories (Most Backward Castes, Backward Among Forward Castes, Forward Among Backward Castes) and eventually by regional categories (for example, the demands for the new state of Uttarakhand). The ethnic categories that define politics in Uttar Pradesh continually changed throughout the 1990s.

In Gujarat, by contrast, the lines of ethnic identification have hardened along the single dimension of religion. The overt importance of caste, region, and tribe has declined, and none has been used to redefine political identities based on religion in Gujarat as in Uttar Pradesh, even though each of these identities has been prominently employed in politics in Gujarat in recent years.[20] The hardening line of religious divisions in Gujarat also has been accompanied by repeated outbursts of violence.

One explanation for the different patterns of ethnic politics in Uttar Pradesh and Gujarat compares the different sizes of the private sector in the two states. Uttar Pradesh has one of the largest public sectors in the country, which provides more than 80% of the jobs in the organized economy even after the economic reforms of 1991. Gujarat, by contrast, has the largest private sector of all the states in the country, and this private sector has been growing at a faster rate than in Uttar Pradesh. Consequently, political parties have different incentives and resources in both states. In Uttar Pradesh, the Janata Dal and the Samajwadi parties undermined the BJP's attempt to create a majority based on religion by identifying a new category as the beneficiary of patronage: Other Backward Castes. The BJP in this state jumped on to the same bandwagon, further subdividing the Backward Castes into Upper and Lower Backward Castes and favoring the Lower Backwards in its own distribution of state largesse. In Gujarat, by contrast, much of the BJP's social base, with roots in the private sector, is less susceptible to promises of state assistance. Furthermore, given the much smaller size of the public sector in Uttar Pradesh, there is less largesse to distribute. Consequently, although the BJP has tried to attract the same social groups in Gujarat as in Uttar Pradesh—the Lower Backward Castes—it has done so not by using the state to create new identity categories but by maintaining a continual state of polarization between Hindus and Muslims.

Conclusion

I have focused here on some of the implications of a single change in the nature of India's patronage-based economy—the expansion of the private sector. I have not paid attention to other simultaneous changes that may well offset the trends I explore here. In particular, the decentralization of patronage-democracy in India through the introduction of Panchayati Raj (elected governments at the village level) may have independent effects entirely different from the effects of the expansion of the private sector.

While not claiming to provide a complete argument about the relationship between patronage, democratic participation, and ethnic politics in India, the main point I wish to make in this article is that it is critically important to theorize about the nature of these linkages. A great deal has been written on the link between the reform of the state-dominated, patronage-driven nature of India's economy and its consequences for economic performance—generally benign—but not enough about its political consequences.

By suggesting that the decline of India's patronage economy, if and where it occurs, can transform and weaken the basis of democracy in India, I do not intend to make an argument in favor of patronage. My purpose instead is to draw attention to the paradox of benign political outcomes resting on malign economic structures that has sustained democracy in India so far and therefore to point out that the reform of those economic structures can now generate the opposite result. Benign economic structures may now be accompanied by malign political consequences.

NOTES

1. Kanchan Chandra, *Why Ethnic Parties Succeed* (New York: Cambridge University Press 2004); Kanchan Chandra, "Ethnic Parties and Democratic Stability," *Perspectives on Politics* 3, no. 2 (June 2005): 235–52.

2. Samuel Huntington, *The Third Wave: Democratization in the Late Twentieth Century* (Norman: University of Oklahoma Press, 1991), 7.

3. See, for instance, William Riordon, *Plunkitt of Tammany Hall* (Boston: Bedford Books, 1994); Richard Joseph, *Democracy and Prebendal Politics* (Cambridge: Cambridge University Press, 1987).

4. V. A. Pai Panandikar and S. S. Kshirsagar, *Bureaucracy and Development Administration* (New Delhi: Centre for Policy Research, 1978), 170, table G.

5. Yogendra Yadav, "Reconfiguration in Indian Politics," *Economic and Political Weekly* 31, nos. 2 and 3 (Jan. 13–20, 1996): 95–104.

6. See, for instance, "The Maturing of a Democracy," *India Today*, August 31, 1996.

7. Shiv Vishwanathan, "Thinking About Elections." *Seminar 440,* 1996.

8. Yadav, "Reconfiguration in Indian Politics," 96.

9. Adam Przeworski, *Democracy and the Market* (Cambridge: Cambridge University Press, 1991).

10. Pranab Bardhan, The Political Economy of Development in India (Oxford: Oxford University Press, 1984), 217.

11. *India Today*, October 15, 1994, cited in Christophe Jaffrelot, "The BJP and the 1996 General Election" (paper presented at the National Conference on Political Sociology of India's Democracy, November 14–16, 1996).

12. *Economic and Political Weekly*, May 4, 1991.

13. *The Week*, January 18, 1998.

14. See, for instance, Andre Beteille, "Classes and Communities," *Economic and Political Weekly*, March 17, 2007.

15. See, for instance, table 2.2 in *State of Democracy in South Asia* (New Delhi: Oxford University Press, 2008), 244.

16. This is based on data calculated from table 5 in Sanjay Kumar, Anthony Heath, and Oliver Heath, "Determinants of Social Mobility in India," *Economic and Political Weekly*, July 20, 2002, 2986.

17. SDSA Team, *State of Democracy in South Asia* (Delhi: Oxford University Press, 2008), table 1.2, p. 229. If these percentages are recalculated with the *don't know*s removed, there is an increasing attitudinal preference for democracy as we go up the class hierarchy: 62% of the lowest classes, 72% of lower and middle classes, and 76% of upper and highest classes profess a preference for democracy. The report does not provide information about how the class categories were constructed.

18. For turnout rates by class and percentage urban population in the 1971, 1996, and 1998 parliamentary elections, see Yogendra Yadav, "Electoral Politics in the Time of Change: India's Third Electoral System 1989–1999," *Economic and Political Weekly* 34, nos. 34–35 (Aug. 21–Sept. 3, 1999): 2393–99. For turnout rates by class and urban population in the 1998, 1999, 2004, and 2009 parliamentary elections, see Suhas Palshikar and Sanjay Kumar, "Participatory Norm: How Broad Based Is It?" *Economic and Political Weekly* 39, no. 51 (Dec. 18, 2004): 5412–17; and Sanjay Kumar, "Patterns of Political Participation: Trends and Perspective," *Economic and Political Weekly* 44, no. 39 (Sept. 26, 2009): 47–51, table 9, p. 50.

19. Yadav, "Electoral Politics," 2397, table 8.

20. See, for instance, A. M. Shah, Pravin Patel, and Lancy Lobo, "A Heady Mix: Gujarati and Hindu Pride," *Economic and Political Weekly* 43, no. 8 (Feb. 23, 2008): 19–21.

CHAPTER EIGHT

Linking Capital and Countryside

Patronage and Clientelism in Japan, Thailand, and the Philippines

PAUL D. HUTCHCROFT

While patronage is found in a wide range of political systems, it has a differential impact on the territorial character of polities and on their overall quality of governance. James Scott speaks of the capacity of patronage to act as "political cement,"[1] and Robert Putnam observes that late-nineteenth-century patronage practices in Italy rendered "political channels . . . more important than administrative channels" in linking local interests to the capital.[2] Through a comparison of three Asian polities with well-developed systems of patronage politics, this chapter examines the degree to which patronage structures provide this critical "political cement" between the national and local levels. While patronage is ubiquitous, its mere presence does not mean that central-local relations are necessarily defined more by "political channels" than "administrative channels." The relative importance of patronage as a territorial glue, I argue, relates to the nature of the broader institutional context.

The key elements of this context include both linkages between national bureaucracies (commonly but not necessarily Ministries of the Interior or Home Affairs) and local government units, and linkages that can be provided by coherent and well-institutionalized national political parties. The first goal of this chapter is to examine how variations in institutional context help us to understand the territorial impact of patronage flows. In strong institutional contexts, where agencies of the national bureaucracy are effective in extending central authority throughout the territory and political parties are coherent and well institutionalized, patronage flows are relatively less important in linking local interests to the capital. In weak institutional contexts, where agencies of the national bureaucracy are less effective in extending central authority throughout the territory and political parties are less coherent and well institutionalized, patronage flows may act as basic "political cement" in binding the polity together on a territorial basis. In the latter situation, one can speak of a "patronage-based state." A second goal is to put forward a proposition relating to the key criteria determining the character of patronage flows: the weaker the institutional context, the greater the allocation of patronage through direct personalistic ties (and vice versa). My third goal, closely related, is to overcome some longstanding conceptual confusion between the terms "patronage" and "clientelism." After untangling these overlapping yet distinct concepts, I differentiate between impersonal patronage flows and personalistic patronage flows; the latter, I explain, should be termed "clientelistic patronage."

These issues are examined through a broad-brushed analysis of patronage structures in Japan, Thailand, and the Philippines. There is a strong basis for comparison among these three countries. In terms of formal territorial structure, all three are unitary states.[3] Ethno-linguistic differentiation within the three countries is relatively low (in the case of Japan and Thailand) or relatively weakly politicized (in the case of the Philippines). Regional differentiation has salience in all three cases, but it is most contentious in Thailand and the Philippines, where there have been major secessionist conflicts in the southern provinces of both countries.[4] In addition, all three countries are well known for high levels of patronage flows and "money politics" and figure prominently in literatures on patronage and clientelism. Yet while patronage is widespread in all three cases, it exists in very distinct institutional contexts. The 2 x 2 matrix in table 8.1 seeks to capture major differences among the three countries in the institutional context of patronage flows linking capital and countryside, beginning with the presumption that there are three major types of linkages between national and subnational units of government: an effective bureaucratic apparatus, coherent and well-institutionalized political parties, and patronage flows.

To sharpen the contrast, I am examining the nature of patronage structures in the three democratic settings circa the early and mid-1990s. Japan very clearly combines a strong national bureaucracy and strong political parties—from the creation of the Liberal Democratic Party (LDP) in 1955 until the 1994 electoral reform and the relative demise of the LDP. Thailand falls in the "strong-weak" quadrant, combining a strong and powerful Ministry of the Interior able to trace its influence back to the late nineteenth century with the emergence of notoriously weak political parties in recent decades. My focus is on the period after the fall of a military government in May 1992 and prior to the 1997 Thai Constitution and the subsequent 2001 ascension to power of Thaksin Shinawatra and his Thai Rak Thai Party—a new type of political formation far more cohesive than nearly all previous Thai political

TABLE 8.1.
Institutional contexts of patronage flows linking capital and countryside

National bureaucracy linkages with local
governments (via Ministries of
Interior / Home Affairs or other agencies)

		relatively stronger	*relatively weaker*
Parties	*relatively stronger*	Japan	
	relatively weaker	Thailand	Philippines

parties. And in the Philippines, regardless of which period of post-1986 democracy one focuses on, there is a weak national bureaucracy combined with weak political parties. Drawing on the argument stated above, the weak institutional context in the Philippines makes patronage flows especially important for linking capital and countryside. Among the three cases, it is the only one that can be classified as a "patronage-based state."

Patronage and Clientelism: Untangling Overlapping but Distinct Concepts

The conceptual foundations of this analysis lie at the intersection of two key bodies of literature: (1) state formation and central-local relations, to be discussed in the following three sections in relation to the cases of Japan, Thailand, and the Philippines; and (2) patronage and clientelism, the primary focus of this section. Patronage and clientelism are sometimes treated as synonymous, hence the need to begin with clear definitions that highlight their distinctiveness.

Patronage is a *material resource,* disbursed for particularistic benefit for political purposes and commonly (but not always) derived from public sources. A foundational definition can be found deep in the footnotes of Martin Shefter's seminal work, *Political Parties and the State:* "Patronage . . . involves the exchange of public benefits for political support or party advantage" and is given out by politicians to "individual voters, campaign workers, or contributors." It is a benefit that is "divisible" (i.e., particularistic) rather than "collective" (i.e., programmatic) in nature.[5] This definition should be amended to reflect the fact that politicians can give huge quantities of patronage to other politicians, for example, pork-barrel funds provided to national legislators and local politicians.[6] Clientelism, on the other hand, describes a *personalistic relationship of power.* Persons of higher social status (patrons) are linked to those of lower social status (clients) in face-to-face ties of reciprocity that can vary in content and purpose across time. As James Scott explains, "There is an imbalance in exchange between the two partners which expresses and reflects the disparity in their relative wealth, power, and status."[7]

Kitschelt and Wilkinson are among those who use the terms *patronage* and *clientelism* interchangeably, favoring the use of the term clientelism. This is defined as "a form of direct, contingent exchange" that is "between electoral constituencies . . . and politicians . . . in democratic systems" and "focused on particular classes of goods."[8] My definition resurrects what they see as an older definition of clientelism, namely "a durable, *face-to-face,* hierarchical and thus asymmetrical relation between patrons and clients supported by a normative framework."[9] Based on my usage of the terms, one can further note that patronage, as an adjective, modifies resources and flows, whereas clientelistic, as an adjective, modifies linkages and ties.[10] Untangling the definitions of patronage and clientelism, I argue, allows us to achieve greater analytical precision. Not all patronage involves clientelism, because some patronage flows are impersonal and others are personal. And not all clientelism involves patronage, because the exchange of goods and services (as described by Scott) may or may not involve the "exchange of public benefits" (as described by Shefter). Indeed, the classic clientelistic tie, between landlords and tenants, exists largely outside the state.

With patronage thus defined as a material resource derived from public sources and disbursed for particularistic benefit, and clientelism defined as a personalistic relationship of power, we can differentiate between two major types of patronage: impersonal and clientelistic. Going one step further, comparative reflection on this distinction suggests the need to rethink the usual dichotomy of government outputs, namely, that which is programmatic and policy-based versus that which is particularistic and oriented to patronage. Given that some patronage is impersonal and some is clientelistic, it is useful to expand the usual programmatic vs. particularistic dichotomy into a broader continuum of (1) programmatic; (2) meso-particularistic, involving patronage disbursed on an impersonal basis; and (3) micro-particularistic, involving clientelistic (i.e., personalistic) patronage. These distinctions are summarized in table 8.2.

With these conceptual foundations in place, we can examine the three countries in comparative perspective—beginning with Japan, where patronage politics are played out in the most highly institutionalized context.

TABLE 8.2.
A heuristic continuum of programmatic and particularistic politics

	Programmatic	Meso-particularistic	Micro-particularistic
Target	Universalistic categories	Specific intermediate-level targets, as in sectors/districts/cities shading into villages and neighborhoods	Individuals and households
Character	Impersonal policies	Impersonal patronage	Personalistic/clientelistic patronage
Examples	National healthcare system, revenue sharing based on uniform models, environmental protection, etc.	Targeted infrastructure/skewed apportionment of districts/agricultural subsidies/U.S.-style pork barrel (via legislation) shading into Philippine-style pork barrel (via grants to legislators)	Spoils system, personal networks of candidates, buying of individual votes, etc.
Key actors and relationships	Bureaucrats, parties, politicians, interest groups, citizens	Bureaucrats, parties, politicians, interest groups, citizens	Revolves around various patron-client (or boss-retinue) ties: oligarchs and officials, oligarchs and politicians, politicians and officials, politicians of higher and lower levels, politicians and constituents, etc.
Source of benefits	General public revenue	Mostly general revenue	A combination of general public revenue as well as private and quasi-public sources, including legislator-controlled pork barrel, casual employee payroll, personal wealth of the politician and his/her supporters, kickbacks on public infrastructure projects, profits from illicit or semi-illicit activities

Japan: Strong Bureaucracy, Strong Ruling Party

After the Meiji Restoration of 1868, the new regime consolidated its hold over the realm by establishing a prefectural system—the state-of-the-art means of administrative centralization associated with the Napoleonic reforms instituted earlier in the century in France.[11] Within each prefect, a single official had a wide range of responsibilities, including public order (aided by control of the police), tax assessment, infrastructure, census, land registration, and so forth. As W. G. Beasley explains, these officials "effectively . . . replaced feudal lords" and were subordinate to a Home Ministry established in 1873. "They thus became part of a bureaucracy which depended on national, not local, connections."[12]

As important as this legacy of centralization is to understanding the modern Japanese state, the Home Ministry itself experienced a major interruption in its influence after the country's defeat in the Pacific War. Tainted by its major role in the political repression of the 1930s and 1940s, and perceived to be obstructing attempts to empower local governments and provide for the election of governors and mayors, the ministry was abolished by the American occupation government in 1947, and the police force was soon thereafter decentralized.[13] In the end, however, such efforts to undercut the power of the national bureaucracy did not endure far beyond the end of the American occupation in 1952. Portions of the old Home Ministry were brought back together that same year, and a new Home Ministry was put in place in 1960.[14] Amid a broader "recentralization of power" in the 1950s, the Americans' decentralization of police was reversed and there was even some consideration (albeit unsuccessful) of abolishing the direct election of governors.[15]

As conservative forces amalgamated in the creation of the LDP in 1955, patronage flows were critical to the party's electoral successes and an important element of ties between the national and the local levels. As Abe et al. explain, local governments "had always lacked the political–and especially the financially independent—basis of real autonomy." Within this context of fiscal centralization, local candidates sought to convince the voters that they had a clear "pipeline to the center" capable of attracting state projects and subsidies to their localities.[16] As Chalmers Johnson characterizes the overall system, "what counts is whether [a local politician] gets results in pressuring the central government to send some resources to the region."[17] As part of this logic, Fukui and Fukai explain, "Candidates in elections at all levels routinely swear to help their constituents get more attention and help from Tokyo—to bring pork from the national treasury. Diet members . . . are constantly visited at their Tokyo offices by delegations of politicians from back home, and spend a great deal of time trying to arrange appointments for them with bureaucrats in key ministries and agencies."[18]

In essence, intermediation between the central and local levels came primarily through an intertwined system of central agencies and the LDP. The Ministry of Finance played a particularly important role in allocating central government subsidies to local governments, some of the most important of which (especially in an era of major infrastructural spending) were through the Ministry of Transport and the Ministry of Communications.[19] Local problems or demands were typically filtered through local LDP units up to "particular LDP Diet members and taken by them to the appropriate sections of various ministries and agencies in Tokyo."[20]

The exemplar of postwar patronage politics was Tanaka Kakuei, who served as prime minister in the early 1970s. Between 1972 and 1985, writes Chalmers Johnson, Tanaka "either totally dominated the Japanese political world or was the primary opponent of the political leader in power."[21] Tanaka understood "that money was indeed the mother's milk of politics and that whoever controlled the largest amounts of it in the political system, controlled the system. Everybody needed money—for the reelection campaigns, for his faction, for entertaining and cultivating the bureaucrats who made the vital decisions—and everybody needed more of it than was allowed under the various laws that controlled political funds." During this period, as well, there was an apparent shift in the relative power of the bureaucracy and the LDP, as "it was Tanaka who first showed [party policy specialists] how to bring the bureaucracy to heel."[22]

The foundation of Tanaka's influence was at the local level, in his home prefecture of Niigata, where he formed a personal support organization, or *kōenkai,* that became "the model for all Diet members' local organizations."[23] These organizations thrived within the single nontransferrable vote (SNTV) electoral system,[24] whose multimember districts fostered fierce intra-party competition. As Matthew Carlson explains:

> With many politicians facing both intraparty and interparty competition, they devised candidate-centered campaign strategies, such as the use of . . . *kōenkai.* Politicians offered a variety of constituency services to the members of their *kōenkai;* these supporters typically returned the favor at election time by providing a stable base of votes. Politicians incurred high financial costs to operate and maintain their *kōenkai,* which contributed to a system where nearly four times more money per capita was spent on politics than in Germany, the United States, or the United Kingdom. . . . With scant emphasis on policy and issue debates in election campaigns, politicians maintained *kōenkai* by spending exorbitant amounts of time and money holding regular meetings with supporters, attending funerals and weddings, and organizing karaoke parties, golf tournaments, and bus trips to hot spring resorts.[25]

Aside from merely voting, as Ethan Scheiner further explains, *kōenkai* members helped to campaign and expand campaign networks.[26] Politicians enjoying the greatest clout with the national government were able to build the largest *kōenkai* at the local level and thus enhance their chances of reelection.[27]

Patronage was thus the dominant vehicle for the differentiation of candidates, and there was a large amount of money greasing a political system that linked national bureaucrats and LDP legislators in Tokyo with local (mainly LDP-affiliated[28]) politicians around the country. Quite clearly, patronage flows in Japan took place within the context of strong institutions—both the bureaucracy and the ruling party. Fukui and Fukai's highly textured study of "pork barrel politics" in two Japanese prefectures, based on research conducted in 1994, explains that general account funds provided by the national government to localities were distributed in two categories: (1) roughly two-thirds via a revenue-sharing scheme distributed by "very rigid 'objective' rules"; and (2) roughly one-third via a public works fund that is anything but objective. Decisions on the distribution of the latter, they note, "are subject to the subjective judgments of bureaucrats in the various ministries with jurisdiction over the particular types of projects involved and, therefore, amenable to interventions by politicians and special interest groups capable of influencing those bureaucrats. This category of funds is the primary target of lobbying activities by local governments and allied Diet members."[29] Other very large sources of government resources, aside from general account funds, were allocated in a similar way.[30]

The process of lobbying took place to a large extent within LDP party networks, which reached from local governments to the prefectures and then to the national level. Personalistic ties, called *keiretsu,* commonly linked national legislators to local politicians.[31] In exchange for the support they obtain from their national legislative patrons, local politicians were expected to deliver the vote at election time. Contention over the allocation of central government funds was largely an intra-party matter, and LDP members of the Diet served as the critical intermediary between local constituents and national bureaucrats. "It is . . . widely believed, though not documented, that voters know without being told which Diet members from their district deliver the most pork from Tokyo."[32] Another important element of intermediation between national and local actors was performed by "middle-level ministry officials who are temporarily assigned to local government offices on routine two- or three-year tours of duty."[33]

As further evidence of the institutionalized context of patronage flows in Japan, the LDP played a central role in managing intraparty competition among its members of the Diet. As Rosenbluth and Theis explain, the party put "same-district co-partisans" on different parliamentary committees and thus "[enforced] a functional division . . . by means of nonoverlapping policy specialization."[34] Intraparty competition at election time was managed through the imposition of campaign rules favorable to the LDP.[35]

It was proposed at the outset that the stronger the institutional context, the less patronage will be allocated through direct personalistic ties. To use the terms introduced in my description of the framework above, one would thus expect to see in the Japanese context of the early 1990s a substantial level of "meso-particularism" relative to "micro-particularism." We shall see that this was indeed the case, but by no means is micro-particularism unimportant. The *kōenkai* are an obvious example, enabling politicians to seek the personal support of voters. While there may have been very little direct vote buying in the Japanese system, cash gifts were common at weddings and funerals and "copious amounts of money" were disbursed at election time to mobilize support.[36] Also highly personalistic are the networks of the *keiretsu*, which nurtured enduring connections between Diet members in Tokyo and politicians at the prefectural and local levels.

The terms "clientelism" and "particularistic" are common in the literature on Japanese politics, and are in many cases entirely appropriate. Based on my definitions, however, much patronage in the Japanese context is in fact not clientelistic and not especially particularistic. This leads me into an analysis of meso-particularism, which on the continuum above lies between programmatic outputs (targeted at universalistic categories) and micro-particularism (targeted at individuals, households, and firms). Indeed, it is striking how much of the literature on Japanese patronage describes flows that are targeted at quite large categories of voters. Ethan Scheiner, drawing on Herbert Kitschelt's work, defines clientelism as "benefits that are awarded to people who supported the party and withheld from those who are found, on the basis of some kind of monitoring, not to have supported it."[37] Through monitoring, parties are able to "keep the provision of benefits very specific and tightly targeted." In terms of empirical examples, however, it becomes clear that the beneficiaries fall into categories that are not very specific or strict: farmers, small business persons, regions, and an entire industry (construction).

Scheiner acknowledges that "the discretionary provisions of benefits are often not targeted as tightly as is necessary to ensure that the correct group is receiving them" and that "some practices and relationships . . . walk a fine line between universalistic and clientelistic arrangements."[38] Gregory Noble's 2010 analysis of the Japanese political economy convincingly argues a broad shift from particularistic to programmatic politics (and critiques Scheiner's use of the term *clientelism*). The examples of past particularism, however, are in fact not very particular: "programs and agencies for farmers, small business owners, and construction companies."[39] Further examples of meso-particularistic public benefits in Japan involve the very substantial political and economic advantages granted to the broad rural population, including not only agricultural protectionism but also the malapportionment of legislative districts in their favor.[40]

In sum, very substantial elements of both meso-particularism and micro-particularism exist side-by-side within a highly elaborate system of Japanese "money politics."[41] As is to be expected in a strongly institutionalized context, patronage flows are often not clientelistic and often not very particularistic.

Thailand: Strong Bureaucracy, Weak Parties

In consolidating his dynastic rule in the late-nineteenth and early-twentieth century, King Chulalongkorn of Thailand worked to centralize the realm by using the same strategy of prefectoralism earlier employed in Meiji Japan. As part of an effort to avoid formal colonization, the Thai monarch was in fact emulating the dominant form of administration found in colonial systems throughout the world. His half-brother, Prince Damrong, set up the Interior Ministry in 1893 and proceeded to strengthen central authority through the creation of prefects that were headed up by resident commissioners sent out from Bangkok. The power of entrenched families was challenged in many localities, and revenue collection was greatly enhanced. As Baker and Pasuk explain, "a new centralized pyramid of bureaucratic administration . . . [replaced] the local lords."[42] The Interior Ministry constituted a vital bulwark of the new Thai state, and to this day it continues to be among the government's most powerful ministries.

After the end of the absolute monarchy in 1932, civilian and military bureaucrats in Bangkok were the backbone of a polity that experienced repeated coup attempts. Authoritarian military regimes were rarely interrupted by civilian rule over the subsequent half-century, and the term "bureaucratic polity" was coined to describe a system that seemed to give little scope for the emergence of countervailing social forces.[43] The Ministry of the Interior was a key institution in safeguarding the power of the Bangkok-based bureaucratic and military elite, and local power was highly circumscribed. In addition to appointing provincial governors and controlling "all aspects" of provincial administration, district administration, and community development, the Ministry of the Interior also managed the election process.[44] "Until the 1970s," explains Arghiros, various "government parties" that were in fact formed by the bureaucracy "could rely on the control of the Ministry of the Interior to win elections and the government party directed local state representatives to mobilize rural voters on its behalf."[45] Provincial governors could dismiss elected officials within their provinces and had oversight as well over the field offices of central ministries.[46]

As Cold War aid and foreign investment began to pour into Thailand in the 1960s and early 1970s, the economy began a period of sustained growth that shook the very foundations of the bureaucratic polity. New social forces emerged in Bangkok and the provinces, contributing to the fall of the military regime in 1973 and an unprecedented level of democratic freedom as well as student and lower-class mobilization. Such freedoms were brutally restricted after 1976, but in the process of reimposing authoritarian rule, the military itself came to rely on patterns of social mobilization (of right-wing forces and fearful middle classes) not previously necessary in the heyday of the bureaucratic polity.[47] A new constitution, drawn up in 1978, reintroduced semi-democratic institutions able to balance the enduring power of the bureaucratic elite with that of an increasingly assertive Bangkok business class. Even though its powers as a part-elected and part-appointed body were limited in many respects, Parliament's very ability to remain in place for such a relatively long period of time (at least by Thai standards, and specifically up until the next military coup in 1991) enabled it to grow in stature.[48] In the well-known 1990 analysis of Benedict Anderson, there came to be "murder and progress in modern Siam" after "the institution of MP . . . achieved solid market value" in the 1980s. As he further explained, "not only does being an MP offer substantial opportunities for gaining wealth and power, *but it promises to do so comfortably for the duration.* It may thus be worth one's while to murder one's parliamentary competition—something inconceivable in the 1950s and 1960s, when parliament's power and longevity were very cheaply regarded."[49]

By virtue of being head of a parliamentary faction, one could take control of those ministries (e.g., Public Works or Communications) that had been given over to the politicians as a trough for patronage. At the beginning of the 1980s, Bangkok business interests dominated the major political parties and enjoyed the spoils that came with their newly obtained control of the patronage-oriented ministries. By mid-decade, Bangkok business was increasingly displaced, in the parties and in the Parliament, by the rise of provincial notables. Since the Vietnam War boom of the 1960s, business interests had prospered throughout the provinces and built up strong bases of local socioeconomic power. As Pasuk and Baker explain, election to the Parliament enabled them "to crown their local leadership, to build contacts in Bangkok, and to tap the government's central funds both for personal gain and for developing their constituencies. Their goal was a seat in the Cabinet or at least access to Cabinet authority."[50] As the post of MP thus acquired "solid market value," the patterns of vote buying for which Thailand has achieved such notoriety became well established (in contrast to earlier decades, when elections were somnolent affairs and vote buying quite rare). With over three-quarters of seats representing provincial areas, it was only a matter of time before the top political positions in the kingdom would come under the control of the so-called rural godfathers (whom Anderson describes as "mafioso-like politician capitalists who, by the use of violence, political connections, and control of local markets and rackets, become feared political bosses").[51]

The rise of provincial politicians constituted a major shift in power away from Bangkok, and by 1990 provincial businesspersons constituted almost half of the cabinet.[52] As Anderson explains, it is through Parliament that they were given "the opportunity to short-circuit the Ministry of the Interior's powerful, territorially based hierarchy, and to make themselves felt, on their own terms, in the metropolitan home base of the bureaucracy itself."[53] Out of the new power arrangements came new networks of influence as those provincial capitalists who formerly operated within the constraints of the bureaucratic polity developed their own connections at all levels of the state—and were able to use these new connections to their political and economic advantage.[54] Budget expenditures were spread around the country more broadly, and a slush fund for MPs ballooned in size after the advent of civilian rule in 1988.[55] The exemplar of the sleazy provincial politician, Banharn Silpa-archa (also known as "Mr. ATM" for his mastery of money politics), became prime minister in 1995–1996.[56]

Thai political parties were weak and heavily factionalized, centered around "senior patrons" competing to gain a cabinet post. Parties commonly enjoyed strength in particular regions and were unable to claim truly national bases.[57] In the post-election jockeying among multiple parties, the ultimate goal of an ambitious politician was to use control of a faction (commonly from four to seven MP's) as a stepping stone to control of a ministry, which could in turn be used "to recoup election expenses, establish war chests for future elections, and distribute favors to supporters.[58] A multi-member district electoral system promoted substantial intra-party competition at the local level, and—not unlike Japan—members of the same party distinguished themselves from each other by virtue of their capacity to distribute patronage resources. Unlike Japan, however, there was no longstanding ruling party with either the stature or the coherence necessary for effective management of intraparty competition among its patronage-oriented politicians. Also quite unlike Japan, coercive techniques were not uncommon and votebuying was rampant. The "key to electoral victory" was the mobilization of *hua khanaen*, "vote canvassers" who worked for individual candidates in mobilizing voters by directly purchasing votes (of individuals and sometime of entire villages), dispensing of patronage, and intimidation.[59] Networks of *hua khanaen* extended from regional and provincial levels down to "every village and every neighborhood," and the most effective canvassers were "those involved in crime and corruption."[60]

Amid major power shifts from bureaucrats to politician-capitalists, and Bangkok to the provinces, the Ministry of the Interior faced a much more complex terrain of power in the countryside. Its influence over provincial administrations, however, remained (and remains even today) very substantial in nearly all the ways described.[61] As appointed officials, the provincial governors danced to the tune of the Interior Ministry, and it is the Ministry that controlled all staffing at the provincial level.[62] There was an elected provincial-level council, whose major role is to approve and allocate infrastructural development budgets.[63] As this became a lucrative trough of patronage for those in the construction industry, the provincial legislatures came to be known as "contractors' councils." Strategically located between national and local politics, the provincial councilors also became the primary vote canvassers for national politicians, "mobilizing the lower-level networks on their behalf."[64] As important as the councils were in political terms, they can be viewed as a mere "playground" for local politicians. The councilors seemed to have extremely little influence on the administration of the province, and the vast bulk of the provincial budget was beyond their reach.[65] In other words, even after the rise of provincial politician-capitalists, the Ministry of the Interior continued to dominate nearly all aspects of provincial administration.

This can perhaps be seen as a reflection of the dualistic nature of the institutional context of patronage flows in Thailand. The territorial bureaucracy first put in place by King Chulalongkorn and Prince Damrong in 1893 continued to have enormous power in the early 1990s, the period examined in this chapter. The political parties that emerged in the latter decades of the twentieth century, by contrast, were weak and factionalized. Far more important than parties in the allocation of patronage were individual politician-capitalists, now linked in an extensive set of quite informal and non-institutionalized networks stretching from the national level through the provincial level and down to every locality. The role of the newly empowered provincial MP's, Baker and Pasuk explain, "attached the provinces politically to the centre more tightly than decades of administrative plans."[66] The old administrative grid, however, has by no means disappeared. In Thailand's well-elaborated and well-financed system of "money politics," patronage flows within the larger context of a strong territorial bureaucracy and weak parties. While patronage serves as an important new "glue" for the polity—or at least for the emerging political-economic elite building myriad new "extrabureaucratic networks"—it co-exists with a much longer-standing bureaucratic network that first united the realm one hundred years ago.[67]

As proposed at the outset of this paper, it is expected that stronger institutional contexts are associated with less personalistic allocation of patronage. What of intermediate cases, such as Thailand, with a strong bureaucracy and weak parties? The answer to this question would require careful empirical work, but it is worth noting that scholars have long been confounded by the Thai polity's combination of quite substantial institutionalization with quite substantial personalism. There are indeed examples of both micro-particularistic and a meso-particularistic patronage, i.e., that which is clientelistic versus that which is relatively more impersonal. The former category includes patronage flows from prominent politicians downward to the members of their faction, the purpose of which is to secure or safeguard a coveted position in the cabinet and its accompanying control of a ministry. A second prominent example is the networks of *hua khanaen,* or vote canvassers, with clientelist ties stretching from the regional and provincial levels downward to individual voters in villages and neighborhoods.

As for patterns of meso-particularism, one clear example is the capacity of an individual MP to support infrastructural pork-barrel projects of benefit to an entire electoral constituency (with Banharn Silpa-archa once again the prime example[68]). Despite obvious parallels between Banharn and Tanaka, one must nonetheless note a marked contrast between Thailand and Japan, where a well-institutionalized ruling party devised multiple ways of nurturing and maintaining key constituencies. In the absence of any such party in Thailand (at least until Thaksin's Thai Rak Thai in first years of the new century), one finds the best examples of relatively more impersonal patronage coming forth from the institution of the monarchy. After 1957, as King Bhumibol sought to reestablish a strong position for the royal family after a quarter-century of relative political marginalization, he projected himself as "the paternal, activist king of a childlike, quiescent peasantry."[69] His efforts were actively supported both by Field Marshal Sarit Thanarat, who was not of the generation that ended the absolute monarchy in 1932, as well as by the United States. As the Communist Party of Thailand gained strength in the 1960s and 1970s, counterinsurgency goals figured even more prominently. His rural projects elicited the support not only of military regimes at home and the U.S. overseas but also of the increasingly prominent business class.[70] While this was not a patronage oriented to gaining votes, it did have clear political purposes and outcomes.

In sum, Thai-style "money politics" existed in the early 1990s within a moderately institutionalized environment: strong bureaucratic involvement in central-local intermediation but a decidedly weak role for political parties (which remained highly unstable, faction-ridden, and lacking in coherence). There are high levels of patronage in both Thailand and Japan, and one finds well-developed networks linking both national and local politicians as well as local campaign organizations and voters. With the presence of a strong ruling party in Japan, however, one finds much more coherent use of meso-particularistic patronage—targeted not at individuals but at broader social categories, with the purpose of capturing and maintaining long-term support for the party as a whole. In addition, Japan's LDP was much more effective than any Thai party in its ability to referee intra-party competition over patronage resources at the local level.

The Philippines: Weak Bureaucracy, Weak Parties

Unlike Japan and Thailand, the Philippines has never relied upon a prefectoral strategy of territorial organization and never had an Interior Ministry of substantial bureaucratic continuity, authority, or coherence. This can be traced to the origins of the modern Philippine state, in an American regime of the early twentieth century that was quite distinctive in the annals of colonialism. The key formative period was under the leadership of William Howard Taft, who between 1900 and 1913 (first as Philippine governor-general, then as U.S. secretary of war, and later as president) played a central role in constructing a new polity—building on the residual architecture of the previous Spanish colonial state and responding to a major revolutionary challenge from supporters of Philippine independence. Four policies, in particular, helped to nurture the territorial dispersal of power throughout the archipelago as well as strong patronage ties linking the national and local levels.[71]

First, Taft and other architects of American colonial rule arrived in the Philippines with a clear desire to promote as much local autonomy as possible (central intervention in local affairs "is foreign to American practice," declared one early report[72]). With fond reference to New England, Taft proclaimed "town government" to be "the practical way of building up a general government."[73] This involved the systematic organization of municipal elections (restricted to a small elite electorate) in 1901, and the election of provincial governors (by municipal officials) in 1902. In promoting local arenas of political endeavor, American colonials were motivated both out of expediency (seeking to undercut elite support for the guerrilla struggle for Philippine independence) and ideals (replicating the spirit of local self-rule practiced at home). In essence, Taft's so-called policy of attraction involved providing greatly expanded opportunities for *political* power to elites who had already developed a strong *economic* base throughout major regions of the Philippines in the latter decades of the Spanish era. One thus finds a major contrast not only between the Americans and other contemporaneous colonial powers, but also between the Americans and the policies taken by late-nineteenth-century Japan and Thailand in their successful efforts to *avoid* colonialism. While other regimes were commonly employing the very effective technique of prefectoralism to enhance central control and subdue provincial rivals, American colonials were inclined to promote local politics and local politicians.

Second, the American colonial system also differed from its counterparts in giving far more attention to elections and the creation of representative institutions than to the creation of a modern bureaucratic apparatus. As Anderson explains, "Unlike all the other modern colonial regimes in twentieth-century Southeast Asia, which operated through huge, autocratic, white-run bureaucracies, the American authorities in Manila . . . created only a minimal civil service, and quickly turned over most of its component positions to the natives."[74] Taft's policy of "political tutelage" involved ever-greater opportunities for Philippine elites to seek electoral office— first at the municipal and provincial levels, as noted above, and later in the National Assembly and Senate (formed in 1907 and 1916, respectively). Taft did not neglect the goal of constructing a reliable civil service, but for reasons of historical timing the effort failed. Because representative institutions in the Philippines emerged *before* the creation of strong bureaucratic institutions, it was easy for patronage-hungry politicos to overwhelm the nascent administrative agencies of the colonial state.[75] While other colonial powers generally set up strong interior (or home affairs) ministries, with the clear goal of promoting administrative control of the territory, the U.S. colonials in the Philippines had only a weak Executive Bureau with little institutional continuity over time. It was more successful in instituting formalistic reporting and approval requirements than in implementing effective supervision.

Third, Taft actively promoted the rise of provincial politicians, with the explicit goal of strengthening American colonials' "hold on the entire archipelago."[76] The two leading provincial governors to emerge, Sergio Osmeña of Cebu and Manuel Quezon of Tayabas, had been quick to see that it was possible to combine a *provincial* base with access to *national* power. They were the major figures in the newly formed Nacionalista Party, a purportedly pro-independence party that was to dominate Philippine politics for much of the next four decades. Along with the other provincial elites-turned-national politicos who were elected to the National Assembly in 1907, they very deftly responded to the new opportunities created by American colonials and achieved a level of political authority capable of obstructing the goals of the U.S. governor-general.[77] The interaction of elites in the new political institutions in Manila led to the emergence of what Anderson calls a "solid, visible 'national oligarchy.'"[78]

Fourth, political party formation is not a normal activity for most colonial masters, but in the Philippines Taft considered it an important element of his larger project of "political education."[79] Not surprisingly, these political parties had many similarities to the patronage-based party system from which Taft, the highly successful Ohio politician, had emerged. At times, the promotion of patronage was a very conscious policy. More important, however, was how the creation of legislative institutions created a logic for patronage at a point when bureaucratic structures had barely had a chance to consolidate their strength. Unlike political parties in most of the colonial world, which were excluded from the corridors of power as they pressed for the goal of national independence, the Nacionalista Party (NP) enjoyed ready access to patronage resources and increasing influence over appointments within the bureaucracy.[80] The patronage basis of Philippine political parties, which can be traced to the early American period and endures through the present, reinforces the territorial dispersal of power throughout the archipelago. As in other settings where democratic structures are infused with a strong element of patronage, there are many informal avenues for the promotion of local interests and the diminution of central supervisory structure. Most proximately, in the late-nineteenth-century U.S. political system that had shaped Taft, patronage-based parties promoted the "broad dispersion of particularistic benefits downward to the localities."[81]

In sum, four policies of the Taft era led to a pronounced dispersal of power throughout the archipelago combined with strong patronage linkages between national and local levels: the promotion of local autonomy; greater attention to elections and legislative institutions than to the creation of a modern bureaucratic apparatus; the nurturing of provincial politicians; and the emergence of patronage-based political parties. Together, they contributed to a process I have termed patronage-based state formation. Defined more formally, this type of state formation (1) occurs within settings that lack strong political institutions, notably effective bureaucracies and/or well-institutionalized political parties; (2) devolves important elements of state administrative functions to local power holders throughout the country; and (3) displays high levels of interconnectedness among the different territorial layers of government via a patronage system that has its apex in the national capital. The devolution of administrative functions that comes forth from patronage-based state formation has an important analogue in the revenue sphere, specifically in the system of tax farming found in many eighteenth- and nineteenth-century colonial and colonial-era states, including the Netherlands East Indies, British Malaya, and Siam. Just as tax farming involved the subcontracting out of the revenue functions of the state (to private merchants who served as collectors of tax throughout the realm), patronage-based state formation involves a subcontracting out of the administrative functions of the state.

Systems of patronage can be very effective in binding a country together, providing the "political cement" described by James Scott at the outset of this analysis and orienting elites in different regions to look to the center for resources. In the Philippines, this is best exemplified at the sociocultural margins of the polity, in the Muslim Mindanao region. Abinales traces the late colonial "transformation of Muslim datus from Malay men of prowess into provincial politicians," eventually becoming "Muslim counterparts to the northern caciques."[82] At the same time, the dominance of patronage necessarily involves major compromises in the quality of governance. To return to the analogy of revenue farming, local politicians resemble private merchants in that they are acting both on behalf of the state and on behalf of their own political (and financial) interests. Some exhibit devotion to public goals, but others find private goals more compelling. In his analysis of state-society relations in Mindanao in the early post-independence years, Abinales explains that "the parameters of governance are negotiated and determined." Local strong men "exemplified the administrative capability of this political fusion by their respective roles as strongmen and state actors, here defending their local turf, there executing imperatives of state on their constituencies."[83] The quality of democracy suffers as well in a patronage-dominated system, as competition centers primarily around the disbursement of pork and patronage, and voters rarely have any clear choice between contending programmatic or ideological perspectives.

Once in place, the patronage-based state in the Philippines has proven difficult to dislodge—despite certain historical junctures at which this might have occurred.[84] As he enjoyed largely uncontested executive authority and effectively one-party rule within the Philippine Commonwealth after 1935, President Manuel L. Quezon was more interested in centralizing control over patronage resources than in building more effective institutions of central government supervision. There was an impulse toward administrative centralization during the Japanese Occupation of 1942–1945 when a Ministry of Home Affairs was put into place, but these efforts did not get off the ground amid multiple challenges to Japanese control over the archipelago. When democratic structures were reestablished after the war, the dominance of the Nacionalista Party under the Commonwealth was replaced with a two-party system in which patronage resources were dispersed in a far more decentralized manner. While "loose firearms" had already been considered a problem in the colonial period, the country became awash in guns during the Japanese Occupation—with many now in the hands of the "new men" that had emerged in the course of a highly decentralized guerrilla struggle. Compared to the immediate prewar years, politicians in the provinces were in a much stronger position relative to those at the center.

Due in large part to its distinctive American colonial heritage, the Philippines in the initial decades after independence displayed a complex web of central-local ties in which Manila could seem to be at once overlord and lorded over. Certain aspects of central-local relations were highly centralized: even the most trifling of administrative decisions had to be approved in Manila, and many local and provincial authorities chafed at restrictions on their autonomy. At the same time, Manila displayed weak capacity for sustained supervision of provincial and local officials—indeed, central supervision of local governments was almost entirely ad hoc, oriented to punishing political opponents while providing political allies with effective autonomy. Both local police and the national Philippine Constabulary were highly politicized, frequently deployed in electoral battles on behalf of the local politicians who controlled them. The heightened postwar prevalence of firearms fostered "warlord" armies that were especially active at election time.

National politicians commonly relied heavily on local power (and the brokering of arrangements with local bosses and their private armies) in order to succeed in electoral contests. Local leaders delivered blocs of votes in exchange for benefits from allies in Manila, while "national" politics were often dominated by the need of congresspersons to consolidate local bailiwicks (through such means as rampant pork-barrel spending). The two national parties—the Nacionalistas and the Liberals—were virtually indistinguishable, and it was not uncommon for politicians to switch parties in search of more favorable access to patronage resources. Carl Landé, in his landmark study of Philippine politics in the 1960s, explained how local political factions enjoyed "considerable bargaining power in their dealings with the national parties" through their ability to deliver blocs of votes.[85] National politicians, however, were able to balance this system by virtue of "the great quantity of material rewards at their disposal," with the result being the "functional interdependence of local, provincial, and national leaders," albeit "unstable" and constantly shifting throughout the electoral cycle.[86]

With his declaration of martial law, in 1972, President Ferdinand Marcos shifted the balance dramatically in favor of his own power and at the expense of local politicians. It was not until 1978 that the regime replaced the closed Congress of pre-martial-law days with an Interim National Assembly. In preparation for the 1978 elections, the Marcos regime launched its own ruling party, the Kilusang Bagong Lipunan (New Society Movement, or KBL). The rhetoric of a "new society" and the emergence of new faces notwithstanding, the old informal patronage politics of the pre-martial-law years remained the fundamental basis of the KBL.[87] Throughout much of the country, politicians flocked to the KBL for the benefits that it could dispense. Local officials, who could be replaced at will by the regime, were particularly anxious to join the ruling party. (The head of the KBL, not coincidentally, was simultaneously the Minister of Local Governments.) Three major cronies of Marcos became regional party chairmen, tasked with ensuring KBL victory and at the same time given the opportunity to achieve political dominance over other power holders in their respective regions of the country. The patronage dispensed by this political machine was an important bulwark for the regime, complementing its elaboration of hollow democratic structures and extensive use of coercion.

Since the fall of Marcos in 1986, many patterns of pre-martial-law Philippine politics have returned. The reopening of Congress marked the return of democratic institutions after nearly 15 years of highly repressive and crony-infested authoritarianism. At the same time, however, it has given many old provincial dynasties new opportunities to reassert their influence over national politics. In 1991, a highly respected election commissioner estimated that enough illegal weapons had been smuggled into the country over the previous five years to supply two additional national armies.[88] As in the pre-martial-law era, political parties have remained weak and poorly institutionalized, seeking to build a national base through ever-shifting and commonly ad hoc alliances with patronage-hungry politicians throughout the archipelago. Political scientist Nathan Quimpo provides perhaps the best description of contemporary Philippine political parties: "convenient vehicles of patronage that can be set up, merged with others, split, resurrected, regurgitated, reconstituted, renamed, repackaged, recycled, or flushed down the toilet anytime."[89]

The often beleaguered administration of Corazon Aquino showed itself to be highly accommodating to local power in the provinces (including many "warlord" figures associated with the previous regime) and very responsive as well to long-standing sentiment in favor of providing more authority to municipal and provincial bodies. In part out of a strong reaction against previous authoritarian excesses, the 1987 Constitution promised greater degrees of autonomy to local governments and "a just share . . . [of] national taxes which shall be automatically released to them." This created the mandate for the most innovative political reform of the Aquino years, the Local Government Code (LGC) of 1991, an ambitious decentralization initiative gave greater authority and resources to a range of local politicians—some of whom had a genuine agenda of democratic reform (commonly in alliance with civil society organizations), and some of whom sought merely to further entrench their control of local authoritarian enclaves.[90]

The most important provision of the LGC required the central government to provide local units with automatic and greatly increased allotments of internal revenue. The stated goal was to reduce the central government's discretionary power over local governments, and the outcome was a more than quadrupling of transfers (in real terms) between 1991 and 1997.[91] In political terms, this quite obviously strengthened the position of local politicians vis-à-vis congresspersons. While some may claim that the Code has promoted local autonomy and "radically transformed the very nature of the Philippine political-administrative system,"[92] it can be viewed more cynically as a mere re-slicing of the patronage pie in favor of governors, city mayors, town mayors, and *barangay* (barrio) captains.[93]

This shift was viewed as a major threat by many congresspersons, particularly if the governors and mayors in their districts were major political rivals. Not to be outdone, congresspersons have enjoyed lavish pork-barrel allocations through programs given such names as "Congressional Initiative Allocation" and "Countrywide Development Fund." Unlike the U.S. pork-barrel system, in which pork is appropriated through national legislation, pork-barrel resources in the Philippines are highly discretionary grants directly controlled by national legislators, that is, legislator slush funds. The dispersal of these funds in the House of Representatives is mediated through the president and the speaker of the House, giving each legislator a particular incentive to be allied with the president. In the wake of every presidential election, not surprisingly, one can observe a flood of party-switchers moving toward the president's coalition—thus guaranteeing each president a majority in the lower house. The 24 members of the Senate also enjoy large quantities of pork, but hold more independent stature by virtue of their election from a single nationwide district.

Another reform under President Aquino was the reorganization of the Marcos-era Ministry of Local Governments into a Department of the Interior and Local Governments. As in earlier years, however, this agency has continued to play a key role in forging local political alliances for whoever occupied the presidential palace. There is also continuity in how supervision of local government units remains a highly politicized process: those allied with the Palace can anticipate special favors, while those out of favor are not uncommonly given harsh treatment.

Returning to the framework developed at the outset of this analysis, it was proposed that a weak institutional context is associated with a greater degree of allocation of patronage through direct personalistic ties. In the Philippine context, therefore, one would thus expect to see a substantial level of "micro-particularism" relative to "meso-particularism." The latter is not absent, however, and can be found in pork-barrel projects that benefit a large group of constituents (such as an entire congressional district). A second example would be regional development programs, likely funded by a foreign donor and often with counterinsurgency goals, seeking to improve infrastructure across a much more extensive territory. All too often, however, even these larger projects can be partly hijacked by local politicians able to skim off percentages (via kickbacks and bribes) for themselves and their allies.

Examples of micro-particularism are too plentiful to fully enumerate and are best conceptualized as a pyramid of personal ties that extend from the Presidential Palace down to the *barangay* (barrio) level—with enormous competition for resources at every level. Through its significant discretion in budgetary matters, the Office of the President disburses funds not only to legislators but also to local politicians. As economist Emmanuel de Dios explains, the "assured revenue transfers" of the Local Government Code "have not weaned local politics away from the imperative of securing additional resources through typical networks of patronage and vertical transactions with the centre. The patronage relationship remains intact."[94] Pork-barrel projects of congresspersons can range from larger-scale projects, as mentioned above, to micro-level projects benefiting particular neighborhoods (e.g., the ubiquitous basketball courts found throughout the archipelago, each backboard labeled with the name of the politician who financed it). On a purely personalistic level of exchange, one can note political positions that are a prominent element of local government,[95] sponsorship of weddings, funerals and baptisms, and vote buying.

In sum, the Philippines exhibits not only high levels of patronage but a flow of patronage resources within a very weakly institutionalized environment: ineffective supervisory structures in the national bureaucracy and largely incoherent political parties that are dominated by the agendas of individual politicians. Based on cursory observation, one can note that substantial elements of patronage are allocated on the basis of clientelistic ties (what I am terming "micro-particularism"). A large degree of authority and power is farmed out to local politicians, who deliver up the votes in exchange for patronage resources from the center. They commonly enjoy substantial autonomy, albeit within an ever-shifting and unstable bargaining relationship with higher levels of the political system, and those who can accumulate control over substantial coercive and economic resources are able to build substantial and often enduring local authoritarian enclaves.

Linking Capital and Countryside

As stated at the outset, the goal of this analysis is to examine the degree to which patronage structures provide a critical "political cement" between national and local actors and levels. Through analysis of three cases—Japan, Thailand, and the Philippines—I have argued, first, that patronage serves an especially important "political cement" or territorial glue in a weakly institutionalized political environment. While Japan has high degrees of patronage, these resource flows were mediated from the center to localities amid strong political institutions: central government bureaucracies with a deep reach throughout the territory, thoroughly intertwined with a powerful and longstanding ruling party, the LDP. Thailand is the intermediate case, with the Interior Ministry playing a dominant role in overseeing local government but very weak and unstable political parties often unable to claim a national base of support. In the Philippines, patronage flows within a particularly weak institutional environment and thus constitutes a critical glue for the polity as a whole. The national bureaucracy that oversees local government has little supervisory capacity, and is most effective in forging ad hoc ties with local politicians on behalf of the presidential palace. Political parties are generally national in scope but notoriously weak in terms of their programmatic and institutional coherence. Of the three cases, only the Philippines can be classified as a patronage-based state.

Second, I have proposed that the weaker the institutional context, the greater the allocation of patronage through direct, personalistic ties (and vice versa). While it is beyond the scope of this paper to provide concrete empirical evidence of the relative importance of these two types of patronage flow in each of the three cases, cursory examination based to a large extent on a broad-brushed analysis of secondary sources demonstrates that relatively more impersonal patronage and relatively more personalistic patronage clearly exist in all three cases. It also suggests that impersonal patronage is of most importance in Japan and personalistic patronage is strongest in the Philippines. Thailand is an intermediate case, with high levels of personalistic patronage seemingly balanced at least in part by impersonal patronage benefiting entire electoral constituencies.

Third, I have asserted the virtues of distinguishing between patronage and clientelism. Patronage is a *material resource* disbursed for particularistic benefit for political purposes and commonly (but not always) derived from public sources, whereas clientelism is a *personalistic relationship of power.* By untangling the two concepts, it is possible to give more nuance to the usual dichotomy of programmatic and particularistic. This is highlighted in the continuum above, which shades from programmatic and universal on the left through an intermediate category of "meso-particularism" (involving patronage disbursed on an impersonal basis) to "micro-particularism" (involving clientelistic or personalistic patronage) on the right. In other words, some types of particularism are more particular than others; and some types of patronage are personalistic, while others are not. By giving attention to the larger context in which patronage flows occur and more clearly distinguishing among types of patronage, we can better understand the differential impact of patronage on the territorial character of polities and on their overall quality of governance.

ACKNOWLEDGMENTS

The author is grateful to Frank Fukuyama, Larry Diamond, Diego Abente Brun, Marc Plattner, and others who provided valuable comments on this analysis when it was first presented at the NED-Grupo FARO conference in Quito in November 2010. The author has also benefited from additional comments provided while presenting this work to seminars at the University of Wisconsin Center for Southeast Asian Studies in January 2011, the Griffith University Centre for Governance and Public Policy in May 2011, and the Department of Political and Social Change at the Australian National University in August 2011. His colleagues in the Southeast Asia "money politics" project, Edward Aspinall, Allen Hicken, and Meredith Weiss, have provided much-valued encouragement, as has Donald Emmerson. Thanks also to Erik Kuhonta for his inputs on the Thailand section and to Thuy Pham and Allison Ley for their research assistance.

NOTES

1. James C. Scott, "Corruption, Machine Politics, and Political Change," *American Political Science Review* 63 (December 1969): 1151.

2. Robert D. Putnam, *Making Democracy Work: Civic Traditions in Modern Italy* (Princeton, NJ: Princeton University Press, 1993), 19.

3. One important difference in governmental structure, with implications for territorial politics to be explained below, is that Japan and Thailand have parliamentary systems and the Philippines has a presidential system.

4. These involve a diffuse secessionist movement arising within the Muslim Malay minority in southern Thailand and two major secessionist movements arising in recent decades among the diverse Muslim ethnic groups of the southern Philippines. See Joseph Chinyong Liow, "Muslim Resistance in Southern Thailand and Southern Philippines: Religion, Ideology, and Politics," *Policy Studies* 24 (East-West Center, Washington, DC, 2006). Other regional differences are also politicized in all three countries, specifically where there is a sense of marginalization within the larger polity: Okinawa in Japan, the Northeast of Thailand, and the Cordillera region in the northern Luzon mountain range of the Philippines.

5. Martin Shefter, *Political Parties and the State: The American Historical Experience* (Princeton, NJ: Princeton University Press, 1994), 283. Elsewhere, Shefter associates "collective" with orientation to public policies and/or ideology (p. 23).

6. In addition, workshop consultation with fellow scholars of Southeast Asian politics

has highlighted the degree to which patronage resources are derived not just from "public benefits" but also from private and quasi-public sources—whether it be the personal wealth of the politician and his/her supporters, earnings from kickbacks on public infrastructure projects, or profits from illicit or semi-illicit activities (e.g., gambling syndicates, prostitution rings, and drug-running, etc.). This is highlighted further in table 8.2.

7. James C. Scott, "Patron-Client Politics and Political Change in Southeast Asia," *American Political Science Review* 66 (March 1972): 93.

8. Herbert Kitschelt and Steven I. Wilkinson, eds., *Patrons, Clients, and Policies: Patterns of Democratic Accountability and Political Competition* (New York: Cambridge University Press, 2007), 7.

9. Kitschelt and Wilkinson, eds., *Patrons, Clients, and Policies,* 4–5 (emphasis added).

10. Differentiation can also be found in basic dictionary definitions. *The Concise Oxford Dictionary* defines patronage as "support or encouragement given by a patron." Neither clientelism nor clientelistic is in the *Shorter Oxford English Dictionary,* but client is defined as "One who is under the protection or patronage of another, a dependant."

11. Paul D. Hutchcroft, "Centralization and Decentralization in Administration and Politics: Assessing Territorial Dimensions of Authority and Power," *Governance* 14 (January 2001): 23–53.

12. W. G. Beasley, *The Rise of Modern Japan* (New York: St. Martin's Press, 1990), 66.

13. Beasley, *Rise of Modern Japan,* 220–21; Hitoshi Abe, Muneyuki Shindō, and Sadafumi Kawato, *The Government and Politics of Japan* (Tokyo: Tokyo University Press, 1994), 59.

14. Beasley, *Rise of Modern Japan,* 229.

15. Abe, Shindō, and Kawato, *Government and Politics of Japan,* 60.

16. Abe, Shindō, and Kawato, *Government and Politics of Japan,* 61; and Ethan Scheiner, *Democracy without Competition in Japan: Opposition Failure in a One-Party Dominant State* (New York: Cambridge University Press, 2006), 4.

17. Chalmers Johnson, "Tanaka Kakuei, Structural Corruption, and the Advent of Machine Politics in Japan," *Journal of Japanese Studies* 12 (Winter 1986): 4.

18. Haruhiro Fukui and Shigeko Fukai, "Pork Barrel Politics, Networks, and Local Economic Development in Contemporary Japan," *Asian Survey* 36 (March 1996): 278.

19. Johnson, "Tanaka Kakuei," 8; see also Fukui and Fukai, "Pork Barrel Politics," 276.

20. Fukui and Fukai, "Pork Barrel Politics," 277–78.

21. Johnson, "Tanaka Kakuei," 22.

22. Ibid., 11, 26.

23. Ibid., 4.

24. Within this system, used from 1947 to 1993, "voters were allowed to cast a single vote for a candidate in a multimember district; each multimember district typically returned three to five members to the Lower House. These votes could not be transferred to a party or to another candidate" (Carlson 2007, 4). As Rosenbluth and Thies further explain, the multi-member districts force "majority-seeking parties . . . to field multiple candidates in direct competition with one another" and "[shift] electoral competition away from programmatic appeals to personal loyalty." The LDP, by virtue of its ability to "milk [business interests] for campaign financing, was the hands-down favorite to dominate such a system" (Frances

McCall Rosenbluth and Michael F. Thies, *Japan Transformed: Political Change and Economic Restructuring* [Princeton, NJ: Princeton University Press, 2010], 176).

25. Matthew Carlson, *Money Politics in Japan: New Rules, Old Practices* (Boulder, CO.: Lynne Reinner, 2007), 5.

26. Scheiner, *Democracy without Competition in Japan,* 71.

27. Fukui and Fukai, "Pork Barrel Politics," 282.

28. While local politics in many municipalities were ostensibly nonpartisan, explains Allinson, "most local politicians, in some communities as many as 80%, were LDP supporters. They shared the party's goals, and they achieved them by supporting LDP Diet members" (1997: 95). Gary D. Allinson, *Japan's Postwar History* (Ithaca, NY: Cornell University Press, 1997).

29. Fukui and Fukai, "Pork Barrel Politics," 274.

30. Ibid., 274–75.

31. Electoral *keiretsu* (line) are essentially patron-client pyramids with a Diet member at the apex and prefectural and local officials below. "Many local politicians are former aides to Diet members," explain Fukui and Fukai, and it is also notable that "politicians elected from the same [prefectoral] district don't belong to the same Diet member's *keiretsu*" (280–81, quotes at 281).

32. Fukui and Fukai, "Pork Barrel Politics," 279.

33. Ibid., 277; see also 276–81.

34. Rosenbluth and Thies, *Japan Transformed,* 56.

35. Ibid., 56–57, 66–67.

36. Ibid., 56; see also Scheiner, *Democracy without Competition in Japan,* 73.

37. Scheiner, *Democracy without Competition in Japan,* 15.

38. Ibid., 15 and 71; see also 15–16, 70–73.

39. Gregory W. Noble, "The Decline of Particularism in Japanese Politics," *Journal of East Asian Studies* 10, no. 2 (2010): 239–74, at 243.

40. Rosenbluth and Thies, *Japan Transformed,* 135–36.

41. It is beyond the scope of this chapter, of course, to demonstrate the relative importance of these two types of patronage flow. The goal here is to establish a conceptual framework, drawing on secondary sources. Other scholars may wish to establish means of measurement based on in-depth use of primary sources.

42. Chris Baker and Pasuk Phongpaichit, *A History of Thailand* (Melbourne: Cambridge University Press, 2005), 52–58; see also Tej Bunnag, *The Provincial Administration of Siam, 1892–1915: The Ministry of the Interior under Prince Damrong Rajanubhab* (Kuala Lumpur: Oxford University Press, 1977).

43. Fred W. Riggs, *Thailand: The Modernization of a Bureaucratic Polity* (Honolulu: East-West Center Press, 1966).

44. Daniel Arghiros, "Political Reform and Civil Society at the Local Level: Thailand's Local Government Reforms," in *Reforming Thai Politics,* ed. Duncan McCargo (Copenhagen: Nordic Institute for Asian Studies, 2002), 226.

45. Ibid., 226–27.

46. Surin Maisrikrod and Duncan McCargo, "Electoral Politics: Commercialisation and Exclusion," in *Political Change in Thailand: Democracy and Participation,* ed. Kevin Hewison

(New York: Routledge, 1997), 134; and Arghiros, "Thailand's Local Government Reforms," 226.

47. Benedict Anderson, "Withdrawal Symptoms: Social and Cultural Aspects of the October 6 Coup," *Bulletin of Concerned Asian Scholars* 9 (July–September 1977): 13–30.

48. After eight years of "semi-democracy," from 1980 to 1988, the country transitioned to civilian rule in 1988. This was ended by a coup in 1991, but the resulting military regime was removed after a Bangkok-based uprising in May 1992.

49. Benedict Anderson, "Murder and Progress in Modern Siam," *New Left Review* (May/June 1990): 14 (emphasis in original).

50. Pasuk Phongpaichit and Chris Baker, *Thailand: Economy and Politics* (Oxford: Oxford University Press, 1995), 354.

51. Daniel Arghiros, *Democracy, Development and Decentralization in Provincial Thailand* (Richmond, Surrey, UK: Curzon Press, 2001), 17, 20, 166–67; and Anderson, "Murder and Progress in Modern Siam," 10.

52. John Sidel, "Bossism and Democracy in the Philippines, Thailand, and Indonesia: Towards an Alternative Framework for the Study of 'Local Strongmen,'" in John Harriss et al., eds., *Politicising Democracy: The New Local Politics of Democratisation* (Basingstoke, Hampshire, UK: Palgrave MacMillan, 2004), 59.

53. Anderson, "Murder and Progress in Modern Siam," 9.

54. Yoshinori Nishizaki, "Provincializing Thai Politics," *Kyoto Review of Southeast Asia* 1 (March 2002). Available online at http://kyotoreview.cseas.kyoto-u.ac.jp/issue/issue0/article_31.html

55. The "MP Development Fund" grew from 5 million baht per MP per year in the 1980s to 20–30 million baht after 1988 (Allen Hicken, "Constitutional Reform and Budgetary Politics in Thailand," unpublished manuscript, University of Michigan, 2011, pp. 5–6). The MP budget for projects of "rural and local development" was 1.5 million baht per MP per year in 1980 and peaked at 20 million baht in 1995 (Achakorn Wongpreedee, "Decentralization and Its Effect on Provincial Political Power in Thailand," *Asian and African Area Studies* 6, no. 2 [2007]: 454–70, at 461). Both sources note that these types of budget expenditures were prohibited by the 1997 constitution.

56. On Banharn's origins and achievements, see Yoshinori Nishizaki, "The Moral Origin of Thailand's Provincial Strongman: The Case of Banharn Silpa-archa," *South East Asia Research* 13 (2005): 184–234.

57. Allen Hicken, "The 2007 Thai Constitution: A Return to Politics Past," *Crossroads* 19 (2007): 128–59.

58. William A. Callahan and Duncan McCargo, "Vote-Buying in Thailand's Northeast: The July 1995 Election," *Asian Survey* 36 (April 1996): 378, 381.

59. Maisrikrod and McCargo, "Electoral Politics," 136, 138–39; and Arghiros, *Democracy, Development and Decentralization in Provincial Thailand*, 96–97, 190.

60. James Ockey, "The Rise of Local Power in Thailand: Provincial Crime, Elections, and the Bureaucracy," in *Money and Power in Provincial Thailand*, ed. Ruth McVey (Honolulu: University of Hawaii Press, 2000), 84.

61. One substantial diminution of the Ministry's power came with the 1997 Constitution, which transferred responsibility for electoral administration to a new Election Commission.

See Erik Martinez Kuhonta, "The Paradox of Thailand's 1997 'People's Constitution': Be Careful What You Wish For," *Asian Survey* 48, no. 3 (2008): 373–92, at 379.

62. Michael H. Nelson, *Central Authority and Local Democratization in Thailand: A Case Study from Chachoengsao Province* (Bangkok: White Lotus Press, 1998), 68.

63. While the councils had been elective since the 1950s, their role expanded after they were put in charge of a lucrative provincial development fund in the 1980s. See Katherine A. Bowie, "Vote Buying and Village Outrage in an Election in Northern Thailand: Recent Legal Reforms in Historical Context," *Journal of Asian Studies* 67, no. 2 (2008): 469–511, at 488.

64. Arghiros, *Democracy, Development and Decentralization in Provincial Thailand,* 24–25.

65. Nelson, *Central Authority and Local Democratization in Thailand,* 65–80.

66. Baker and Phongpaichit, *A History of Thailand,* 240.

67. Albeit quite imperfectly, of course, as demonstrated most dramatically by secessionist pressures in the Muslim South and deep resentments in a marginalized Northeast. In comparative perspective, however, Bangkok has had substantial success in extending its authority throughout the realm. As Arghiros asserts, "The Thai state is extremely strong and has effective reach into all provinces and districts, no matter how far they are from Bangkok" (*Democracy, Development and Decentralization,* 21). The term "extrabureaucratic networks" comes from Bowie, "Vote Buying," 488.

68. See Nishizaki, "The Moral Origin of Thailand's Provincial Strongman."

69. Baker and Phongpaichit, *A History of Thailand,* 178.

70. Ibid., 175–80, 183–83.

71. This analysis draws on Paul D. Hutchcroft, "Colonial Masters, National Politicos, and Provincial Lords: Central Authority and Local Autonomy in the American Philippines, 1900–1913," *Journal of Asian Studies* 59, no. 2 (2000), and Paul D. Hutchcroft and Joel Rocamora, "Patronage-Based Parties and the Democratic Deficit in the Philippines: Origins, Evolution, and the Imperatives of Reform," in Richard Robison, ed., *Routledge Handbook of Southeast Asian Politics* (London: Routledge, 2012).

72. Hutchcroft, "Colonial Masters, National Politicos, and Provincial Lords," 283.

73. Glenn A. May, *Social Engineering in the Philippines: The Aims, Execution, and Impact of American Colonial Policy, 1900–1913* (Quezon City, Philippines: New Day Publishers, 1984), 41.

74. Benedict Anderson, "Cacique Democracy and the Philippines: Origins and Dreams," *New Left Review* (May–June 1988): 11.

75. See Shefter (1994), who explains that the historical timing of the creation of modern bureaucracies and the emergence of mass political participation is of critical importance in determining the relative strengths of a "constituency for bureaucratic autonomy" versus a "constituency for patronage."

76. Ruby R. Paredes, "The Origins of National Politics: Taft and the Partido Federal," in Ruby R. Paredes, ed., *Philippine Colonial Democracy* (New Haven, CT: Yale University Southeast Asia Studies 1989), 60.

77. Michael Cullinane, *Ilustrado Politics: Filipino Elite Responses to American Rule, 1898–1908* (Quezon City, Philippines: Ateneo de Manila University Press, 2003).

78. Anderson, "Cacique Democracy and the Philippines," 11.

79. Hutchcroft, "Colonial Masters," 287.

80. This analysis draws on Shefter's distinction between "internally mobilized" and "externally mobilized" parties. The NP are in the former category, defined as parties "founded by elites who occupy positions within the prevailing regime and who undertake to mobilize a popular following behind themselves in an effort either to gain control of the government or to secure their hold over it" (1994, 29–36, quote at 30; see also his specific analysis of the NP on 23).

81. Stephen Skowronek, *Building a New American State: The Expansion of National Administrative Capacities, 1877–1920* (Cambridge: Cambridge University Press, 1982), 39.

82. Patricio N. Abinales, *Making Mindanao: Cotabato and Davao in the Formation of the Philippine Nation-State* (Quezon City, Philippines: Ateneo de Manila University Press, 2000), 67, 130.

83. Abinales, *Making Mindanao,* 184.

84. See Paul D. Hutchcroft, "Dreams of Redemption: Localist Strategies of Political Reform in the Philippines," in *Social Difference and Constitutionalism in Pan-Asia,* ed. Susan H. Williams (New York: Cambridge University Press, forthcoming 2014), 82–83.

85. Carl H. Landé, *Leaders, Factions, and Parties: The Structure of Philippine Politics* (New Haven, CT: Yale University Southeast Asia Studies, 1965), 24.

86. Ibid., 79, 82.

87. Indeed, "KBL" has evolved into a popular moniker for the overall system of patronage, recast as an abbreviation for three events that are commonly frequented by vote-seeking politicians: *Kasal* (wedding), *Binyag* (baptism), *Libing* (funeral).

88. Marites Dañguilan-Vitug, "Ballots and Bullets: The Military in Elections," in Lorna Kalaw-Tirol and Sheila S. Coronel, eds., *1992 and Beyond: Forces and Issues in Philippine Elections* (Quezon City: Philippine Center for Investigative Journalism and the Ateneo Center for Social Policy and Public Affairs, 1992), 90–91, quoting COMELEC Commissioner Haydee Yorac.

89. Nathan Gilbert Quimpo, "The Left, Elections, and the Political Party System in the Philippines," *Critical Asian Studies* 37 (March 2005): 4–5.

90. On the political dynamics of the passage of the law, see Paul D. Hutchcroft, "Paradoxes of Decentralization: The Political Dynamics Behind the Passage of the 1991 Local Government Code of the Philippines," in *KPI Yearbook 2003,* ed. Michael H. Nelson (Bangkok: King Prajadhipok's Institute, 2004). Unlike in Japan and Thailand, both parliamentary systems, national legislators in the Philippines' presidential system have fewer opportunities to gain power over a central ministry through the successful formation of a party faction. In the Philippines, there is relatively more focus on building up a local political bailiwick and cultivating allies at the level of the congressional district—quite commonly by trying to install one's own relatives in key local gubernatorial and mayoral positions. With the bailiwick as a foundational source of power, there is thus relatively more inclination to promote decentralization rather than grab posts in the central government. To the extent that a congressperson faces major rivals in the congressional district, however, s/he is likely to view decentralization as a threat rather than an opportunity.

91. Steven Rood, "Decentralization, Democracy, and Development," in *The Philippines: New Directions in Domestic Policy and Foreign Relations,* ed. David G. Timberman (New York: Asia Society, 1998), 118–19.

92. Aquilino Q. Pimentel Jr., "Pursuing our Collective Struggle for Local Autonomy: Amending the Local Government Code of 1991," statement delivered at the Opening Cer-

emonies of the Public Consultations on the Proposed Amendments of the Local Government Code of 1991, in San Fernando City, La Union, Philippines, August 4, 2000.

93. Hutchcroft, "Dreams of Redemption," 99–100.

94. Emmanuel S. de Dios, "Local Politics and Local Economy," in *The Dynamics of Regional Development: The Philippines in East Asia,* ed. Arsenio M. Balisacan and Hal Hill (Quezon City, Philippines: Ateneo de Manila University Press, 2007), 196. See also Paul D. Hutchcroft, "Re-Slicing the Pie of Patronage: The Politics of the Internal Revenue Allotment in the Philippines, 1991–2010," *Philippine Review of Economics* 49, no. 1 (2012): 109–34.

95. Hal Hill, Arsenio M. Balisacan, and Sharon Faye A. Piza, "The Philippines and Regional Development," in *Dynamics of Regional Development,* ed. Balisacan and Hill, 36, 47.

CHAPTER NINE

Eastern European Postcommunist Variants of Political Clientelism and Social Policy

LINDA J. COOK

Experiences with political clientelism in Eastern Europe's postcommunist states differ from those of the other regions discussed in this volume. From the end of the Second World War until 1989, Eastern Europe was governed by monopolistic communist political regimes. Authoritarian and politically stratified, these regimes featured non-competitive, ritualized elections and pervasive patronage relationships. Nevertheless, they brought to the region socioeconomic development, basic social welfare, and comparatively egalitarian income distributions. Following the collapse of communism in 1989, the region's economies were mostly privatized, inequality grew, and inherited social sectors underwent retrenchment and reform. All postcommunist states initially legalized political competition and held elections. The East-Central European (ECE) states quickly consolidated democratic institutions, while most former Soviet states relapsed into forms of electoral-authoritarianism that preserved constricted electoral competition.[1] For the first time in decades, politicians in the region had to appeal to populations for political support and compete for votes.

It might seem that this region would provide fertile ground for the development of political clientelism, particularly the exchanges of support and votes for social goods (i.e., electoral clientelism) that other chapters have described in Latin America and India. However, I will argue that this type of electoral clientelism has been limited in the postcommunist space. Rather, after the early stages of transition, these states have differentiated into three distinct categories:

1. In poor, monoindustrial, rural and isolated postcommunist spaces, including some parts of the Former Soviet Union (FSU) and Southeastern Europe, political clientelism remains common.

2. In the consolidated East Central European democracies, where most elections since 1989 have met "free and fair" criteria, levels of electoral clientelism are low.
3. In post-Soviet electoral-authoritarian regimes, elites have relied mainly on other, non-clientelistic strategies for manipulating and controlling electoral outcomes.

All three groups of states began the transition with a susceptibility to electoral clientelism because Communist political elites controlled access to all resources, including employment. As studies of early postcommunist elections have shown, when these elites first confronted electoral competition, they used such control to deliver votes to party candidates.[2] In some of the less-transformed postcommunist spaces, where local economies remain state-dominated and electorates mainly state-dependent, politicians continued to rely on such clientelistic mechanisms. However, throughout most of the region economies were privatized during the 1990s, depriving politicians of monopolistic control.

As the ECE states consolidated democracy, three sets of factors largely undermined the conditions for electoral clientelism. First, the socioeconomies of these states, already relatively developed at the end of the Communist period, grew and diversified, providing populations with resources, mobility, and opportunities that undercut demand for political clientelism among ECE electorates. Secondly, the political parties that emerged were weakly rooted in society and fluid. Most lacked the capacity to build or supply stable clientelistic networks of exchange with societal constituencies. Thirdly, in ECE states nearly universalist systems of social welfare provision had been established before the emergence of political parties and competitive elections. Professionalized welfare bureaucracies stood as obstacles to politicians who might raid the welfare state and use social benefits for electoral gain (though the much larger spoils to be had in the privatizing economies and financial sectors of these states was perhaps a more important factor here).

In the Russian Federation and other post-Soviet states that developed electoral-authoritarian regimes, politicians adopted different, perhaps more cost-effective methods of manipulating electoral outcomes. These states began and remained at lower levels of socioeconomic development than the ECE states and provided weaker political rights (see table 9.1). Here corruption of the electoral process became widespread, but mechanisms other than electoral clientelism dominate political life. Researchers and election observers have documented a multitude of methods that are used by post-Soviet governing authorities to constrict electoral choice, pressure voters, manipulate or falsify turnout and voter preferences, and so forth.[3] Discrete vote-buying and a "bread and circuses" approach to elections are also widespread,

TABLE 9.1.

Levels of socioeconomic development and democratization in postcommunist Europe

Category / country	GNI per capita (PPP, 2007)	EU accession	FH political rights scores 2008
ECE Early EU accession			
Czech Republic	22,160	May 2004	1
Hungary	17,470	May 2004	1
Poland	15,600	May 2004	1
Slovak Republic	19,220	May 2004	1
Slovenia	26,230	May 2004	1
ECE Late EU accession			
Bulgaria	10,790	January 2007	1
Romania	12,350	January 2007	2
Post-Soviet E-A			
Ukraine	6,830	Non-member	3
Russian Federation	14,330	Non-member	6
Belarus	10,790	Non-member	7

Sources: World Development Indicators (for GNI); EU Accession at www.eu.org; Freedom House at www.freedomhouse.org/template.cfm?page=363&year=2008

Note: For political rights scores: 1 = most free, 7 = least free.

but these methods usually do not entail electoral clientelism's stable exchanges or networks of relations between voters and politicians. Usually, abuse of electoral processes and control over outcomes in postcommunist electoral-authoritarian polities provide few payoffs for rank-and-file voters.

Political corruption is certainly present in postcommunist polities, but exchanges are predominantly intra-elite and largely exclude or marginalize societal actors. Corrupt exchanges are concentrated among government officials and employees in state administration. While these exchanges may have clientelistic features, they are more accurately conceptualized in the work of scholars such as Grzymala-Busse and Gimpelson, and Treisman. Grzymala-Busse characterizes corruption among ECE's political elites as "strategies of exploitation" that are distinct from electoral clientelism because they do not involve redistribution to voters. Gimpelson and Treisman write about the "fiscal games" played between Russian central and regional officials over allocations of state social and other expenditures. My research on postcommunist welfare states found patterns of heavily elite-dominated bargaining over control of social expenditures.[4] These elite strategies will be discussed toward the end of the chapter.

Table 9.2 summarizes the argument so far. The advent of democracy and elections in Eastern Europe after 1989 and the marketization of most economies produced three divergent patterns of electoral politics and clientelism across the post-

TABLE 9.2.
Socioeconomic development, democratization, and political/electoral clientelism
in postcommunist East European states

Low SES, Statist, Low Democracy	*Medium SES, Market, Low Democracy*
Outcome: High Electoral Clientelism Examples: Rural Russia, Poland SE ECE: Bulgaria Romania Albania	Outcome: Non-clientelistic electoral manipulation Examples: Former Soviet States Russian Federation Ukraine
Low SES, High Democracy (No cases)	*High SES, Market, High Democracy* Outcome: Low Electoral Clientelism Examples: ECE States Poland Hungary Czech Republic Slovenia

communist space: high electoral clientelism, high democracy, and non-clientelistic electoral manipulation. This divergence is best explained by the intersection of structural factors, primarily levels of socioeconomic development, and institutional factors, specifically levels of market transition, democratization, and political competition. Electoral or "benefit for vote" clientelism persisted in places where populations remained poor and state-dependent and politics noncompetitive, including some rural areas in Russia and Poland as well as less-developed regions in Southeast European states, that is, parts of Bulgaria and Romania (Quadrant 1). Throughout most of ECE, where levels of socioeconomic development and market transition were higher and democracy quickly became institutionalized, levels of clientelism remained low (Quadrant 4). In post-Soviet electoral-authoritarian regimes, where socioeconomic development and market transition were intermediate and political/electoral competition constricted, non-clientelistic methods of controlling and manipulating electoral outcomes came to dominate.

The chapter proceeds as follows: Part I presents a brief discussion of the concept of political clientelism, its role in the early stages of postcommunist transition, and its persistence in statist backwaters. Part II explains the limits of electoral clientelism in the ECE democratic context. Part III focuses on alternative methods of electoral manipulation in post-Soviet electoral-authoritarian polities. Part IV discusses the prevalence of intra-elite bargaining, specifically "exploitation" and "fiscal games," in postcommunist politics. The conclusion considers what broader lessons may be taken from these cases, particularly the success of ECE postcommunist states in largely escaping political clientelism.

I. Conceptualizing Clientelism and Communism

While there is no broad consensus on the meaning of political clientelism, the definition used most often, both in the political science literature and by authors in the present volume, focuses on politicians' delivery of social goods to the poor in exchange for electoral support or votes.[5] Scholars have analyzed clientelism's pre-conditions, causes, processes, and consequences for economic development, distribution of public goods, and the quality and strength of democracy. Electoral clientelism is driven by poverty and scarcity of public goods. As Auyero explains in chapter 5 of this volume, it relates to "the daily life of the dispossessed" and "to poor people's problem-solving strategies that revolve around offering votes and support." It typically relies on stable networks of asymmetric relations, established and maintained by political parties that are rooted in stable communities, with agents who can monitor clients' political behavior, ideally including their casting of ballots. Politicians, for their part, engage in clientelistic exchanges because they need constituents' support, voter turnout, and votes. While analysts recognize that electoral clientelism may contribute to some increase in welfare provision, its effects are judged to be largely negative. According to Susan Stokes, writing in the authoritative *Oxford Handbook of Comparative Politics,* most scholars take the view that "political clientelism . . . slows economic development by discouraging governments from providing public goods and by creating an interest in ongoing poverty and dependency of constituents. . . . It vitiates democracy by undermining the equality of the ballot . . . it keeps dictators in power by allowing them to stage elections in which competition is stifled."[6]

The concept of political clientelism set out in this volume's introduction is broader and includes provision of preferential access to, or exchange of, excludable public goods as part of a stable network of asymmetric relationships that are intended to affect political choices and behavior.

Under this definition, clientelism does not require a context of competitive elections; it can function in conditions of concentrated political power, absence of democracy, or weakness of formal political competition. This conception of clientelism is perhaps most broadly specified by Nicolas van de Walle in chapter 10 of this volume as "the discretionary use of state resources and authority for political ends, insofar as the primary objective of actors is control of the state and its resources." This broader type of political clientelism is well illustrated in van de Walle's pre-1989 African cases, where it supports corrupt and autocratic polities while also serving to promote cross-ethnic elite accommodation.

Under such a broad definition, communist-era political economies qualify as clientelistic, particularly at the elite level. The state controlled all employment. Every position carrying status and authority required Communist Party membership and was formally subject to a political loyalty test through the *nomenklatura* system. The primary goal of the party-state elite was to buy and enforce political loyalty by controlling and manipulating access to jobs, goods, and services. Access was stratified according to individuals' and groups' political status and importance to the state, and a system of ethnic balancing of political elites was used to promote inter-ethnic accommodation.

While communist administrative and professional elites were subject to strict political demands in exchange for their positions and privileges, this was less the case for society below the elite level. Electoral mobilization and turnout, particularly in rural areas and in the many single-industry cities and towns, had a clientelistic aspect, but benefits were generally non-excludable, distributed to collective farms and massive enterprises as guaranteed state support. Reliance on connections, corruption, bribes, and side payments to obtain goods and services was pervasive in communist societies, including in the social sector (such as gratuity payments to medical personnel). Such exchanges were, however, primarily the products of shortage economies with prices set below market-clearing levels, low wages, and broad cynicism, rather than of electoral politics or competition. Overall, then, the more specific concept of electoral clientelism as an exchange of excludable goods for votes between political elites and constituents provides limited analytical leverage in understanding communist polities. Significantly for the analysis here, the majority of those in employed in low-status, low-paid health and education sectors, the social sector workers who are often enmeshed in clientelistic networks in the other cases, were less subject to political demands as a condition for employment, and more to requirements for formal education and professional qualifications.

Electoral Clientelism in the Early Postcommunism and Regions with Persistent Underdevelopment

A number of studies have found evidence of electoral clientelism—stable networks of "benefit for vote" exchanges between politicians and constituents—in elections during the early postcommunist period, and more persistently in regions and states that retain strong elements of state-dominated political economies. In the first republic-level Gorbachev-era (1990) competitive elections (in what was then still the Soviet Union), managers of large enterprises and agricultural collectives delivered their workers' votes to communist candidates, who promised to preserve socialist job security and welfare. Market-oriented reformers, who threatened workers' security, made inroads mainly in major urban areas. Old communist elites, facing electoral competition for the first time, adapted to the rules of competitive politics by developing clientelistic electoral strategies, using control over jobs and benefits to mobilize constituents for the party's candidates, especially where they could monitor voting. According to one study, it was easier to "get the vote out" in the rural areas where the boundaries of electoral districts and workplaces (collective and state farms) were by and large the same.[7] Such strategies continued to be used effectively in rural and other less-developed regions through the early 1990s. Other fraudulent electoral practices were also used, but leaders in rural regions were able to rely mainly on their state-dependent workers to control electoral outcomes.[8]

Studies of politics in the poorest regions of Russia and ECE show that electoral clientelism survived well into the postcommunist period. These ECE regions, found mainly in Southeastern Europe, feature less-educated electorates that are often distinct from the region's dominant ethnicity and retain strong neo-patrimonial features.[9] A study of electoral politics in Albania, the poorest of the ECE postcommunist states, for example, shows that constituents in the north and south of the country engage in clientelistic voting, as demonstrated by their strong attachment to regionally based, ethnically identified parties regardless of those parties' performance in office. The study's authors conclude that long-established informal institutions of clientelism "in the democratic era has taken the form of clientelistic voting."[10] Similar clientelistic practices persisted in rural areas of Poland and Russia, under the auspices of the Polish Peasant Party and Russia's Agrarian Party, and in single-industry towns. Henry Hale's comparative study of Russia's gubernatorial elections throughout the 1990s showed that politicians disproportionately controlled constituents' votes through clientelistic linkages in regions that had low levels of economic development and political competition as well as strong ethno-cultural networks. Most of these regions were agricultural or relied on a single industry or enterprise, with "clientelistic forms of linkage strongest in Russia's remote rural regions."[11]

Hale's analysis of the Russian case provides insights into both the potential strength and the weakness of electoral clientelism in specific postcommunist contexts. His research shows that, where the Russian state continued to control, supply, and subsidize collective farms and massive industrial enterprises that dominated communities, farm chairmen and enterprise managers acted as political brokers.

With strong community roots, they were able to distribute goods and monitor voters' compliance. Hale concludes: "Greater effective state control over key economic resources facilitates strong clientelistic linkages between politicians and voters. . . . The greatest divergence among postcommunist countries/in levels of clientelism/ in the shorter run is likely to involve variation in levels of political competitiveness and control over political economy. . . . Those that adopt market-oriented reforms are likely to dismantle the fonts of clientelism in transition."[12]

II. East-Central Europe's Democracies: Escaping Electoral Clientelism

As noted at the beginning of this chapter, three sets of structural and institutional factors militated against clientelistic linkages between emerging political parties and electorates in postcommunist ECE states. First, successful economic development progressively undermined the conditions for clientelism. As ECE postcommunist governments privatized and established diversified market economies, structures of statist economic control and local monitoring broke down. As Hale expected, these changes effectively dismantled the "fonts of clientelism" in the more developed, democratized states. Especially in Poland, Hungary, the Czech Republic, and Slovenia, relatively high levels of per capita GNP, rapid privatization, and early integration into the European Union (see table 9.1) created electorates that are well educated, substantially middle class, and mobile, with access to diverse private sectors and relatively adequate supplies of public goods. ECE electorates are, in sum, comparatively well equipped materially and intellectually. In the terms of Andrew Roberts, a scholar of voting behavior in the region, the "level of material security gives citizens the ability to resist clientelistic appeals based on vote-buying."[13] While socially weak groups that might be vulnerable to selling their votes are certainly present, relatively egalitarian income distributions in these states limited poverty, especially after the early 1990s.[14] It is also the case that the most dispossessed groups, those who typically populate clientelistic networks elsewhere, are in ECE comprised mainly of ethnic Roma and other transient populations that are largely demobilized and ignored by political parties.[15]

Secondly, ECE political parties are neither structured nor positioned to supply clientelistic institutions. That is, these parties generally lack the organizational capacity to either maintain clientelism's stable networks of asymmetric dyadic relationships or monitor constituents' political behavior. Most parties either formed after 1989 or were revived from the pre–World War II period after lying dormant for decades. The long period of suppression of political parties under communism, followed by rapid transitions to democracy after 1989, left parties without deep roots or links to their societies. Communist Parties (CPs) that successfully reformed in social-democratic directions, such as the Democratic Left Alliance in Poland and the Socialist Party in Hungary, soon declined and lost support, while CPs that remained hard-left withered. New parties, as well as those revived from the interwar period, frequently fragmented or disappeared, rendering most of them too unstable or ephemeral to credibly commit to the particularistic exchanges or contracts that clientelism entails.[16] In sum, incumbents generally lacked partisan political machines that would allow them to monitor the electoral behavior of constituents.

Commensurately, postcommunist ECE electorates have remained extremely volatile regarding their partisan preferences. Even twenty years after communism's collapse, electorates are still fluid and politically unattached, with only about 2% on average identifying as members of any party.[17] In addition, ECE parties emerged (or re-emerged) primarily in well-educated, urbanized, economically complex societies, where vote-buying would likely be expensive and illegitimate. As Anna Grzymala-Busse, a prominent scholar of the region concludes, given these conditions, politicians "offering selective goods to supporters is inefficient and implausible."[18]

Research on public preferences and voters' behavior in ECE states confirms the relatively low significance of electoral clientelism. In a recent empirical study of postcommunist elections in the Czech Republic, Hungary, and Poland, for example, Andrew Roberts shows that voters judge officials and reward or punish them at the polls on the basis of these officials' policy performance in office. Though ECE parties generally do not articulate clear programmatic alternatives among which voters can choose before elections, voters hold parties and politicians accountable for their policy successes and failures in office. Roberts presents compelling evidence that ECE voters are well informed about politics, that public opinion surveys accurately predict votes, and that politicians pay attention to these surveys when making policy decisions even between elections. In a study of 34 elections across 10 ECE states from 1994 to 2004, he found that incumbents were consistently held accountable for economic performance, especially unemployment.[19] Public opinion surveys also show that corruption is viewed as illegitimate by large majorities,[20] while Robert's review of 28 ECE election reports in *Election Studies* found that 14 had listed corruption as a major issue. There is, in Roberts's terms, a substantial "degree of agency among citizens, a capacity to understand politics and to act on their understanding. Vote shares of governments are highly affected by their economic performance. . . . This result counters some of the pessimism about the quality of new democracies. If politicians are being held accountable . . . they have strong incentives to deliver good economic policies."[21] ECE electorates, in short, have the "structural capacity" to effectively hold politicians accountable.

Moreover, ECE politicians strongly fear "electoral retribution" from these citizens. The frequent defeats and implosions of parties and coalitions in these states speak to the degree and effectiveness of public dissatisfaction, which is partially directed at high levels of corruption among political and economic elites (much of it linked to the privatization processes). The continuing instability and volatility of both parties and electorates and the broad popular disapproval of corruption should prove inimical to clientelism In sum, clientelistic exchanges between parties and electorates appear to play a limited role in ECE polities.

A third set of factors distinguishes postcommunist ECE from regions of high clientelism considered in this volume: the social sectors of postcommunist states were extensively developed and institutionalized before the transition to democracy.[22] At first consideration, it might seem that state control over a large pool of social resources—public employment, social transfers, placements in schools and universities, and so forth—would lend itself to clientelistic exchanges. There is evidence, however, that the size, high level of professionalization, and structure of inherited welfare states has impeded development of clientelistic strategies. Benefits in communist-era welfare states were poor but broadly distributed, with provision of pensions, child payments, basic health care, and education approaching universalism. Very few benefit programs were means-tested, and while access was stratified by political status, social position, and place of residence, by the end of the communist era no social group was excluded.[23] Moreover, very high percentages of electorates continued to hold their governments responsible for social security and provision well into the postcommunist period; public expectations of clean, effective, broadly distributive welfare programs were high.[24]

Haggard and Kaufman's (2008) major comparative study of Asian, Latin American, and ECE welfare states shows that ECE public welfare sectors were far broader in coverage and better financed than those in Latin America (or East Asia) at similar periods and levels of development (see table 9.3).[25] In terms of coverage, most Latin American welfare states concentrated benefits on civil servants and urban workers in the formal state sector. Benefit coverage generally excluded the urban poor and much of the rural population. In fact, the recent extension of benefit programs to these poorer strata in Latin America and the use of means-testing and conditional cash-transfer programs have contributed to the growth of clientelism in the region. Though there was great social need in postcommunist societies, especially outside the developed ECE states, the universalist structure and program design of inherited

TABLE 9.3.

Total Social Security, education, and health spending as percentage of GDP for ECE states (1990), Latin America (1976–1980), and the Soviet Union (1976)

	Social security	Health	Education	Total government spending
ECE States				
Poland	20.7%	4.0%	3.5%	39.7%
Hungary	14.9	4.1	1.7	49.8
Czechoslovakia	9.9	n/a	4.1	36.1
Romania	10.6	2.9	0.9	33.5
Bulgaria	12.1	0.9	1.3	42.2
ECE Average	13.6	4.4	2.3	40.3
Soviet Union	15.6	2.6	3.7	—
Latin American* Average	4.9	1.4	3.4	22.0

Source: Haggard and Kaufman 2008, 29; Kornai, *Socialist System* (1992), 314.

*Latin America = Argentina, Brazil, Chile, Columbia, Costa Rica, Mexico, Peru, Uruguay, Venezuela

welfare programs left them much less susceptible to the kinds of parcelization and discretionary distribution that are found prominently in studies of clientelism in Latin America, India, and elsewhere.[26]

Finally, postcommunist welfare programs and benefits were administered by professional bureaucracies that had long been staffed mainly on the basis of educational qualifications. A landmark study by Tomas Inglot (2007) showed that although ECE welfare states often developed in response to emergencies, administration was professionalized and routinized, and entrenched practices carried over into the postcommunist period in a path-dependent fashion.[27] Professionalization stood as a barrier to political colonization of social sectors. Similarly, in his study of patronage-based "runaway state building" in ECE, Conor O'Dwyer found that while political patronage was rampant in state administration, there was much less such patronage in the social sector. O'Dwyer concluded from interview evidence that "Welfare agencies . . . were less directly linked to the *nomenklatura* system. Moreover, even lower-level positions in the welfare system—such as nurses and teachers—require more specialized knowledge and professional expertise than those in administration, which serves as a barrier to patronage."[28] O'Dwyer concluded that patronage relations were not absent from the social sector, but less common than in other sectors of state administration. In addition, strong specialized state-bureaucratic institutions such as pension funds and public health administrations fought to preserve their control over financing and distribution of most entitlement programs in the postcommunist period.

One might still puzzle over the apparent limits of ECE politicians' efforts to use these large inherited social programs for electoral gain. Inherited universalist systems came under intense financial and ideological pressures for retrenchment and liberalization in the postcommunist period. Social expenditures were cut back, and some programs, especially family and poverty benefits, were subject to means tests and targeted to the poor. Why didn't ECE politicians try to gain control over distribution in these programs and use them to trade benefits for electoral support as many have done in Latin America and elsewhere?

First, the universalist inheritance itself proved a serious obstacle. In Latin America and Africa, means-tested antipoverty programs that have been established over the past two decades usually extend state welfare benefits to previously excluded groups. In the ECE context, means-testing almost always meant restricting established benefits, that is, cutting out previously included groups. Such cuts are seldom popular with voters, and politicians often resisted cuts of long-established benefits that could antagonize pensioners and other constituents. Despite their commitment to market reforms and welfare retrenchment, for example, Poland's Democratic Left Alliance legislated a massive expansion of the pension system to new categories of beneficiaries. The center-right Hungarian Democratic Forum, which won the 1990 election on a strongly pro-market program, substantially increased spending on universalist family benefit programs.[29] In fact, my field interview revealed that means-testing was mostly championed but by technocratic specialists who were committed to poverty relief, and supported by international financial institutions such as the World Bank. Politicians were more often interested in resisting retrenchment, which could be politically costly. Reformed, means-tested programs were in some cases (i.e., child benefits in Hungary) returned to universalism by decisions of courts and legislatures, because means-testing violated established norms and legal entitlements.[30]

Secondly, politicians would have had difficulty politicizing and parcelizing welfare states because social sector bureaucrats and professionals *did* seriously fight to retain control over budgets and policy. In practice, those fights were mainly with finance and economic development ministry officials who wanted to privatize programs and create social security markets, rather than with politicians. And the most intense were over pension funds, the "big prize" of the inherited social security systems, mostly earned-entitlement programs that could not have been subjected to means-testing. In Russia these struggles were largely intra-elite; in ECE participation was broader, including representatives of political parties, labor unions, professional groups, and societal constituencies. Overall, though, welfare politics were dominated by officials from social sector funds and social and economic ministries. Another aspect of the opportunity structure in postcommunist polities may also have mattered here. Economic privatization and marketization were ongoing during this period, and the big spoils were to be had in these states' production and finance sectors. Indeed, that is where analysts such as Grzymala-Busse, Treisman, and others find corruption to be concentrated (see below). Perhaps it was so much more lucrative to raid other sectors of the economy that the resources of the professionalized, bureaucratized social sector were not worth the fight for most politicians.

III. Controlling Electoral Outcomes in Post-Soviet Electoral-Authoritarian Polities

Like their ECE counterparts, post-Soviet states experienced democratic moments in the early 1990s, but from the outset most were dominated by strong executives and failed to consolidate democratic institutions. Open and fair competitive elections had ended by 2000, in many cases sooner. Most post-Soviet states evolved into various types of semi-authoritarian or electoral-authoritarian regimes that continue to hold elections but under very restrictive conditions.[31] "Parties of power," which depend on the political executive and administrative resources of the state, dominate electoral-authoritarian (E-A) regimes. Though weakly linked to mass societal constituencies, these parties often succeed in winning large electoral majorities in successive elections. Candidates make few commitments to societal constituents, either programmatic or clientelistic; instead, authorities rely on a range of formal-legal rules and informal-corrupt practices to limit competition and to control electoral outcomes. These typically include manipulating electoral rules to limit competition, directing media and administrative resources to candidates favored by the authorities, and/or simply falsifying ballot counts in elections. Clientelistic practices are present, but play a relatively minor role. While the specific political arrangements of post-Soviet E-A regimes vary, the Russian Federation is the most important and will serve as a representative case of this type of political system.

In Russia, the competitive electoral arena of the 1990s had given way by 2000 to the dominance of a single "party of power," United Russia, which is subordinate to the presidential administration and until 2011 won increasing majorities in the national legislature (Duma).[32] The consolidation of United Russia's electoral and legislative dominance was accomplished by a variety of means, including changes in electoral rules that favor the ruling group, manipulation of mass media, arbitrary disqualification of non–United Russia candidates, persecution of business elites who used their resources to support non-UR candidates, and a variety of procedural irregularities before, during, and after elections.[33] Though United Russia enjoyed broad and genuine popularity in its early years, in part because it and President / Prime Minister Vladimir Putin governed during a long period of strong economic recovery and growth, the party has developed other mechanisms to maintain political control. According to Grigorii Golosov, a prominent expert on Russia's electoral politics,

> The United Russia "party of power" . . . in the past gained support by providing the voters with a constantly rising standard of living, now [i.e., after the 2008 recession] it must rely on a new mechanism. The components of this political system include limited competition among a small number of political parties, falsification of results when necessary, placing the regional election commissions under the regional leaders . . . governors have built up political machines to ensure sufficient turnout to demonstrate the population's loyalty to the authorities. These machines operate through the regional media, material enticements, and election day entertainment at the polls.[34]

Of these mechanisms, the last two may be considered in some measure clientelistic, and I will return to them below. The majority, however, entail political authorities' efforts to restrict voters' choice of candidates, manipulate electoral processes, or falsify outcomes. They are designed to limit, distort, or falsify voters' preferences rather than to bribe or incentivize constituents. Unlike clientelism, these mechanisms do not rely on exchange with constituents to influence electoral outcomes.[35]

Reports by election observers as well as forensic statistical analyses of Russian and other E-A elections show the systematic falsification of turnouts and outcomes in recent years and increases in blatant forms of electoral fraud such as ballot-box stuffing and misreporting results. The OSCE and other election monitoring organizations assert that misconduct has worsened during the postcommunist period and effectively gave up efforts to monitor Russian elections after 2007 because of conflicts with Russian authorities and obstruction of observer missions. Some official election reports strain credulity. In the mountainous, conflict-ridden republics of the Caucasus, where evidence of anti-Moscow political sentiments is strong, for example, official turnout is regularly reported at more than 90%, while a Russian journalist familiar with the region estimates actual turnout at about 5%.[36] One fairly typical recent survey showed that a plurality of respondents throughout Russia felt alienated from politics, were pessimistic about the possibility of influencing decision making, and believed that ordinary Russians had no mechanism to exercise control over national politics.[37]

Forensic statistical analyses of Russian elections over the postcommunist period confirm evidence of substantial and growing fraud. One authoritative study concludes that electoral fraud, though present to a limited extent in the mid-1990s, increased significantly after 2003 and spread to regions that previously had little such experience. In the metaphor used by the authors of the study, fraud "metastasized across the country" to affect many regions (*oblasts*) during Putin's second presidential term.[38] Statistical analyses indicate manipulation of electoral registers, including stuffing them with "dead souls" (i.e., improbable or impossible increases in the number of registered voters in districts that strongly supported incumbents). Statistically abnormal distributions of turnout, consistently stronger support for incumbents in high-turnout districts, and numerical patterns that signify "rounding up" of vote tallies without regard to actual cast ballots, all indicate large-scale falsification. It is estimated that these methods affected millions of votes by 2007–2008 and helped to deliver a super-majority to United Russia in the federal legislature as well as a majority in 81 of 83 regional legislatures.[39] Electoral fraud and manipulation in Russia do not appear to be closely controlled by Moscow; rather, elections may constitute a competition in which governors manufacture results in order to demonstrate their loyalty to the federal center.[40] Varying combinations of methods are used in different regions. Similar, and in some cases more egregious, distortions in electoral practice are present in the politics of other post-Soviet E-A regimes.[41]

Vote-buying with rewards, bribes, or pay-offs to constituents is also used to motivate turnout and influence voters' electoral choices in Russia. Such cases have been described by both analysts and OSCE election monitoring missions. The most commonly reported involve one-time, election-day incentives to come to the polls or vote for a particular candidate—money, buffets, entertainment for adults and children, lotteries, or small consumer goods given out at polling places. In some cases selected categories of voters, such as state and municipal employees and pensioners, receive gifts or groceries at polling places. These practices are in part holdovers from the Soviet period, which featured ceremonial and festive elections, although use of such incentives is reported to be growing.[42] No broadly representative data on their incidence is available, and reports present divergent pictures. A detailed 2008 Golos Election Monitoring Report covering five diverse regions and districts, for example, found voter bribery to be one of the less frequent violations, well behind violations of rights and voting procedures, pressure on voters, fraud, and illegal campaigning. By contrast, a well-informed observer of the 2009 regional elections reported that the provision of goods and entertainment at the polls had become "a central form of turning out the vote."[43] While politicians distributing money or goods conforms to the clientelistic model in exchanging tangible, excludable benefits for votes, it does not involve sustained connections between voters and candidates or parties (as described in OSCE reports), nor do such handouts appear to be connected to formal social sector programs or access to services.

Finally, with the 2008 economic downturn evidence emerged of growing pressures—both in the general population and among public sector workers—to actively support and deliver votes for United Russia. There were an increasing number of reports of constituents being "pressured" to vote by their managers, supervisors, and other authority figures. In various polls, between 2 and 17% of respondents reported being subjected to some type of election-related pressures, including by representatives of local administrations, workplace managers, election commissions, or other officials bribing or threatening them to participate.[44] Sources report instances of work collectives being required to cast ballots inside their factories or to provide cell-phone pictures of their completed ballots to managers.

It remains uncertain whether Russia's social sectors are becoming explicitly politicized and to what extent appointed and tenured professional positions now depend on political support for United Russia at both the federal and regional levels. Some analysts assert that politicians colonized education and health professions with political appointees beginning in the early 1990s, but evidence for this claim is limited and indirect, and as in ECE, the effects appear to be much smaller for social sector workers than for state administrators.[45] In recent elections, though, there is at least anecdotal evidence of social service professionals being pulled into political machines that systematically support and mobilize on behalf of the "party of power." Administrators of medical facilities are reportedly responsible to local administrations for "delivering" the votes of those employed in their clinics and hospitals. University students are pressured by administrators to vote and support United Russia. The most detailed account of such mobilization is provided by Grigorii Golosov's study of the 2009 regional elections, which described the role of public sector employees:

> Their importance for the political machines is not only in their own votes, but in their ability to convince large groups of others to participate in the elections (and vote for United Russia). In schools, this campaigning takes place at parent meetings, through personal contacts with the parents, and especially by telephone. The practice of having class leaders systematically and repeatedly call parents on election day, summoning them to vote, has become widespread. It is well known that in hospitals, there is almost 100 percent participation in elections and 100

percent support for United Russia. . . . Most of these machines are relatively new
. . . they were first widely tested in the 2007 Duma elections and brought to full
force only in the 2008 presidential elections.[46]

Electoral clientelism, as we have seen in Latin America, India, and elsewhere,
is driven by politicians' needs to generate political support, electoral turnout, and
votes. In Russia and other E-A polities, I have presented evidence that efforts to influence voters' behavior and choices through clientelistic exchanges constitute only
one of many methods used to control election outcomes. Other types of electoral
manipulation and outright falsification dominate. Some analysts see this behavior as
strongly influenced by the Soviet inheritance, with elites seeking to manipulate elections, "min[ing] their institutional heritage and exploit[ing] familiar practices."[47]
It is also easier and cheaper to manipulate and falsify outcomes, if the political
and institutional context allows, than to influence or incentivize voters. In more
democratic, competitive, law-governed polities, such corrupt methods could not
proliferate. In E-A political systems there are no effective legal disincentives against
committing fraud. Many of the methods used simply marginalize voters rather than
involve them in exchanges. There may be systemic internal pressures in E-A systems
to develop clientelistic networks, particularly among public sector workers, as a
hedge against declining political support or to maintain acquiescence. This question
merits further research.

IV. Beyond Clientelism: Postcommunist Elites, Exploitation, and Fiscal Games

I have argued that clientelism, especially electoral clientelism, has not become a
dominant political strategy in postcommunist polities. This is not to deny, however,
that levels of corruption in postcommunist states are extremely high, both as measured in international comparative terms and as perceived by the region's electorates.
Much of the corrupt exchange, however, takes place among political, economic, and
bureaucratic-administrative elites. In postcommunist cases, state (or party-state)
and economic modernization preceded the emergence of competitive political parties. This sequence affected the development of postcommunist political exchange.
The expansive state-administrative apparatuses inherited from the communist era
provided abundant opportunities for political elites' patronage, rent-seeking, exploitation, and further expansion of state-administration. This sequence also set the
stage for the massive postcommunist privatizations of state-owned property, which
provided vast opportunities for elites' corruption and misuse of political authority.

Political corruption less frequently reached social sector professionals or involved exchanges with electoral constituents. Several social scientists have developed conceptual categories for the intra-elite bargaining and corrupt networks in these politics and usefully distinguished this behavior from clientelism.

In her major study of ECE's postcommunist politics, Anna Grzymala-Busse argues that politicians in the region have mainly pursued strategies of "exploitation," in which they appropriate resources from the state and keep these resources within the political-administrative elite. This behavior is distinct from clientelism in that elected officials do not distribute to constituents in exchange for political support. In Grzymala-Busse's analysis, politicians who win competitive ECE elections extract resources from the state for their own (political and personal) uses. Voters receive few or no selective goods. According to her argument, the weak supply of electoral clientelism's conditions discourages strategies of exchange with voters and encourages parties to try to win and retain office while extracting as much as possible from the state and distributing it narrowly. Political competition, which includes the risk of losing office through poor policy performance or corruption scandals, sets limits to the extent of politicians' exploitation of state resources. She notes that exploitation is "most likely in new democracies where parties arise in an age of mass media versus mobilization and organizational investments, and voter loyalties and party identities are fluid."[48] The salience of corruption as an election issue and source of voter dissatisfaction in ECE states, discussed earlier, complements this claim of pervasive exploitation by political elites. This overall political picture buttresses Grzymala-Busse's argument that the concept of clientelism does not fit well the political realities of ECE, that is, that politicians exploit and hoard state resources rather than engaging in clientelistic exchanges for voters' support.

Grzymala-Busse's arguments find resonance in the research of other scholars. Several find that official corruption has very high salience as an electoral issue in the region. Vladimir Gimpelson and Daniel Treisman find a related strategy of "fiscal games" as a major form of bargaining and exchange between central and regional political elites in Russia. The authors claim that once elected, politicians colonize state and public administration with their clients and that Russian regional authorities over-expanded public sectors to pressure Moscow for transfers of funds. Over-expansion contributed systematically to wage arrears and often provoked public sector strikes, especially in education. Regional authorities were willing to risk strikes as part of their "fiscal game" to pressure the center for additional transfers of social funds. Even when additional transfers came from central authorities, as they usually did, only part went to pay down wage arrears. In Gimpelson and Treisman's view, public sector workers serve as clients but also as pawns in a game between regional and central political authorities, often remaining unpaid for extended periods as part of a bargaining strategy in which they have little agency or rights of exchange. As in ECE, exchanges are concentrated at the elite level.[49]

My research on postcommunist welfare state politics also shows widespread domination by state and social sector elites. The politics of social sector reform in Russia and other post-Soviet states show a pattern of intra-elite bargaining in which social ministries, national pension fund managers, university rectors, health sector administrators, and others have sought to preserve and expand allocations, institutions, and staffing levels in their sectors in order to maintain their own control over resources, and the resulting political influence.[50] Clientelistic distribution at local and regional levels may well have taken place, with some of these social goods reaching the population in the form of jobs, benefits, and services, but not as part of a structured exchange between political elites and constituents.

The work that comes closest to a clientelistic interpretation of postcommunist politics is Conor O'Dwyer's *Runaway State Building* (2006). While he does not use the language of clientelism, O'Dwyer argues that ECE polities experienced explosive patronage-based administrative growth in the postcommunist period and provides compelling evidence of such expansion for selected cases. However, both O'Dwyer (for ECE) and Treisman and Gimpelson (for Russia) claim that most of this patronage did not take the form of clientelistic colonization of public or social sectors. O'Dwyer's interviews showed that the professionalization of the social sector insulated it from the rapid patronage-based turnover that affected much of ECE state administration. Gimpelson and Treisman's data likewise show that most of the clientelistic expansion of Russian regional governments took place in the administrative sector, and much less in the social sector.[51] In sum, the politicization of public sector employment and distribution of social benefits that characterize clientelism in Latin America and South Asia is less present in postcommunist states, while corruption and patronage developed differently and became more elitist in form.

Conclusion: Lessons and Comparative Implications

My chapter examines the utility of the "political clientelism" framework for understanding politics and social policy in the postcommunist states of East Central Europe and Russia. I conclude that, except for some poorly developed regions, electoral clientelism has not played a major role in either the relatively affluent postcommunist democracies of East Central Europe or in the poorer, electoral-authoritarian post-Soviet states, of which Russia serves as a representative case.

Three main sets of conditions militate against the development of electoral clientelism in most ECE states. First, electorates are predominantly middle-class, educated, and mobile. They have access to diverse economic opportunities and relatively adequate supplies of public goods. Electorates are informed about politics, broadly politically competent, and hold parties responsible for their policies and performance in office. Voters generally disapprove of corruption and punish politicians for both policy failures (particularly high unemployment) and egregious corruption. These factors, taken together, limit electorates' need or demand for, and tolerance of, electoral clientelism. Secondly, ECE political parties are shallowly rooted, unstable, and lack the organizational means to monitor electoral clients. In sum, they have weak capacities to supply clientelistic institutions. Finally, inherited universalist, professionalized, and bureaucratized welfare states proved difficult to parcelize and politicize; professionals and bureaucrats stood in the way, and means-testing reforms required politically unpopular claw-backs of previously universal benefits.

Post-Soviet states are governed by strong executives and "parties of power" that are supported by state-administrative resources. These parties—United Russia is taken here as the representative case—use and abuse various formal rules and informal mechanisms and administrative resources to control electoral outcomes. Political authorities systematically falsify voter lists and statistics on electoral turnout as well as outcomes. Voters face increasingly limited choices, lack the means to hold politicians accountable, and receive little in exchange for their electoral participation. There is some recent evidence of bribery and pressure or coercive mobilization, including the use of social sector workers and administrators for partisan electoral mobilization. This may indicate a tendency for electoral-authoritarian systems to build clientelistic networks as they age or face declining performance. It is too early to tell.

The postcommunist cases can be usefully compared with the Latin American cases in which electoral clientelism is much more evident. Several features of Latin American societies, polities, and welfare states distinguish them from the postcommunist regions and supply the conditions for electoral clientelism. First, most Latin American societies have substantially lower levels of socioeconomic development, education, and basic welfare than the postcommunist cases (see table 9.3). Levels of inequality are higher, middle classes smaller, and severe poverty and social exclusion more common in both rural and urban areas. These conditions produce a large supply of potential clients—voters who confront the poverty, basic need, and limited opportunity that can make selling one's vote a good option. Secondly, because Latin America has weaker authoritarian legacies, its re-democratizing states inherited more intact party systems, and the transition to democracy was less wrenching than in the postcommunist states. These parties had organizations that could penetrate and monitor localized constituencies, and those constituencies were relatively more stable, locally oriented, and available for mobilization than their postcommunist counterparts. Finally, Latin American welfare states were much more limited in scope; they concentrated benefits on civil servants and urban workers in the formal sector and excluded poorer rural and urban strata. Clientelistic politicians could build support by including these strata selectively in new welfare programs, particularly conditional cash transfer programs, and colonizing expanding public sectors. By contrast, in the postcommunist context the extensive development, routinization, and professionalization of inherited welfare states has limited the political colonization of social sectors, which were in any case contracting during democratization.

The contrast of the institutionalized, universalistic Chilean welfare state with the Argentinean system presented in this volume by Calvo and Murillo and Luna and Mardones, respectively, are relevant and instructive here.[52] In the Chilean case, institutional constraints, voters' distributive expectations, and program design all contributed to the maintenance of relatively "clean" social programs. According to Calvo and Murillo (chap. 1), in Chile, social benefit distribution was carried out by bureaucratic agencies with civil service rules, in contrast to Argentina, where there were limited institutional constraints over discretion in delivery of publicly financed private goods and use of political networks for their delivery. Furthermore, according to Luna and Mardones (chap. 2), the amount of discretionary spending available to incumbents is a function of each program's design, which shapes capacity to allocate and oversee allocation. Distributive expectations, particularly universalism, also contribute to politicians' behavior. Some political targeting takes place even in "clean" systems such as Chile, but the degree of political distortion is much lower, resonating with the arguments of O'Dwyer and others concerning postcommunist systems.

Can the ECE cases, as new democracies that largely "escaped" electoral clientelism, tell us anything about how to keep clientelism from developing in other new democracies? This is a complex question, because several sets of factors mattered in ECE: high levels of socioeconomic development and growth that undermined societal demand for clientelistic benefits; weakly rooted, unstable political parties that lacked the capacity to supply clientelistic networks; and inherited universalistic welfare states that were resistant to politicization and parcelization. However, the significance of these different factors can be distinguished. The institutional factors here are relatively malleable—at least hypothetically, stronger parties might have been built, and welfare policies targeted, if politicians' incentives to supply clientelism had been stronger. It is the structural factors producing weak "demand" from electorates for clientelistic benefits that matter most. The requirement here is not just for economic growth, but for socioeconomic development that produces high levels of literacy, numeracy, education, economic opportunities, and social inclusion as well as relative freedom from basic needs. Such an outcome is, necessarily, the product of a long-term development program. If and when societies experience such development, both demand for, and supply of, clientelism are likely to decline.

It should be clear from this chapter that comparatively low levels of electoral clientelism in ECE do not translate into high-quality democracy. As noted above, levels of economic and political corruption have remained quite high, with periodic scandals bringing down governments and undermining public confidence. The instability of political parties and the weakness of their links to the electorate are also problematic for democracy. Electorates cannot rely on parties to articulate coherent programs or represent societal interests. Nevertheless, ECE politics hold critical advantages over highly clientelistic ones. In ECE the political arena remains open and competitive, and electorates can use the ballot to hold political officials and parties accountable for their performance in office.[53] Electorates can place some limits on the degree of governmental corruption and failure and can reward or punish as competent voters with informed opinions. These polities come much closer to maintaining the equality and integrity of the ballot, giving politicians incentives to promote development and provide public goods, and preventing concentrations of political power. Perhaps electoral-authoritarian polities, which regularly corrupt and falsify elections without involving voters in even clientelistic exchanges, provide the least benefit to their voters.

ACKNOWLEDGMENTS

The author thanks the participants in the Conference on Political Clientelism, Social Policy, and the Quality of Democracy: Evidence from Latin America, Lessons from Other Regions, in Quito, Ecuador, October 2012, as well as Tomas Inglot, Mitchell Orenstein, and two anonymous reviewers from Johns Hopkins University Press for comments on various drafts of the chapter.

NOTES

1. The three Baltic states of Estonia, Latvia, and Lithuania are exceptions here; like the ECE states, all three have democratic polities, market economies, and EU membership.

2. See Henry Hale, "Correlates of Clientelism: Political Economy, Politicized Ethnicity, and Postcommunist Transition," in *Patrons, Clients, and Polities: Patterns of Democratic*

Accountability and Political Competition, ed. Herbert Kitschelt and Steven Wilkinson (Cambridge: Cambridge University Press, 2007), 227–51; Gavin Helf and Jeffrey W. Hahn, "Old Dogs and New Tricks: Party Elites in the Russian Regional Elections of 1990," *Slavic Review* 51, no. 3 (1992): 511–30.

3. See, for example, Mikhail Myagkov, Peter Ordershook, and Dimitri Shaikin, *The Forensics of Election Fraud: Russia and Ukraine* (Cambridge: Cambridge University Press, 2009); Sarah Birch, "Post-Soviet Electoral Practices in Comparative Perspective," *Europe-Asia Studies* 63, no. 4 (2011): 703–55; Derek Hutcheson, "Elections, International Observers, and Politicisation of Democratic Values," *Europe-Asia Studies* 63, no. 4 (2011): 685–70; Sarah Birch, "Electoral Systems, Campaign Strategies, and Vote Choice in the Ukrainian Parliamentary and Presidential Elections of 1994," *Political Studies* 46 (1998): 96–114: V. Gel'man, "Out of the Frying Pan, into the Fire: Post-Soviet Regime Change in Comparative Perspective," *International Political Science Review* 29, no. 2 (2008): 157–80; Keith Darden, "Blackmail as a Tool of State Domination: Ukraine under Kuchma," *East European Constitutional Review* 10, nos. 2/ 3 (2001): 67–71; OSCE Report Archive at www.osce.org/odihr/elections; Index of Electoral Malpractice database available at www.essex.ac.uk/government/electoralmalpractice/data.htm.

4. See Anna Grzymala-Busse, "Beyond Clientelism: Incumbent State Capture and State Formation," *Comparative Political Studies* 41, nos. 4/5 (2008): 638–73; Linda J. Cook "Negotiating Welfare in Postcommunist States," *Comparative Politics* 40, no. 1 (2007): 41–62; Vladimir Gimpelson and Daniel Treisman, "Fiscal Games and Public Employment: A Theory with Evidence from Russia," *World Politics* 54:2 (January 2002): 145–83.

5. Susan C. Stokes, "Political Clientelism," *The Oxford Handbook of Comparative Politics,* ed. Charles Boix and Susan Stokes, 604–27 (Oxford: Oxford University Press, 2007); Javier Auyero, "Lessons Learned While Studying Clientelistic Politics in the Gray Zone" (chap. 5 in this volume); Simeon Nichter, "Political Clientelism and Social Policy in Brazil" (chap. 6 in this volume); Kanchan Chandra (2010) "Patronage, Democracy, and Ethnic Politics in India" (chap. 7 in this volume); see also Susan C. Stokes, "Perverse Accountability: A Formal Model of Machine Politics with Evidence from Argentina," *American Political Science Review* 99 (2005): 315–25.

6. Stokes, "Political Clientelism," 604.

7. Helf and Hahn, "Old Dogs and New Tricks," 526.

8. Helf and Hahn, "Old Dogs, New Tricks"; Hale, "Correlates of Clientelism."

9. Neo-patrimonialism is the tendency to preserve state-dependent populations through state ownership of productive resources and state-financing and distribution of social benefits.

10. Klarita Gerxhani and Arthur Schram, "Clientelism and Polarized Voting: Empirical Evidence," *Public Choice*, no. 141 (2009): 305–17, quote p. 315.

11. Hale, "Correlates of Clientelism," 233. Gubernatorial elections in Russian regions were ended by Putin in 2004, when they were replaced by presidential appointments of governors to be confirmed by regional legislature, though such confirmation was largely a formality.

12. Hale, "Correlates of Clientelism," 247.

13. Andrew Roberts, *The Quality of Democracy in Eastern Europe: Public Preferences and Policy Reforms* (Cambridge: Cambridge University Press, 2009), 170.

14. Linda J. Cook (2010) "Eastern Europe and Russia," in *The Oxford Handbook of the*

Welfare State, ed. Frances Castles, Stephan Leibfried, Jane Lewis, Herbert Obinger, and Christopher Pierson (Oxford: Oxford University Press, 2010), chap. 46.

15. Thanks to Tomasz Inglot (personal communication) for this point about the Roma.

16. Anna Grzymala-Busse, "Political Competition and the Politicization of the State in East Central Europe," *Comparative Political Studies* 36 (December 2003): 1123–47, p. 1129.

17. Ibid., 1130.

18. Grzymala-Busse, "Political Competition," 1145.

19. Andrew Roberts, "Hyperaccountability: Economic Voting in Central and Eastern Europe," *Electoral Studies* 27 (2008): 533–46.

20. Tatiana Kostadinova, "Abstain or Rebel: Corruption Perceptions and Voting in East European Elections," *Politics and Policy* 37, no. 4 (2009): 691–714.

21. Roberts, "Hyperaccountability," 534; see also Andrew Roberts, "What Kind of Democracy Is Emerging in Eastern Europe?" *Post-Soviet Affairs* 22 (2006): 37–64.

22. Thanks to Mitchell Orenstein for suggesting this comparative logic and line of argument.

23. Cook, "Eastern Europe and Russia."

24. Cook, "Negotiating Welfare in Postcommunist States"; Christine S. Lipsmeyer, "Welfare and the Discriminating Public: Evaluating Entitlement Attitudes in Post-Communist Europe," *Policy Studies Journal* 31, no. 4 (2003): 545–64.

25. Stephan Haggard and Robert Kaufman (2008) *Development, Democracy, and Welfare States: Latin America, East Asia and Eastern Europe* (Princeton, NJ: Princeton University Press). Haggard and Kaufman's study covers only East Asia; it does not, unfortunately, include comparative data on India or South Asia.

26. Linda J. Cook, *Postcommunist Welfare States: Reform Politics in Russia and Eastern Europe* (Ithaca, NY: Cornell University Press, 2007). Neo-liberal policy advisors from the World Bank and other global institutions pressed for the introduction of means-tested programs in postcommunist states, and some such programs were implemented, but they proved politically controversial in ECE and difficult to administer effectively in the post-Soviet cases, and many were dismantled or abandoned.

27. Tomasz Inglot, *Welfare States in East-Central Europe 1919–2004* (Cambridge: Cambridge University Press, 2008).

28. Conor O'Dwyer, "Runaway State Building: How Political Parties Shape States in Postcommunist Eastern Europe," *World Politics* 56, no. 4 (2004): 520–53, quote on p. 523; Conor O'Dwyer, *Runaway Statebuilding: Patronage Politics and Democratic Development* (Baltimore: Johns Hopkins University Press, 2006).

29. Peiter Vanhuyesse, *Divide and Pacify: Strategic Social Politics and Political Protests in Post-Communist Democracies* (Budapest: Central European University Press, 2006).

30. Cook, "Negotiating Welfare in Postcommunist States"; Mitchell Orenstein (World Bank report on Pension Reform).

31. For recent important discussions of electoral-authoritarianism, see A. Schedler, ed., *Electoral Authoritarianism: The Dynamics of Unfree Competition* (Boulder, CO: Lynne Reiner, 2006); Stephen Levitsky and Lucan Way, *Competitive Authoritarianism: Hybrid Regimes After the Cold War* (Cambridge: Cambridge University Press, 2010); Valerie Bunce and Sharon Wolchik, *Defeating Authoritarian Leaders in Postcommunist Countries* (New York: Cambridge

University Press, 2011); Dan Slater, *Ordering Power: Contentious Politics and Authoritarian Leviathans in Southeast Asia* (New York: Cambridge University Press, 2010).

32. See especially, Thomas Remington, "Patronage and the Party of Power: President-Parliament Relations under Vladimir Putin," *Europe-Asia Studies* 60, no. 6 (2008): 959–87; V. Gel'man, "From 'Feckless Pluralism' to Dominant Party Politics? The Transformation of Russia's Party System," *Democratization* 13, no. 14 (2006): 545–61.

33. Ian McAllister and Stephen White, "Public Perceptions of Electoral Fairness in Russia," *Europe-Asia Studies* 63, no. 4 (2011): 663–83. In one population survey, conducted in 2007 by the independent and critical Levada Center, respondents reported the following list of "expected departures from electoral propriety" (though only small proportions reported direct experience with these irregularities: leaking of compromising materials; manipulation of media access and coverage; bias by electoral commissions in registering candidates, manipulation of party lists, and ballot papers at polling stations; falsification of results in election commissions; bribery of electors by parties; pressures on electors by local authorities to persuade them to vote for a particular party).

34. Grigorii Golosov, "Building a New Political Machine," *Russian Analytical Digest*, no. 57, March 17, 2009, p. 2.

35. Myagkov et al., *Forensics of Election Fraud.*

36. See *Radio Free Europe*, Nov. 29, 2009.

37. Stephen White and Valentina Feklyunina, "Russia's Authoritarian Elections: The View from Below," *Europe-Asia Studies* 63, no. 4 (2011): 602–79.

38. Evgeniya Lukinova, Mikhail Myagkov, and Peter C. Ordeshook, "Metastasised Fraud in Russia's 2008 Presidential Elections," *Europe-Asia Studies* 63, no. 4 (2011): 603–21.

39. Cameron Ross, "Regional Elections and Electoral Authoritarianism in Russia," *Europe-Asia Studies* 63, no. 4 (2011): 641–61; Birch, "Post-Soviet Electoral Practices"; Stephen White and Olga Kryshtanovskaya, "Changing the Russian Electoral System: Inside the Black Box," *Europe-Asia Studies* 63, no. 4 (2011): 557–78; see also Walter R. Mebane and Kirill Kalinin, "Electoral Fraud in Russia: Vote Counts Analysis Using Second-digit Mean Tests" (paper presented at the Annual Meeting of the Midwest Political Science Association, Chicago, April 2012). Supporters of United Russia also dominated election commissions at all levels.

40. Lukinova et al., "Fraud in Russia's 2008 Presidential Elections," 621.

41. See, for example, Birch, "Electoral Systems," 718; Myagkov et al., *Forensics of Election Fraud;* and various OSCE reports.

42. A. S. Avtonomov, Yu. A. Buzin, V. A. Ivanchenko, A. V. Kristov, V. I. Kynev, and A.E. Lyubarev, *Vybory v Kontekste Mezhdunarodnykh Izbiratel'nykh Standartov* (Moscow: Nezavisimaya Institut Vyborov, 2006) at http://vibory.ru.; Ross, "Regional Elections."

43. Ross, "Regional Elections" (2011), citing Golosov, "Building a New Political Machine" (2009), 5.

44. McAllister and White, "Public Perceptions of Electoral Fairness in Russia." In a 2007 poll from the critical Levada Center, 17% of respondents reported that they or a member of their family had such an experience (pp. 669–70).

45. Gimpelson and Treisman, "Fiscal Games and Public Employment," 179. The authors argue that newly elected regional officials in Russia during the 1990s regularly increased public sector employment as a means of building patronage machines, but their statistics

show that hiring was concentrated in public administration and affected the social sector much less. "Between 1992 and 1998," they write, "employment in health, sport, and social protection increased by 226,000, and that in public administration grew by an estimated 1,049,000" (p. 179).

46. Golosov, "Building a New Political Machine," 4–5.

47. Birch, "Post-Soviet Electoral Practices," 722.

48. Grzymala-Busse, "Beyond Clientelism," 647.

49. Gimpelson and Treisman, "Fiscal Games and Public Employment."

50. Cook, *Postcommunist Welfare States.*

51. Gimpelson and Treisman, "Fiscal Games and Public Employment."

52. Chile, along with Costa Rica and Uruguay, are somewhat exceptional in Latin America in that they have considerably more developed and egalitarian welfare states than do the rest of the region.

53. Roberts, "Hyperaccountability."

CHAPTER TEN

The Democratization of Clientelism in Sub-Saharan Africa

NICOLAS VAN DE WALLE

Sub-Saharan Africa[1] developed a reputation for bad governance and corruption in the 1970s and 1980s when political leaders from the region such as President Mobutu Sese Seko of Zaire or President Kenneth Moi of Kenya became notorious for their egregious corruption even as their populations endured dreadful poverty. This negative reputation was enhanced by the region's declining levels of human rights and woeful lack of economic growth. While these leaders and their close followers amassed impressive personal fortunes, African economies underperformed relative to other regions.[2] Between 1960 and 1989, Africa's share of global GDP fell by close to two-thirds. By the late 1980s, levels of absolute poverty often exceeded two-thirds of the total population.

In some regions of the world, notably in East Asia, authoritarian politics appeared to go hand in hand with excellent economic results, and the term "developmental dictatorship" applied to them recognized that their economic success was related to their regimes' authoritarian characteristics.[3] In Africa, on the other hand, between independence in 1960 and 1989, the average citizen actually became poorer, in some countries by a significant amount.[4] The ways in which African governments ruled was widely held to be a primary cause of this developmental failure. In particular, a number of scholars argued from different theoretical perspectives that pervasive political clientelism was largely to blame for the patterns of low economic growth and persistently high levels of poverty.[5]

Until 1989, Botswana and Mauritius were the only African countries that regularly convened competitive multiparty elections, and after 1970, only a handful of countries convened even a single such election. A substantial wave of democratization swept through Africa after 1989,[6] resulting in the generalized adoption of multiparty electoral politics. Between 1989 and 2010, 132 presidential elections in which more than a single candidate ran were held in 39 of 48 African countries, and 164 multiparty legislative elections were held in which more than one party won representation in the legislature. In sum, multiparty electoral politics have become the norm.

How have these political changes influenced political clientelism? Have the changes had a meaningful impact on the economic welfare of African citizens? In recent years, the public policy literature has become increasingly concerned with the negative impact of political clientelism on economic growth in low-income democracies.[7] Too often, it is argued, democratic governments in low-income countries provide "targeted goods," such as expensive social services and public works, to political supporters who are economically suboptimal but help leaders win elections. The political repression of popular participation in authoritarian regimes allows them to take the long view and focus on public investment. Regular competitive elections place more pressure on politicians to maintain popular support with wasteful short-term expenditures, and the result is an increase in political corruption and clientelism with negative consequences for economic growth. The implication is that this risk is particularly high for fledgling democracies in low-income countries.

These arguments do not sit well with Africa observers who still remember the pervasive and deeply dysfunctional levels of these practices that existed before democracy. Was this the same kind of clientelism that now threatens the new democracies even more? How could things get any worse? This chapter argues that regime type does indeed have an impact on the form and political function of clientelism. The nature of African economies, the types of regimes, and state capacity all shaped the form and function of clientelism after independence. Today, these practices are undergoing a profound shift with democratization. I further argue that at least some of these changes are likely to have a positive impact on the welfare of people in the region. Far from the model of "developmental dictatorship," most African authoritarian systems did not promote economic development with high levels of public investment. Instead, they were both highly clientelistic and non-redistributive, with highly regressive patterns of public expenditure.

By promoting greater political participation and rewarding governments who bring about economic development, democratization potentially increases the incentive for politicians to broaden the benefits of clientelism to larger segments of the population. In Africa, this has the potential to create, for the first time, the political conditions for states to provide greater social services to a larger proportion of the population. The effect on welfare could be significant.

Theoretical Issues

Several propositions can be advanced in order to understand the current evolution of political clientelism in sub-Saharan Africa. First, some definitions: I favor an admittedly broad definition of the term to make it as comparative as possible. In that spirit, I define political clientelism as *the selective distribution of goods and services by politicians to favored constituencies in exchange for their political loyalty.* For the most part, clientelistic relationships concern the discretionary use of state resources and authority for political ends, insofar as a primary objective of political actors is the control of the state and its resources. Political parties in power rely on these state resources to remain in power, while opposition parties seek to gain support at least in part based on the promise of eventual control of the state. This definition excludes much of the routine corruption by state agents, for example when a school teacher charges a "fee" for school books or when policemen stop cars on the highway for bribes.[8] In at least some cases, the two practices are linked, as when certain offices are allocated to political supporters with the knowledge that they will generate revenues from bribes. But in many cases they have different causes and are not related.

The relationship between the traditional village-level clientelism and the post-colonial political clientelism of the modern African state is complex. A large anthropological literature discusses dyadic exchanges in rural societies that serve as insurance mechanisms for highly vulnerable peasants, notably to protect them from significant production shocks.[9] Much of the modernization literature tended to view the political clientelism that emerged in late industrializers as the anachronistic relic of the traditional version that would progressively disappear with urbanization, greater education, and the development of a middle class.[10] To be sure, African politicians have often adopted the rhetoric and cultural repertoires of traditional forms of tribute to legitimate the clientelistic practices they want to pursue, but their clientelism is fundamentally different; indeed, the references to specific cultural traditions are not necessarily historically accurate but are often "invented" fairly recently in Terence Ranger's sense.[11] In other words, there is no reason to believe that the level or manner of political clientelism in an African country today is causally related to cultural traditions that may or may not have existed in that country's past. As I argue below, other structural factors explain the incidence and form of political clientelism much more compellingly.

Second, political clientelism should be understood as an inevitable and omnipresent feature of the modern state. The fiscal and regulatory capacity of the modern state will always generate discretionary resources, which its agents will seek to manipulate in order to gain political advantage[12] and which opposition groups will inevitably covet. Fiscal capacity provides state agents with resources to redistribute, while the ability to regulate the provision of goods and services in the economy will provide them with discretion over the allocation of those goods and services. In sum, as broadly defined above, political clientelism is inherent to the modern state.

Third, though ubiquitous, the manifestations and precise function of political clientelism vary enormously because it is endogenous to regime type, state capacity, and economic structure. As defined above, political clientelism exists in all modern states in one form or another, but just as clearly, its precise manifestations vary enormously. Clientelism in a democratic regime is likely to be different than in an authoritarian system; the size of the economy and of the fiscal resources available to the state also shape the importance of clientelistic payoffs, and so on. This endogeneity of clientelism has long been recognized in different contexts,[13] but students of clientelism have typically linked such practices to specific economic and sociopolitical institutions and as a result have not theorized the factors that shape it. Very little attention has been given to the impact of changes in these structures on clientelism, which is the main aim of this chapter. I will examine how political and economic changes in Africa since independence are altering the patterns of political clientelism that we observe.

Clientelism in Postcolonial Africa

Before examining the impact of recent changes, it is useful to identify patterns in political clientelism in Africa in the decade after independence. At the risk of excessive generalization, several regime and state characteristics can be claimed to have powerfully affected the nature of clientelism in most African states following independence. First, as I have argued elsewhere,[14] these regimes were marked by extreme presidentialism. Though many African states inherited parliamentary rule at independence, power was soon concentrated in a relatively powerful presidency, whose considerable formal powers as defined by the constitution were in fact often dwarfed by their even greater informal and de facto ones. Powers of appointment, control of the national budget, and discretion over policy implementation with little oversight were not only concentrated in the office of the presidency but were often actually controlled by the president himself along with a tiny cadre of top politicians who were often above the law for all intents and purposes. Similarly, the executive branch dominated the other branches of government, with a subservient and pliant legislature and a weak, unprofessional, and politicized judiciary.

Second, Africa's postcolonial regimes were authoritarian. With the notable exceptions of democratic Botswana and Mauritius, the 48 countries in the region convened very few competitive elections, and civil and political rights were rarely observed, as is attested to by the very low democracy ratings for these countries in regime databases such as Freedom House or Polity. To be sure, significant differences existed between, say, the personal tyranny of a President Macías Nguema in Equatorial Guinea and the relatively mild form of authoritarian rule practiced by Julius Nyerere and his successors in Tanzania. In the former, virtually no political competition existed even within the narrow confines of the presidency; whereas in the latter, significant contestation was allowed under the umbrella of the single party, whose primary elections were quite competitive. Still, the weakness of formal political competition and low political participation are hallmarks of Africa before 1989.

Third, African states were characterized by their weak fiscality and low state capacity. African states were small in size relative to their GDP and were chronically underfunded.[15] Again, there is considerable variation, but African government tax revenues were often under 10% of GDP, averaging roughly about half the levels associated with the rich countries of the OECD. The causes of this low rate of fiscal extraction were complex. Poverty, economic structure, and the difficulty of taxing peasant agriculture were part of the story, as was the low extractive capacity of most states, and, in some states, the very high rates of tax evasion. The state that emerged from colonialism lacked basic competence and legitimacy, and its ability to project power throughout its territory was highly uneven.[16] Among the poorest states in the world, with typically small populations stretched out over a large territory and well over half of the population living in rural areas, African states found it difficult to prevent exit by economic agents.

One consequence was a typically small state that provided relatively few of its citizens with social services or entitlements. On average, state personnel in the region amounted to less than 2% of the total population, compared to almost 8% of the population in OECD countries, and more than 3% in the rest of the developing world.[17] Roughly half of these employees were nurses and school teachers, so the number of positions in the central administration was comparatively quite limited. Access to social services and public infrastructure was similarly comparatively limited. Though there is substantial variation across the continent, many Africans outside of the major cities did not get access to medical care, schooling opportunities, or public utilities, as suggested in table 10.1.[18]

The table suggests the extent of variation in the region. The sole democracy in the region, Botswana, enjoyed both faster economic growth, and a more developed state that provided a far higher level of social services than most other states in the region. Oil states like Angola, Congo (Brazzaville), and Nigeria were considerably richer than the average African country but did not generally translate this wealth

TABLE 10.1.
Social services and public utilities in Africa

Selected countries	Female literacy rate (%) (1990)	Access to clean water (%) (1999)	Hospital beds per 1,000 people (last year avail.)	Paved roads (%) (last year avail.)	Electric power (KWh consumption per capita) (2006)
Angola	—	39	1.7	10.4	153
Botswana	92	93	2.4	33	1,419
Burkina Faso	14	34	0.9	4.2	—
Congo-Br	—	—	1.6	5	155
Malawi	49	41	1.1	45	—
Nigeria	62	50	0.5	15	116
Sudan		64	0.7	36	95
Tanzania	78	49	1.1	8.6	59
SSA average	59	49	—	12	531
Latin America	76	84	7.1	22	1,808
High income countries	99	99	6.1	87	9,675

Source: The World Bank, 2009. World Development Indicators, 2009.

into higher levels of well-being for their citizens. Their oil wealth usually led to a substantially larger number of civil servants and public employees. These political and economic characteristics conditioned the clientelism that emerged in the years following independence in the region. In particular, three stylized facts can be articulated.

First, *political clientelism in the postcolonial era was dominated by the executive branch of government.* In part, this reflects the personal nature of political power in that era. President Ahidjo of Cameroon personally stamped every exit visa granted by the government. In Kenya, President Moi built a presidency of 20,000 employees that effectively constituted a parallel government and took power away from the regular bureaucracy. Presidents such as Mobutu in Zaire or Houphouët Boigny in Cote d'Ivoire routinely squirreled away a substantial proportion of the export revenues coming from commodity exports for their personal use and for clientelistic purposes. In part, this state of affairs reflects the dominance of the executive branch in postcolonial Africa and the lack of an effective balance of powers and of institutional checks on presidential power. The political and financial resources accruing to the legislative branch were typically few and highly dependent on the good will of the presidency. Legislators might be rewarded for their support with access to state resources, but they enjoyed little autonomous access to these resources; and indeed, a position in the legislature was clearly less lucrative and prestigious than a cabinet position, let alone a position in the higher reaches of the presidency itself, which typically came with considerably more financial and political resources.

Second, *political clientelism overwhelmingly favored a highly circumscribed socio-political elite and was rarely economically redistributive in a meaningful sense.* As suggested in the previous section, African states both could not afford extensive political patronage in the form of jobs and services to political clienteles and were not predisposed to it, given the nature of political competition. Instead, political clientelism overwhelmingly favored a relatively small number of people, who were critical to maintaining regime stability. Clientelistic resources did not descend very far down the social pyramid, despite much legitimating rhetoric to the contrary. Instead, they were used to promote cross-ethnic elite accommodation, as presidents sought to build a viable coalition of national elites to support their rule by including key elites from different regions, ethnic groups, clans, and so on in the presidential coalition.[19] A clear ethnic calculus has often been obvious in the construction of government cabinets, in which different groups would be assured a number of seats.[20] The ethnic elites thus brought into the presidential fold were expected to play a kind of "brokerage" role between specific communities and the regime: presidential nomination propelled them to a visible leadership position in exchange for which they were supposed to ensure their group's support for the regime. In the independence era, at least some nationalist parties had built up considerable mobilizational capacity in much of the national territory. But as the regimes became more authoritarian and elections less competitive, political participation waned considerably, and these parties were often marginalized.[21] The brokerage model made sense to national leaders in order to reach out and build legitimacy for their rule away from the capital, at low cost, and in a manner which did not require much capacity.

In theory, brokers brought state resources from the capital back to their communities. Certainly, the social imagery and rhetoric around ethnicity often promoted the illusion of broad redistribution. A Losi minister serving in the Zambian government was said to defend Losi interests at the table of government, which in turn would provide substantial benefits to the Losi community. On the other hand, politicians who opposed the president were accused of ensuring that their communities would suffer irreparable harm in terms of jobs and services.[22]

Nonetheless, the evidence actually suggests that the social benefits of these broad clientelistic alliances around African presidents were rarely substantial. We know this because we see that the large number of elite offices in the capital did not translate into a large number of lower-level patronage positions or extensive social services in the hinterlands, which were generally relatively low (see table 10.1) and more often than not provided by church organizations or western donors rather than the central state. Finally, evidence of the lack of clientelistic redistribution through a proactive state can be gleaned from the region's very high and persistent levels of social inequality.[23]

The postcolonial state's inattention to social services and economic development continued traditions put in place by the colonial state, which viewed the state's primary functions as the maintenance of public order and security and the repression of nationalist ambitions[24] and supported most investments to promote economic development only when they advanced these functions. It was only after World War II, in the brief period before independence, that a more overtly developmental state began to emerge when the colonial governments understood that they needed to prepare their colonies for independence.[25] The nationalist governments that took over after 1956 vowed to accelerate the development process with a strong emphasis on service delivery and infrastructural development, but most of them largely failed to do so and found the colonial state's law-and-order institutions convenient for the maintenance of power.

Third, *political clientelism was often prebendal in nature, was linked to illegal acts, and undermined property rights.* A prebend refers to a public office that is sold for political gain and can claim a long and distinguished historiography, mostly in its manifestation in the early modern state in Western Europe.[26] Officials of the state earn low nominal official salaries, but their positions give them discretionary access to resources because of the rules, regulations, and policies of the state, from which they are expected to profit. The selective implementation and manipulation of their own policies can allow customs officials to gain considerable revenues, ministerial officials to take a cut on state procurement contracts, or the officials of regulatory bodies to extract bribes from the companies they are supposed to regulate. Following independence in Africa, in the absence of adequate resources with which to build large states and substantial patronage, and given the absence of political motivations to do so, most political clientelism took the form of prebends for top state elites.

It should be made clear that these practices are unambiguously illegal, despite their pervasiveness in some regimes. Other clientelistic practices exist that are either legal or in a gray zone of semi-legality. In some cases, they have been codified in specific ways—for instance, the U.S. federal spoils system. In postcolonial Africa, however, there was no question that ministers who appropriated a substantial proportion of their ministry's revenues, for example, were engaged in illegal acts. The actions of regulatory officials preying on successful businesses and thus undermining property rights were similarly unambiguously illegal. Indeed, its very illegality allowed the president to occasionally discipline his barons and assert his preeminence by arresting them for acts of corruption he had himself encouraged them to undertake.[27] This presidential assertion of power helps explain the number of occasional anti-corruption campaigns in the most corrupt countries of the region. The absence of democracy was thus an important factor in allowing this system of clientelism to emerge. No free press or legislative inquiry could shed light on acts of corruption; no investigative magistrate could charge a minister when it was inconvenient to the president.

The variation across the region related to these dynamics should be made clear. In countries like the Zaire of Mobutu or the Central African Republic, where formal institutions were very weak, the personalization of rule around prebendalism and elite cronyism was almost complete. On the other hand, states with stronger formal institutions also exhibited these traits, but alongside more Weberian bureaucratic and policy-making processes and with different societal dynamics such as a more enterprising independent media or political opposition.

Clientelism and Democratization in Africa

What effect, if any, has democratization since 1989 and the generalized turn to regular multiparty elections had on the patterns of political clientelism just described? Democratization has changed some of the key sociopolitical characteristics present in Africa, while leaving others unchanged. At least three major transformations in political clientelism are presently underway in Africa as a result of democratization. In each of these, the processes are still incipient and will necessarily take considerable time.

A preliminary caveat relates to the fact that this essay discusses modal patterns in the continent that contrast with other regions of the world. As a result, it does not really discuss factors that are likely to provide considerable sources of variation in political clientelism within the Africa region. For instance, there is some evidence that ethnic heterogeneity and other social cleavages increase the incidence of clientelism.[28] The degree of state capacity probably matters in significant ways, and the quality of the state bureaucracy and rule of law institutions vary quite widely across the region. Electoral rules and other institutional factors structure individual incentives in the political system and thus also condition the specific forms that clientelism will take.[29]

The first change relates to *the emergence of legislative pork and electoral clientelism.* Democratization and the convening of regular competitive elections are heralding both a relative diminution of presidential power relative to legislative power and an increasing role for political parties. The first transformation that can already be observed in many countries in Africa is thus the movement of the locus of clientelism from the presidency and executive branch to the parties and legislature, particularly during elections. This evolution is the most obvious of the changes underway following democratization, but it has received curiously little notice. With the introduction of competitive elections and the premium put on winning them, the political importance of political parties is dramatically enhanced, and the incentive for political actors to use clientelism to win elections is increased. As a result, relative to the past, we can expect clientelistic practices to change their locus from the executive branch of government to political parties and legislators. The role of political clientelism changes with changes in political regime. Authoritarian presidents once sought to keep a viable coalition together with the judicious distribution of state resources to a relatively small number of elites. With the movement to competitive elections, the nature of remaining in power shifts. Buying off elite support is by no means irrelevant, but funding party structures and campaigns as well as retaining the support of the voters now become the primary objective of politicians. Incumbents need to win elections to be able to stay in power, while opposition parties need to win elections to wrest that power from them. In sum, with democratization, the main instruments of political clientelism move from brokerage and prebendalism to mass patronage and vote buying, while the locus of clientelism starts to migrate from the executive to the legislative branch of government.

This transition is slow for reasons discussed below, and it is far from complete, but the introduction of Constituency Development Funds (CDF) in fledgling electoral democracies as varied as Ghana, Kenya, Malawi, Tanzania, Uganda, and Zambia constitutes an interesting institutional innovation. In each of these countries, legislators have demanded and received allocations from the national treasury to allow them to make grants to their home districts. The amounts are not trivial. In Zambia, each constituency received 400 Million Kwacha in 2008, equivalent to US$80,000, and the government has been considering doubling the amount. In Kenya, 210 parliamentary constituencies each received a little over US$500,000 that same year, and the parliament has passed a law mandating that CDF outlays be equivalent to 7.5% of government revenues. The official intention is to respond to constituency needs and to streamline the development process so that legislators directly address the developmental challenges at the grassroots, which they claim they understand best. In practice, the CDFs constitute incumbency funds, increasing the visibility of legislators in their districts and presumably also their popularity and ability to win reelection, even when these funds are misappropriated and are not used for developmental purposes.

The discussion of CDFs in the local press in these countries suggests that they are in fact routinely abused. In Kenya, for instance, a new watchdog group called the National Taxpayers Association released a well-publicized report in March 2011 castigating 28 parliamentarians for abuses in their CDFs following an audit of their accounts.[30] Legislators in these countries complain of the costs of winning elections, thanks to increasingly pervasive "vote buying" practices, and the subtext in narratives about some of the recent CDF scandals, much described in the local press and publicized by various watchdog NGOs that have started to appear, suggest that at least some incumbents believe that the CDF funds provide a return on their electoral investments.

The implications of these CDFs for political stability, the patterns in their utilization, their actual impact on development, and even their impact on the reelection of incumbents (typically quite low in these countries) merit further investigation.[31] The point should be clear though: in the wake of democratization, we are witnessing an ineluctable evolution of political clientelism away from the presidency (though to be sure, it still controls many clientelistic resources) and toward the legislative branch.

A second evolution that occurs as a result of democratization is what might be called *the codification of clientelism*. I hypothesize that the illegal and prebendal arrangements of the past will progressively disappear; in their place will emerge the kind of patronage politics that we observe in mature democracies, usually focused around party politics and having been the subject of formal agreements among the main political players in the system. These practices may be more or less significant in much the way that variation is observed between, say, Belgium, the Netherlands, and Denmark in the locus and scope of party patronage,[32] but on the whole they will fall far short of the egregious illegality that was characteristic of authoritarian Africa.

First, the need to win elections and finance the political party organizations without which such victories are not possible leads virtually all democracies to tolerate the funneling of public money and functionary positions in the state apparatus to party organizations. Public funding for party foundations are common, for instance, as are generous public allocations for campaigns, typically structured in such a way as to favor the mainstream parties. Second, various mechanisms exist in many older democracies to limit the incumbency advantage of the party in power, both by circumscribing the patronage possibilities for the party that controls the executive branch and by providing at least some similar possibilities for the opposition. In the United States, for instance, the presidential spoils system best exemplifies this dynamic, since the president has enormous discretion over a large number of high-level positions in the federal bureaucracy; but these are formally constrained in number and subject to very explicit rules. Such arrangements have typically evolved organically in democratic polities as political competition and participation have evolved over time.

The evolution of the CDFs suggests the possibility of this kind of path for fledgling African democracies. Though often little more than a slush fund for the local party hierarchy and the elected incumbent, and though the private and corrupt appropriation of these funds appears to happen frequently, the CDFs are the subject of intense negotiation and discussion within the political systems and civil society in countries like Kenya, Tanzania, and Zambia. Civic associations have emerged that are making public arguments for greater public and apolitical control of the funds and less incumbent discretion over them. In Tanzania, for instance, the Policy Forum, a network of NGOs, has been engaging in a spirited debate about how to improve the CDFs in that country, which it views as largely ineffective and corrupt at present.[33] Abuses of the funds are discussed in the press, as are suggestions for alternative projects from the ones chosen.

More than two-thirds of incumbent parliamentarians were defeated in the 2008 Kenyan elections, and much negative publicity in the press surrounding the perceived mismanagement of the CDFs appears to have been a factor in at least some of these defeats. Presumably, this gives the new parliamentarians an incentive to manage the funds differently. In sum, as a result of democratization, public debate is in the process of codifying and circumscribing the use of the funds in a process that I hypothesize will eventually concern most clientelistic practices.

Implications for Social Provision

A final and third impact of democratization is *the emergence of a more redistributive form of clientelism.* As argued above, during the long period of authoritarian rule, Africa's political and economic institutions generated significant social and economic stratification. Again, despite some careless scholarship to the contrary, the elite clientelism of postcolonial Africa was not redistributive, but rather it was directed to an exceedingly narrow elite that accumulated disproportionate wealth. Moreover, the taxation policies, social programs, and public spending patterns of most of the countries in the region were neither progressive nor comprehensive enough to lessen inequality.[34]

Almost by definition, democratic regimes are more responsive to their electorates and empower a larger proportion of the population, since a broad electoral franchise makes decision makers more accountable to the adult population. As the clientelistic networks expand down the social pyramid, thanks to electoral logic, they are likely to result in greater economic redistribution. In sum, the more democratic a country, the greater the participation and the more pressure there is on politicians to make clientelism more redistributive. Even if the logic of clientelism will always be to give a relatively privileged minority access to state resources, the size of this minority increases with competitive politics. Moreover, whether they are clientelistic or not, democracies almost certainly engender greater public expenditure, notably in the social sectors, than do authoritarian states.[35]

What is the evidence for these propositions in sub-Saharan Africa? It is admittedly far from conclusive. Stasavage provides cross-national data suggesting that recent democratization in Africa has resulted in increases in education spending,[36] but his research is almost alone in testing this relationship for Africa. Acemoglu, Johnson, and Robinson[37] and Engerman and Sokoloff[38] find evidence of a global, historical link between social equality and democracy. On the other hand, from a broad contemporary data set, Ross[39] finds no such positive relationship. Keefer[40] is sometimes cited to suggest that democratization does not have positive effects on the quality of governance, but his main argument compares new democracies unfavorably with older ones, not with non-democracies, so it can be viewed as a sanguine endorsement of the future of democratic governance in Africa. Collier[41] similarly ascribes worse policies and greater conflict to democracies in low-income countries, but his data appears to lump together countries with any kind of elections, including highly authoritarian countries, an issue I return to below.

On the other hand, statistics undeniably suggest a significant improvement in social indicators for Africa since the onset of democracy two decades ago. Absolute poverty levels have declined steadily since the late 1990s, the first such sustained decline since independence.[42] Infant mortality rates, malnutrition levels, school attendance rates, and access to improved water all appear to have undergone substantial improvements over the last decade.[43] From the citizens' side, the Afrobarometer survey shows increasingly widespread access to such services as piped water (50% of Afrobarometer respondents), access to the electricity grid (54%), and walking access to a health clinic (63%).[44]

The extent to which these social welfare improvements are related to democratization is unfortunately not unambiguous. At least in part, they have resulted from the increases in foreign aid made possible by the donor-funded Millennium Development Goals (MDG) campaign rather than democratization. In nominal terms, foreign aid to Africa increased from around US$12 billion in 1990 to just under US$40 billion in 2008, and these totals do not include the even larger increases that have occurred for flows by nongovernmental actors. Much of this aid has been directed at increasing and improving public services delivery in order to improve individual welfare.

Donors have increased their funding for targeted cash transfer programs in Africa, following their introduction and popularization in Latin America. In these programs, poor people receive cash, often in exchange for undertaking some activity thought to increase individual welfare and reduce poverty, such as enrolling their children in school, going for medical check-ups, or getting vaccinated. Since the mid-1990s in particular, when these programs began to be perceived as highly effective, they have been introduced in African countries such as Ghana, South Africa, Mozambique, and Uganda. Early evaluations suggest a positive impact on poverty,[45] but little research has been done on the political economy dynamics of the implementation of these programs.[46] Writing about a new conditional cash transfer program in Zambia aimed at encouraging poor people to visit health clinics and enroll their children in schools, Schubert and Slater[47] note that the country typically had one or two welfare officers for a district of 200 to 500 thousand people, and cautioned that success would be dependent on a substantial improvement in the current levels of local state capacity. In sum, the increases in resources for social services may encounter an aid absorption problem in which effectiveness in the short term is limited by implementation constraints.

The welfare improvements brought about by the substantial aid increases under the MDG campaign have occurred in most African countries, not just the most democratic countries, though it is important to note that most aid recipients have undergone some improvement over the last two decades in their level of political and social rights. Radelet[48] does establish a causal link between the general turn to electoral politics in the region, improved governance, and improved economic and social conditions.

Aside from these increases in social spending, various accounts similarly suggest that political changes in the region are engendering the emergence of a different kind of politics. Recent accounts from the region suggest that democratization has increased and broadened participation to previously disempowered groups. How else can one interpret the widespread reports of vote-buying,[49] the growing role of businessmen and their money in electoral politics due to the cost of vote-buying,[50] and the emergence of a political business cycle in which governments increase funding for infrastructure and social services right around election time?[51] Opposition politicians complain of the ability of incumbents to use state resources to gain electoral support,[52] not least thanks to the CDFs described in the previous section of this chapter. Evidence also exists that electoral politics have increased conflict around land property rights, which have become an object of struggle for politicians and their constituents.[53]

Further evidence is offered by the emergence of a new populism currently seeping into African politics in which politicians are more prone to adopt demagogic posturing about foreign businesses making large profits while remaining insensitive to the needs of poor people. For instance, Larmer and Fraser[54] describe the emergence of the Patriotic Front in Zambia, a classic populist party that has won significant representation in parliament and now controls the mayorality of Lusaka based on rhetoric that promises material benefits to voters and fans anti-elite and anti-foreign sentiment as well as other various popular grievances to win elections. Similar dynamics have been noted in countries such as Madagascar, Kenya, Senegal, and Benin.[55]

Moreover, surveys of the attitudes of African citizens suggest a growing assertiveness on the part of voters vis-à-vis their public officials. Afrobarometer data suggest that Africans determine their vote for local officials primarily in terms of their ability to deliver services and increasingly value their ability to engage in direct communication with their elected officials.[56] Unfortunately, we lack longitudinal data to determine how these attitudes have evolved over time, but one study of Ghanaian attitudes toward government performance indicates that citizens' satisfaction with the level of service delivery they receive, particularly in health and education services, has risen consistently since the first survey in 1999.[57]

The link between service delivery and clientelism is complex, particularly in a region in which provision has never been either universal or guaranteed. Nonetheless, these same attitudinal surveys tell us that citizens are both fed up with the petty corruption of the state and tolerant of it if it helps them get access to various services, which they understand as one function of the current political dispensation. As Chang and Clark argue, "The popular distaste of corruption may be neutralized when voters benefit (or expect to benefit) from the actions of corrupt politicians."[58]

Needless to say, these developments may have negative economic and political consequences, and they obviously do not indicate a growing virtuousness in African politics. However, they do suggest that clientelistic strategies are reacting to the growth of political participation by starting to become more socially inclusive. In the African context, this is an important historical change that has significant implications for governance in the coming decades.

A large literature has emerged in recent years to distinguish the economic policy performance of clientelistic regimes from non-clientelistic ones.[59] The former emphasize targeted goods, it is argued, which politicians can then manipulate for political gains; while the latter focus on universal public goods, which are inherently not targetable. Economic growth, it is typically suggested, is fostered by governments that do the latter. Keefer[60] offers secure property rights, the rule of law, or universal education as examples of non-targeted policies. His examples of targeted policies are jobs and public works.

It seems clear that certain kinds of government expenditure are more favorable for economic growth than others. On the other hand, the distinction between targeted and non-targeted policies does not seem completely compelling, particularly when, as in Africa, poverty levels are extraordinarily high and government expenditures have historically been so limited. The building of roads and bridges, for instance, may well have a clientelistic logic and may favor one region or one constituency over another, but they still can have major impacts on welfare and economic growth. Peasants out in the bush are likely to benefit a great deal from a road that allows them to market crops or communicate more readily with the outside world. They may not benefit nearly as much from the property rights of businessmen being protected in the capital, 500 miles away.

In any event, even if targeted public policies are second best, their introduction for the first time in countries with very high levels of poverty have the potential to improve the lot of the poor and should not be dismissed too readily. Clientelistic expenditures that actually expand services or provide some good to the extremely poor can have a positive impact on economic growth, particularly when no government expenditure reached these segments of the population in the past. It is in that sense that I hypothesize that the effect of democratization on clientelistic practices signifies significant progress.

Caveats in Lieu of a Conclusion

I have argued in this chapter that clientelism is endogenous to the nature of the political regime, state capacity, and economic structure. These three factors have shaped the distinctive prevailing patterns of clientelism in Africa in the decades after independence. The previous, more tentative section argued that the significant political transition of the early 1990s is in the process of profoundly altering the dynamics of clientelism, notably with a broadening of its beneficiaries. A significant impact on the delivery of social services to citizens is one likely outcome. I want to conclude with some caveats to temper the optimism informing this last section. A number of political factors suggest that the predicted transformation of political clientelism will be slow and difficult.

First, democratic transitions in Africa are far from complete. Even if Michael Bratton is correct to surmise that multiparty competitive elections have become entrenched enough in popular attitudes that they can now be "regarded as an institutionalized norm of African politics,"[61] the 2010 Freedom House scores for African countries draw attention to the political variation in the Africa region today. Freedom House rates 9 countries in Africa as "free" in 2010, followed by 23 as "partly free," and 16 as "not free." The overwhelming majority of these African states convene regular elections, but, in fact, only a small number of countries in the "free" category appear to have now consolidated fairly robust democratic institutions with genuine checks and balances, a free press, and a reasonably independent judiciary.

Thus, in approximately a quarter of the countries in the region, authoritarian incumbent presidents have adapted to the new rules of the game by instituting "façade democracies"[62] or "electoral autocracies"[63] that undermine neither their hold on power nor the main instruments that buttress their rule. Even in countries that have seen significant democratic progress, the resulting regimes are often best characterized as "hybrid"[64] or "illiberal democracies,"[65] as authoritarian dynamics subsist alongside the new democratic dispensations.

The relative weakening of presidentialism in the region posited in the previous section is occurring in a significant way. Still, none of Africa's new multiparty regimes have abandoned presidential constitutions, for instance, for parliamentary rule, which is in force in just a handful of Africa's 48 political systems. Though democratization has often included concerted efforts to curtail presidential power and empower mechanisms of vertical and horizontal accountability, more often than not presidential prerogatives remain significant. Similarly, the extent to which elections have been competitive varies significantly across the countries of the region, and changes in the logic of clientelism will be smaller in countries in which effective competition is actually quite limited because of presidential manipulation of the process or the weakness of opposition parties.

Even where the formal institutions of democratic rule appear to be taking hold, change may be slowed down by the absence of a concurrent change in political culture and practice. In Jonathan Fox's felicitous phrase, it takes time and effort to transform clients into citizens[66]: civic organizations, the press, and the expectations of the citizenry will not immediately adjust to the new dispensation, but need to be nurtured and encouraged. Moreover, a panoply of well-established informal institutions buttress the democratic order in consolidated democracies and shape both expectations and behaviors of political actors[67]—including norms and informal understandings regarding the relationship between political parties, mechanisms of accommodation, and compromise between the branches of government, and broadly understood standards of not only what is legal—but also what constitutes acceptable behavior in the political game. These informal rules do not immediately emerge in the aftermath of democratization but require the passage of time and the experience of repeated elections, budget cycles, and legislative sessions. In the meantime, the old culture of neopatrimonialism will be repeatedly invoked by actors who find it useful to their ends, and it is far from clear that other actors will always be able to proscribe the resultant behavior. For their part, many politicians and their followers were socialized in the *ancien régime* and bring certain expectations to the new one. It takes time for a new generation of politicians who have been socialized differently to emerge.

One of the key instruments of the new kind of politics that I hypothesize will emerge are political parties. Parties are key because of their role in mobilizing voters and representing societal interests in the policy process but also because they are intrinsic to shaping expectations within elite circles. For instance, strong parties with well-defined policy positions shape public policy debates that are likely necessary for sustainable social policies. In addition, strong parties and well-institutionalized party systems are likely to be a requisite for the process of clientelistic codification that was sketched out in the previous section. Clientelistic abuses are less likely when parliamentarians know that their party's control of the executive branch is not guaranteed in the next election cycle. Credible deals are more likely between stable, well-institutionalized parties who alternate in power.

Unfortunately, for the most part, parties are weak and poorly organized at the present time. Building strong party organizations takes skill and requires the passage of time, if for no other reason than that elections are discrete events that only occur occasionally. Moreover, the lack of access to state resources will provide an inherent disadvantage for opposition parties, who will find it harder to fund their activities unless they rely on private business to compete with state-funded incumbents. This may in part explain why alternation has taken place in few countries in the region.[68] The asymmetry between parties may slow down the transformation in the modalities of clientelism that I have predicted, though it is true that opposition parties in at least some countries can gain access to valuable resources by winning state and local elections. Opposition party promises to expand social services if and when they get power may not always be heard by voters, even when they are credible. Incumbents, for their part, will have less of an incentive to provide more ample services to their constituents when opposition parties are organizationally weak and underfunded. As a result, one can hypothesize that more competitive systems will evolve less slowly in the direction of greater constituency service that I am predicting.

Second, the transformation of political clientelism is likely to be slowed down by the fact that an array of structural factors were not displaced by the regime changes of the early 1990s. Thus, poverty, economic stagnation, and fiscal crisis will militate against attempts to move toward a broader, more democratic clientelism of the kind predicted in the previous section. Fiscality constitutes the Achilles heel of poor democracies. As emphasized above, the advantage of the kind of elite clientelism practiced in authoritarian Africa is its cheapness, and the more ambitious expenditures of a more democratic clientelism will bring with it huge economic risks, particularly in the absence of rapid economic growth. Indeed, the history of post–World War II Latin America is in many respects a history of a failed transition of the kind predicted here. The extension of the electoral franchise resulted in regimes that established political economies that promoted service delivery and the growth of a state apparatus that these economies could not ultimately sustain,[69] leading directly to the economic crises of the 1980s. In Africa, a successful transition will include the ability to shepherd limited resources into productive public expenditures, notably in social sector investments that both promote productivity growth and economic development and accommodate political coalition building.

Thus, sustained economic growth is probably a requisite of the political regime transition that I am hypothesizing can take place. It is, more fundamentally, likely necessary for the very survival of democracy. If Przeworski et al.[70] are correct in suggesting that democracies are unlikely to survive in low-income countries unless they are able to generate rapid economic growth, at least some of these weakly institutionalized democracies will not survive. For a long time, the biggest danger facing them will be their inability to promote economic growth, which could lead to an anti-democratic backlash. Rapid economic growth, on the other hand, can help finance the growth of the state apparatus and the services it provides, fueling both the growth of patronage opportunities and legitimacy for the regime.

NOTES

1. Throughout, Africa is used interchangeably with sub-Saharan Africa and designates the countries south of the Sahara.

2. Nicolas van de Walle, *African Economies and the Politics of Permanent Crisis, 1979–1999* (New York: Cambridge University Press, 2001); and B. J. Ndulu, Stephen A. O'Connell, Jean-Paul Azam, Robert Bates, Augustin Fosu, Jan Willem Gunning, and Dominique Njinkeu, *The Political Economy of Economic Growth in Africa, 1960–2000* (New York: Cambridge University Press, 2008).

3. Stephan Haggard, "Institutions and Growth in East Asia," *Studies in Comparative International Development* 38 (2004): 53–81; and Meredith Woo-Cummings, *The Developmental State* (Ithaca, NY: Cornell University Press, 1999).

4. Shaohua Chen, and Martin Ravallion, "How Have the World's Poorest Fared since the Early 1980s?" *World Bank Research Observer* 19 (2004): 141–69.

5. Robert Bates, *When Things Fell Apart: State Failure in Late-Century Africa* (New York:

Cambridge University Press, 2008); Jean-François Bayart, *L'Etat en Afrique: la politique du ventre* (Paris: Fayard, 1989); Van de Walle, *African Economies and the Politics of Permanent Crisis;* Richard Sandbrook, *The Politics of Africa's Economic Recovery* (Cambridge: Cambridge University Press, 1993); and Michael G. Schatzberg, "Power, Legitimacy and 'Democratisation' in Africa," *Africa* 63 (1993): 445–61.

6. Michael Bratton and Nicolas van de Walle, *Democratic Experiments in Africa: Regime Transitions in Comparative Perspective* (New York: Cambridge University Press, 1997).

7. Philip Keefer, "Clientelism, Credibility, and the Policy Choices of Young Democracies," *American Journal of Political Science* 51 (2007): 804–21; and Paul Collier, *Wars, Guns and Votes* (New York: Harper Books, 2009).

8. On these practices in Africa, see Giorgio Blundo and Jean-Pierre Olivier de Sardan, *Everyday Corruption and the State: Citizens and Public Officials in Africa* (London: Zed Books, 2006).

9. Steffen Schmidt et al., eds., *Friends, Followers and Factions: A Reader in Political Clientelism* (Berkeley: University of California Press, 1977); and Marcel Fafchamps, *Rural Poverty, Risk and Development* (Northampton, MA: Edward Elgar Publishers, 2003).

10. David Apter, *The Politics of Modernization* (Chicago: University of Chicago Press, 1966); and James C. Scott, "Patron-Client Politics and Political Change in Southeast Asia," *American Political Science Review* 66 (March 1972): 91–113.

11. Terrance Ranger, "The Invention of Tradition Revisited: The Case of Colonial Africa," in *Legitimacy and the State in Twentieth-Century Africa: Essays in Honour of A. H. Kirk-Greene,* ed. Terrance Ranger and Olufemi Vaughan (Oxford: MacMillan Press, 1993), 62–111.

12. Christopher Clapham, "Clientelism and the State," in *Private Patronage and Public Power,* ed. Christopher Clapham (London: Frances Pinter, 1982), 1–36; and Simona Piattoni, ed., *Clientelism, Interests, and Democratic Representation* (Cambridge: Cambridge University Press, 2006).

13. Sharon Kettering, "The Historical Development of Political Clientelism," *Journal of Interdisciplinary History* 18 (1988): 419–47; Anna Grzymala-Busse, "Beyond Clientelism: Incumbent State Capture and State Formation," *Comparative Political Studies* 41 (2008): 638–731; and Rene Lemarchand, "The Changing Structure of Patronage Systems," in *The Precarious Balance: State and Society in Africa,* ed. D. Rothchild and N. Chazan (Boulder, CO: Westview Press, 1988).

14. Nicolas van de Walle, "Presidentialism and Clientelism in Africa's Emerging Party Systems," *Journal of Modern African Studies* 41 (2003): 297–321; and *African Economies and the Politics of Permanent Crisis.*

15. Van de Walle, *African Economies and the Politics of Permanent Crisis;* Arthur A. Goldsmith, "Sizing up the African State," *Journal of Modern African Studies* 38 (2000): 1–20; and Arthur A. Goldsmith, "Africa's Overgrown State Reconsidered: Bureaucracy and Economic Growth," *World Politics* 51 (1999): 520–46.

16. Jeffrey Herbst, *States and Power in Africa: Comparative Lessons in Authority and Control* (Princeton, NJ: Princeton University Press, 2000).

17. Salvatore Schiavo-Campo, Giulio de Tommaso, and Amitabha Mukherjee, "Government Employment and Pay: A Global and Regional Perspective" (World Bank Policy Research Working Paper No. 1771, World Bank, Washington, DC, May 1997).

18. It might be added that the most recent data reported in the table incorporates the substantial progress made on social service delivery in recent years.

19. Bayart, *L'Etat en Afrique.*

20. Leonardo R. Arriola, "Patronage and Political Stability in Africa" *Comparative Political Studies* 42 (2009): 1339–62.

21. Ruth Berins Collier, *Regimes in Tropical Africa: Changing Forms of Supremacy, 1945–1975* (Berkeley: University of California Press, 1982); and Nelson Kasfir, *The Shrinking Political Arena: Participation and Ethnicity in African Politics with a Case Study of Uganda* (Berkeley: University of California Press, 1976).

22. On ethnic politics in Zambia, see Daniel Posner, *Institutions and Ethnic Politics in Africa* (New York: Cambridge University Press, 2004). On these dynamics more generally, see Arriola, "Patronage and Political Stability in Africa"; and Kanchan Chandra, *Why Ethnic Parties Succeed: Patronage and Ethnic Headcounts in India* (New York: Cambridge University Press, 2004).

23. Nicolas van de Walle, "The Institutional Origins of Inequality in Sub-Saharan Africa," *Annual Review of Political Science* 12 (2009): 307–27.

24. M. Crawford Young, *The African Colonial State in Comparative Perspective* (New Haven, CT: Yale University Press, 1994).

25. Frederick Cooper, *Africa since 1940: The Past of the Present* (New York: Cambridge University Press, 2002).

26. Gabriel Ardant, "Financial Policy and Economic Infrastructure of Modern States and Nations," in *The Formation of National States in Western Europe,* ed. Charles Tilly (Princeton, NJ: Princeton University Press, 1975).

27. Bayart, *L'Etat en Afrique.*

28. Edward Miguel, "Tribe or Nation? Nation Building and Public Goods in Kenya versus Tanzania," *World Politics* 56 (2004): 327–62; and Mwangi S. Kimenyi, "Ethnicity, Governance, and the Provision of Public Goods," *Journal of African Economies* 15 (2006): 62–99.

29. Stephan Haggard and Mathew D. McCubbins, eds., *Presidents, Parliaments, and Policy* (Cambridge: Cambridge University Press, 2001).

30. "Politics: CDFs Misused in Grassroots Projects," *The Daily Nation* (Nairobi, Kenya), March 28, 2011.

31. Mwangi S. Kimenyi, "Efficiency and Efficacy of Kenya's Constituency Development Fund: Theory and Evidence" (working paper, University of Connecticut, 2005).

32. Herbert Kitschelt and Steven Wilkinson, eds. *Patrons, Clients, and Policies: Patterns of Democratic Accountability and Political Competition* (Cambridge: Cambridge University Press, 2007).

33. Vera Mshana, "Constituency Development Fund in Tanzania: The Right Solution?" (paper presented at the Policy Forum, Dar Es Salaam, Tanzania, 2008).

34. Van de Walle, "The Institutional Origins of Inequality in Sub-Saharan Africa."

35. For a good review, see Michael Ross, "Is Democracy Good for the Poor?" *American Journal of Political Science* 50 (2006): 860–74.

36. David Stasavage, "Democracy and Education Spending in Africa," *American Journal of Political Science* 49 (April 2005): 343–58.

37. Daron Acemoglu, Simon Johnson, and James A. Robinson, "Reversal of Fortune: Geography and Institutions in the Making of the Modern World Income Distribution," *Quarterly Journal of Economics* 117 (2002): 1231–94.

38. Stanley L. Engerman and Kenneth L. Sokoloff, "History Lessons: Institutions, Factors Endowments, and Paths of Development in the New World," *Journal of Economic Perspectives* 14 (2000): 217–32.

39. Ross, "Is Democracy Good for the Poor?"

40. Keefer, "Clientelism, Credibility and the Policy Choices of Young Democracies."

41. Paul Collier, *Wars, Guns and Votes.*

42. Martin Ravallion and Francisco Ferreira, "Poverty and Inequality: The Global Context," in *The Oxford Handbook of Economic Inequality,* ed. Wiemer Salverda, Brian Nolan, and Tim Smeeding (Oxford: Oxford University Press, 2009): 599–639.

43. Steven Radelet, *Emerging Africa* (Washington: Center for Global Development, 2010); and William Easterly, " Can the West Save Africa?" *Journal of Economic Literature* 47 (June 2009): 373–447.

44. "What Can the Afrobarometer Tell Us about Service Delivery in Africa?" Afrobarometer Briefing Paper No. 92 (October 2010), accessed at www.afrobarometer.org.

45. John Farrington and Rachel Slater, "Introduction: Cash Transfers: Panacea for Poverty Reduction or Money Down the Drain?" *Development Policy Review* 24 (2006): 499–511; and Martin Ravallion, *Targeted Transfers in Poor Countries: Revisiting the Tradeoffs and Policy Options,* Vol. 3048, World Bank Publications, 2003.

46. But see L. Pritchett, *The Political Economy of Targeted Safety Nets* (World Bank Social Protection Discussion Paper # 0501, World Bank, Washington, DC, 2005).

47. Bernd Schubert and Rachel Slater, "Social Cash Transfers in Low-Income African Countries: Conditional or Unconditional?" *Development Policy Review* 24 (2006): 571–78.

48. Radelet, *Emerging Africa.*

49. Richard Banégas, "Marchandisation du vote, citoyenneté et consolidation démocratique au Bénin," *Politique Africaine* (1998): 75–87; and Pedro C. Vincente and Leonard Wantchekon, "Clientelism and Vote Buying: Lessons from Field Experiments in African Elections," *Oxford Review of Economic Policy* 25 (2009): 292–305.

50. David Pottie, "Party Finance and the Politics of Money in Southern Africa," *Journal of Contemporary African Studies* 21 (2003): 5–28; and Cedric Mayrargue, "Yayi Boni, Un President Inattendu? Construction de la figure du Candidat et Dynamiques Electorales au Benin," *Politique Africaine* 102 (2006): 155–72.

51. Steven A. Block, "Political Business Cycles, Democratization, and Economic Reform: The Case of Africa," *Journal of Development Economics* (2002): 205–28.

52. Thomas Bierschenk, "The Local Appropriation of Democracy: An Analysis of the Municipal Elections in Parakou, Republic of Benin, 2002–2003," *Journal of Modern African Studies* 44 (2006): 543–71.

53. Catherine Boone, "Electoral Populism Where Property Rights Are Weak: Land Politics in Contemporary Sub-Saharan Africa," *Comparative Politics* 41 (January 2009): 183–202.

54. Miles Larmer and Alastair Fraser, "Of Cabbages and King Cobra: Populist Politics and Zambia's 2006 Election," *African Affairs* 106 (2007): 611–37.

55. Danielle Resnick, "Populist Strategies in African Democracies" (Working Paper No. 2010/114, UNU-WIDER United Nations University–World Institute for Development Economics Research, October 2010).

56. See, for instance, Michael Bratton, "Citizen Perception of Local Government Responsiveness in Sub-Saharan Africa," Afrobarometer Working Paper No. 119, May 2010; "Tanzanians and their MPs: What the People Want and What They Don't Always Get," Afrobarometer Briefing Paper No. 59, February 2009; and "La gouvernance locale au Sénégal: Effet de la proximité de l'élu au Citoyen,"Afrobarometer Briefing Paper No. 95, October 2010, all accessed at www.afrobarometer.org.

57. "How Ghanaians Rate the Performance of the NPP Administration," Afrobarometer Briefing Paper No. 49, June 2008.

58. Eric Chang and Nicholas N. Kerr, "Do Voters Have Different Attitudes toward Corruption? The Sources and Implications of Popular Perceptions and Tolerance of Political Corruption," Afrobarometer Working Paper No. 116, accessed at www.afrobarometer.org.

59. Keefer, "Clientelism, Credibility and the Policy Choices of Young Democracies"; and Haggard and McCubbins, eds., *Presidents, Parliaments, and Policy.*

60. Keefer, "Clientelism, Credibility and the Policy Choices of Young Democracies."

61. Michael Bratton, "Formal versus Informal Institutions in Africa," *Journal of Democracy* 18 (July 2007): 96–110.

62. Richard AJoseph, Africa: States in Crisis," *Journal of Democracy* 14 (2003): 159–70.

63. Andreas Schedler, ed., *Electoral Authoritarianism: The Dynamics of Unfree Competition* (Boulder, CO: Lynne Rienner Press, 2007).

64. Larry Diamond, "Thinking about Hybrid Regimes," *Journal of Democracy* 13 (2002): 21–35.

65. Fareed Zakaria, "The Rise of Illiberal Democracy," *Foreign Affairs* 76 (1997): 22–43.

66. Jonathan Fox, "The Difficult Transition from Clientelism to Citizenship," *World Politics* 46 (1994): 151–84.

67. Gretchen Helmke and Steven Levitsky, eds., *Informal Institutions and Democracy: Lessons from Latin America* (Baltimore: Johns Hopkins University Press, 2007).

68. Matthias Basedau, Gero Erdmann, and Andreas Mehler eds., *Votes, Money and Violence: Political Parties and Elections in Sub-Saharan Africa* (Scottsville, South Africa: University of Kwazulu-Natal Press, 2007); and Lise Rakner and Nicolas van de Walle, "Opposition Parties and Incumbent Presidents: The New Dynamics of Electoral Competition in Sub-Saharan Africa," in *Democratization by Elections,* ed. Staffan Lindberg (Baltimore: Johns Hopkins University Press, 2009).

69. Samuel Huntington and Joan Nelson, *No Easy Choice: Political Participation in Developing Countries* (Cambridge, MA: Harvard University Press, 1976); and Karen Remmer, "Exclusionary Democracy," *Studies in Comparative International Development* 20 (December 1985): 64–85.

70. Adam Przeworski et al., "What Makes Democracies Endure," *Journal of Democracy* 7 (January 1996): 39–55.

Defining Political Clientelism's Persistence

BEATRIZ MAGALONI

Trading selective benefits for political support is common in many democracies. Rather than presenting a summary of each of the chapters in this book, the goal of the following pages will be to provide a synthesis of some conceptual issues, including how to define clientelism, how it shapes poverty relief and social policy in developing societies, and how clientelism can be restrained to give rise to more democratic and accountable forms of electoral exchange.

1. Defining Clientelism

Many developing countries fail to grant entitlements to the poor, often making clientelism the only safety net available to them. A prevalent form of political linkage in the developing societies, clientelism is an informal contractual arrangement between a political "patron" and his or her "clients" wherein the former delivers material benefits, jobs, and other personal favors and the latter respond with desirable forms of political behavior such as voting for the patron, mobilizing to protest on his behalf, or even performing acts of violence to intimidate political rivals.

Most of the existing literature emphasizes the electoral uses of clientelism. Yet this form of political linkage involves more than vote buying. Clientelism is an exchange relationship that entails, on the part of the patron, the delivery of material benefits, including offering privileged access to government jobs and programs, and demands, on the part of the client, a variety of political behaviors, of which voting for the patron is perhaps the most consequential. According to Kitschelt and Wilkinson, a clientelistic exchange relation is characterized by: "[First], a contingent direct exchange that concerns goods from which non-participants in the exchange can be excluded. Second, such exchanges become viable from the perspective of politicians, if voter constituencies respond in predictable fashion to clientelistic inducements without excessive opportunism and free riding. Third, short of con-stituencies' spontaneous and voluntary compliance with the clientelistic deal, poli-ticians can invest in organizational structures to monitor and enforce clientelistic exchanges" (2007, 76).

Clientelism entails an *ongoing* relationship and should be distinguished from vote buying on the spot market. The patron targets material benefits, favors, and services to a core political clientele and excludes from these benefits those who are not loyal. Such a "punishment regime" is a distinctive characteristic of this form of political linkage (Diaz-Cayeros et al. 2001). Core clients remain loyal to their patron in part because of the material benefits they receive and expect to receive into the future, and in part because of the fear of punishment or that they would be removed from the machine's spoils system if they defect to the opposition (Magaloni 2006).

2. Commitment Problems

There has been an important debate within the political science literature about whether it is necessary to violate the secrecy of the ballot to make clientelism work. The key question is what the patron can do to sanction voter opportunism. By voter opportunism, the literature means that the voter will receive the transfer to "vote his or her conscience" (Stokes 2005).

Robinson and Verdier (2002) were the first to highlight the voter's commitment problem. What prevents voters from accepting material rewards and then voting as they wish? In their view, the commitment problem can't be solved if what is ex-changed is cash or other particularistic benefits. This is why machines often privilege the distribution of government jobs, which tie the political machine to the voter in a long-term relationship of mutual convenience. Voters will support the machine to protect their jobs, while the party will create and sustain jobs to keep its power over clients.

However, clientelism as a form of vote mobilization encompasses many more transferable goods than job patronage. Politicians in the developing world often re-sort to the distribution of cash handouts, food baskets, grain and livestock, fertilizer, construction materials, household appliances, medicines, access to health services and hospital beds, and so forth, because they are easy to distribute. However, it is very hard to distribute these kinds of material benefits when political parties do not have an ongoing relationship with their clients. Vote buying on the spot market is basically very risky because it is equivalent to giving cash to a total stranger.

Magaloni, Diaz-Cayeros, and Estévez (2012) argue that machine parties need to invest in creating *political loyalty* to solve commitment problems. Loyalty entails a deeply held commitment that compels voters to stick with their party. Although voter's loyalties might entail a moral sense of obligation (Greene and Lawson 2011), they are essentially conditional, constructed through an ongoing informal contractual relationship wherein parties and voters interact repetitively and are able to monitor each other's mutual compliance. The patron needs to deliver on his promises if he wants to keep its core clients loyal, and they, in turn, need to reciprocate if they want to be given continued access to their patron's spoils system.

These ongoing relationships need to be embedded in a dense organizational network. Parties employ party brokers and local patrons to acquire *local knowledge* about voters: who belongs to the core base, how strong are voters' partisan attachments, and what is the nature of their needs. When clientelism is not sustained by an organizational network, it degenerates into vote buying on the spot market, which is a far more risky strategy.

3. Swing Versus Core Voters

There is a lively debate about whether machines target benefits to "swing" voters (Dixit and Londregan 1996) versus "core supporters" (Cox and McCubbins 1986). Stokes's model with applications to the Argentine Peronist Party generates predictions consistent with swing voter models. Loyal voters do not extract private rewards, because they cannot threaten to vote against the machine. "Such a threat would lack credibility: the party knows that the loyal voter, even without rewards, is better off cooperating forever than defecting forever" (2005, 320). According to her approach, weakly opposed voters and indifferent voters are the target of vote buying because only they can credibly threaten to vote their conscience if they do not receive the transfer.

Nichter (2008) offers an alternative explanation, which he terms "turnout buying," suggesting that parties who reward unmobilized supporters for showing up at the polls can activate their passive constituencies. Nichter's model of turnout buying predicts that parties target strong supporters.

Most of the distributive politics literature has focused on vote buying on the spot—the distribution of transfers during an election in exchange of votes (Dixit and Londgregan 1996; Stokes 2005) or turnout (Cox 2006; Nichter 2008). But clientelism must be conceived as an *ongoing relationship,* a form of political linkage between a political party, its network of brokers, and a core base of support (see Calvo and Murillo in this volume).

Magaloni, Diaz-Cayeros, and Estévez (2012) develop a model of "conditional partisan loyalties," explaining why machines disproportionately target core voters with their favors. Prior models of distributive politics rest on the assumption that a loyal voter's ideological proximity to a party remains unaffected by the history of past redistribution. Given this assumption, the loyal voter is captive or condemned to vote for his party "no matter what." They model the strategic interaction between a core voter and her party as a dynamic game in which a voter's ideological proximity to a party is a function of the history of political exchanges; partisan loyalties are anchored in that history. This form of *conditional party loyalty* is akin to Fiorina's (1981) rational party identification—a running tally of accumulated retrospective evaluations. In their model, poor voters' partisan loyalties are generated and sustained by these material inducements rather than by symbolic appeals.

Magaloni et al. (2012) predict essentially that machines will target the bulk of their investments in core voters, uncovering five compelling reasons why parties continue to invest in core voters even though they are already most likely to support them in any election: (1) Parties expect to interact with voters in an ongoing relationship; (2) core voters' loyalties are conditional on whether their party delivers material benefits and favors; (3) buying votes from swing voters is more expensive because it takes more money to convince voters that are ideologically more distant.; (4) the swing-voter strategy is subject to a strong voter opportunism problem in which the voter will receive the transfer and walk away; and (5) party elites will be able to capture more rents for personal gain when following a core-voter strategy.

Hence clientelism works better for both patron and client when it is embedded in a dense organizational network. Machines such as the Peronist Party in Argentina or the Mexican Institutional Revolutionary Party (PRI) are probably the best examples in Latin America. Although corrupt and often unaccountable, party, brokers, and their core voters in these systems are engaged in an ongoing relationship where mutual obligations are often fulfilled.

Clientelism works very differently when partisan organizations are weak or nonexistent, such as in Peru or Ecuador, to name two clear examples. In these settings, candidates with little or no preexisting linkages with voters often need to buy votes blindly. Community-embedded party brokers can tell who is who in each community, help target benefits to core voters, and mobilize them to the voting booths. When these linkages are weak or nonexistent, vote buying becomes risky, equivalent to throwing a fish net into the open ocean to catch "swing voters" every time an election is held.

Where party organizations are weak, ethnicity and other markers such as religion often serve elites to mobilize voters and to determine to whom to target particularistic benefits. This is why clientelism often goes with ethnic politics in vast areas of the developing world (Chandra 2004).

4. Institutional Design and Clientelism

Clientelism is a prevalent form of political exchange in the developing world. Several reasons can be highlighted as to why clientelism is so prevalent in poor societies. First, as argued by Keefer and Vlaicu (2006), in the developing world programmatic appeals often lack credibility, and consequently parties can't sway voters through ideological appeals or policy issues. Instead, vote maximizing politicians need to mobilize votes through the distribution of particularistic benefits or clientelistic promises rather than promises of public goods (Wantchekon 2003).

Second, poverty further reduces the saliency of ideology because the poor are more responsive to material incentives (Dixit and Londregan 1996). Machines such as the PRI or the Peronist Party have been able to sustain electoral dominance for decades by catering to poor voters who are highly dependent on government programs and the system of spoils for survival (Magaloni 2006).

Third, clientelism can flourish under certain characteristics of the public sector, where lack of state autonomy allows parties and their brokers to politicize public resources for electoral purposes (Geddes 1994, Greene 2007, Grzymala-Busse 2007, Magaloni 2006, Shefter 1977). For example, the hegemony of the PRI was sustained to a large extent through government largesse and the ruling parties' capacity to politicize all social programs, including major poverty alleviation funds. There was no effective separation between the PRI and the state in Mexico. A similar phenomenon characterizes Argentina's relationship between the Peronist Party and the state.

In figure C.1 below, taken from Diaz-Cayeros et al. (2001), major social policy programs in Mexico aimed at helping the poor are mapped along two dimensions. The vertical dimension refers to how targeted to the poor the policy is, ranging from highly regressive programs such as electricity or food subsidies, disproportionately benefiting the middle class, to conditional cash transfer programs (CCTs), which largely benefit the poor. The horizontal dimension is given by what they call government discretion, which they defined as "the leeway politicians have in deciding who receives benefits, when benefits are given and when they are withdrawn." Programs that allow a high of degree of government discretion are vulnerable to political and electoral manipulation, and poverty-reduction efforts suffer as a result. Discretionary programs give politicians the ability to withdraw benefits on the basis of electoral criteria or for political motivations, such as when a beneficiary fails to vote for the incumbent or an election cycle is over.

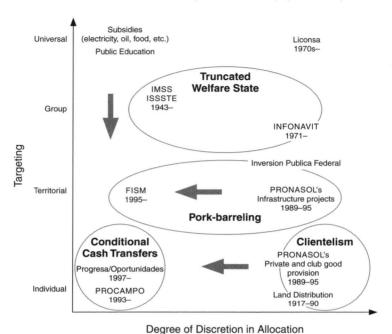

Figure C.1. Types of Anti-Poverty Programs. *Source:* Diaz-Cayeros et al. (2001).

In their study, government discretion is a key explanatory variable accounting for the distortion of anti-poverty programs in Mexico. As long as the PRI controlled the federal bureaucracies—which meant that there was no real separation between party and state—and as long as there remained ample formal discretion for government officials to operate social programs through the party's clientelistic networks, poverty reduction would prove elusive.

Clientelism in Mexico was restrained through the establishment of formula-based programs that provide benefits according to an established eligibility formula and that cannot be withdrawn unless the beneficiary fails to meet the eligibility criteria. What lies behind this progress in poverty reduction is a monumental political transformation. The country transitioned to democracy, which unquestionably empowered poor citizens. "Winning votes became more important for the fate of politicians facing elections. But perhaps most crucially, by introducing veto players in the policy-making arena, the transition to democracy further contributed to better policy design: social policies have been purposefully designed to limit the ability of political parties to manipulate social transfers for electoral reasons, and have pushed bureaucrats to better target social transfers" (Magaloni et al. 2012, 289).

Effective poverty reduction calls for social assistance programs that exhibit both characteristics simultaneously: they are targeted to the poor, and they are not discretionary. Conditional cash transfer programs have become prevalent all over Latin America. Although these programs represent a move in the right direction, it should be emphasized that they are not bulletproof and that they can serve as a mask for clientelism. For example, the program mi Familia Progresa in Guatemala was discredited because of alleged political manipulation by the former incumbent (and his former wife) and was consequently reduced to virtual insignificance with the triumph in 2011 of right-wing Otto Perez Molina.

CCTs put women at the center of poverty reduction. Making sure that the money arrives and stays in their hands and that these resources are destined to improve children's health, nutrition, and education requires monumental organizational capacity and state autonomy. CCT funds are often a major source of monetary income for the extremely poor, and these resources are in constant threat of expropriation by those who interact on a regular basis with the women who receive them.

Essential for the proper implementation of CCTs are state officials on the ground must keep the programs insulated from illegitimate capture by local caciques, power brokers, and political parties. State officials also need to be proximate to the everyday lives of poor women. These programs have transferred a great deal of power to health providers and teachers, who are in charge of certifying whether beneficiaries meet the program's behavioral conditions and hence of determining who stays in the program and who is withdrawn.

Moreover, clientelism is not going to disappear with the introduction of CCTs. It is possible that machine politics will fade as states and bureaucratic agencies gain independence from political parties. Yet clientelism is likely to remain tenacious at election time, with parties and candidates using public funds to buy votes by distributing handouts and other particularistic benefits. As long as clientelism does not entail the systematic manipulation of social programs, in my view, this practice can survive without undermining democracy and effective poverty reduction.

5. The Counterfactuals

Observers agree that clientelistic practices undermine democratic political representation (Stokes 2005), entrenching incumbents who use public resources to retain power (Magaloni 2006; Greene 2007). Clientelism is also thought to retard economic growth (Robinson and Verdier 2002) and to distort poverty reduction (Magaloni et al. 2012).

Yet the consequences of clientelism need to be judged next to the counterfactuals. First, consider the issue of political order. Until the end of the Cold War, authoritarian political institutions prevailed in the overwhelming majority of developing societies. Many dictatorships were highly repressive and also politically unstable. Authoritarian rulers who used clientelism were significantly more stable and often less repressive than rulers that had no established linkages with civil society (see Huntington 1968, for the first formulation of this idea). Corruption and clientelism might hence be conceived as strategies to tame political violence, and in this sense they might not be negative for development.

A second consideration relates to the lack of political linkages that prevails in many young democracies. Clientelism entails a form of electoral accountability, even if limited. Machine and voter are linked through an ongoing relationship that entails mutual obligations. Although this relationship is asymmetrical and based on inequality, it is often better for the poor than having no linkage with an elite patron at all. We need to take voters' strategies more seriously and understand why voters invest or willingly engage in this form of exchange.

6. Voters' Coordination Dilemmas

To be self-sustaining, clientelistic linkages require voters' complicity. Poor voters willingly become loyal to a clientelistic party machine because it gives them access to a stream of benefits and favors. The perverse nature of clientelism is that voters willingly sustain a system that is corrupt and that keeps them poor.

The dilemma is one of coordination. Each voter acting alone has powerful reasons to remain loyal. Whoever defects is likely to be sanctioned and excluded from the spoils system. Rational voters remain loyal to the machine because of the expectation of continuing to receive access to benefits into the future. If everyone reasons likewise, the party machine can be sustained in equilibrium (Diaz-Cayeros et al. 2001).

To exit the system, the voter needs to know that many others like him will vote against the clientelistic machine, for otherwise she alone will bear the costs of defection. The equilibrium is perverse because everyone becomes an accomplice of the system even when it is collectively suboptimal.

Exiting the system requires, then, the capacity of a voter to endure the costs of not having access to the spoils system. These costs are formidable for the poor, who often depend on the machine's favors for survival. In contrast, the middle class can better afford to defect from the system (Magaloni 2006). The poor are therefore particularly vulnerable or predisposed to this form of exchange. Other causes include state capture and the access to valuable resources to buy-off votes (oil, other commodities, non-tax revenues).

REFERENCES

Chandra, Kanchan. 2004. *Why Ethnic Parties Succeed: Patronage and Ethnic Head Counts in India.* New York: Cambridge University Press.

Cox, Gary. 2006. "Core Voters, Swing Voters and Distributive Politics." Paper prepared for the conference on Representation and Popular Rule, Yale University, October 27–28.

Cox, Gary, and Mathew D. McCubbins. 1986. "Electoral Politics as a Redistributive Game." *Journal of Politics* 48 (May): 370–89.

Diaz-Cayeros, Alberto, Beatriz Magaloni, and Barry Weingast. 2001. "Democratization and the Economy in Mexico: Equilibrium (PRI) Hegemony and its Demise." Typescript, Stanford University.

Dixit, Avinash, and John Londregan. 1996. "The Determinants of Success of Special Interests in Redistributive Politics." *Journal of Politics* 58 (November): 1132–55.

Fiorina, Morris P. 1981. *Retrospective Voting in American National Elections.* New Haven, CT: Yale University Press.

Geddes, Barbara. 1994. *Politician's Dilemma: Building State Capacity in Latin America.* Berkeley: University of California Press.

Greene, Kenneth F. 2007. *Why Dominant Parties Lose.* Cambridge: Cambridge University Press.

Greene, Kenneth, and Chapell Lawson. 2011. "Self-Enforcing Clientelism." Typescript.

Grzymała-Busse, A. 2007. *Rebuilding Leviathan: Party Competition and State Exploitation in Post-Communist Democracies.* Cambridge: Cambridge University Press.

Huntington, Samuel P. 1968. Political Order in Changing Societies. New Haven, CT: Yale University Press.

Keefer, Philip, and Razvan Vlaicu. 2006. "Democracy, Credibility, and Clientelism." World Bank Policy Research Working Paper No. 3472.

Kitschelt, Herbert, and Steven Wilkinson. 2007. *Patrons, Clients and Policies: Patterns of Democratic Accountability and Political Competition.* Cambridge: Cambridge University Press.

Magaloni, Beatriz. 2006. *Voting for Autocracy: Hegemonic Party Survival and Its Demise in Mexico.* Cambridge: Cambridge University Press.

Magaloni, Beatriz, Alberto Diaz-Cayeros, and Federico Estévez. 2007. "Clientelism and Portfolio Diversification: A Model of Electoral Investment with Applications to Mexico." In *Patrons, Clients and Policies: Patterns of Democratic Accountability and Political Competition,* ed. Herbert Kitschelt and Steven Wilkinson. Cambridge: Cambridge University Press.

Magaloni, Beatriz, Alberto Diaz-Cayeros, and Federico Estévez. 2012. *Strategies of Vote Buying: Democracy, Clientelism and Poverty Reduction in Mexico.* Cambridge: Cambridge University Press.

Nichter, Simeon. 2008. "Vote Buying or Turnout Buying? Machine Politics and the Secret Ballot." *American Political Science Review* 102 (February): 15–28.

Robinson, James, and Thierry Verdier. 2002. "The Political Economy of Clientelism." Paper presented at the Political Economy of Clientelism Conference, Stanford University, May.

Shefter, Martin. 1977. "Party and Patronage: Germany, England, and Italy." *Politics and Society* 7(4).

Stokes, Susan. 2005. "Perverse Accountability: A Formal Model of Machine Politics with Evidence from Argentina." *American Political Science Review* 99(3): 315–25.

Wantchekon, Leonard. 2003. "Clientelism and Voting Behavior: Evidence from a Field Experiment in Benin," *World Politics* 55 (April): 399–422.

Page numbers followed by f indicate figures and those followed by t indicate tables.